BOTH SIDES OF THE FENCE

REG FEARMAN

The
History
Press

For my late wife Joan, my parents Arthur and
Sally and my sister Doreen who were always
there for me. Also to my son, Gary, for his great
assistance to me in my speedway promoting career.

First published 2014

The History Press
The Mill, Brimscombe Port
Stroud, Gloucestershire, GL5 2QG
www.thehistorypress.co.uk

© Reg Fearman, 2014

The right of Reg Fearman to be identified as the Author
of this work has been asserted in accordance with the
Copyright, Designs and Patents Act 1988.

British Library Cataloguing in Publication Data.
A catalogue record for this book is available from the British Library.

ISBN 978 0 7509 5848 6

Typesetting and origination by The History Press
Printed in Great Britain

CONTENTS

FOREWORD

INTRODUCTION TO FOREWORDS

Reg Fearman's autobiography is aptly named. His experience of the speedway world truly comes from both sides of the fence. Indeed, the title of this book is really a considerable understatement.

Philip Dalling.

His involvement in speedway has encompassed not merely being a terrace fan in his early teens and an England Test rider just a few short years later, but just about every other role imaginable. Promoter, track constructor and curator, publicist, international team manager, top-level administrator, enthusiastic mainstay of the veterans' organisation – the list goes on and on.

However, a title is a title and the reference to his activities on both the sharp and the comfortable (?) sides of the safety barrier which separates the riders from everyone else merits a double appreciation in the form of this Foreword.

There can be no more suitable contribution to reflect on Reg's life in speedway on the riding side of the fence than perhaps the greatest rider the sport has ever known (and one of Reg's oldest and greatest friends within speedway), the legendary five-times World Champion Ove Fundin.

Crossing over to the other side of the fence, it is equally fitting that an appreciation should come from John Berry, one of the men whose entry to the ranks of the promoters/administrators of the sport came via the British League Division Two competition that Reg Fearman did so much personally to make possible.

Philip Dalling, 2014

FOREWORD BY OVE FUNDIN

I first met Reg Fearman in 1954 when we spent five weeks together sailing on the SS *Oronsay* from London to Australia.

Reg's father and mother were also on board. I had met Mr and Mrs Fearman before I met Reg. Back in 1954, we speedway riders from the Continent, after taking part in World Championship qualifying rounds at European venues, then had to do it all again in the championship rounds held in the UK.

My first race in one of these meetings was at Norwich where I met the Australian ace Aub Lawson. He took a liking to me and, as both of us were scheduled to ride at West Ham in the next round, he arranged for me to stay with Reg's mum and dad at their Plaistow home, where Aub had lived during his days with West Ham and where he still stayed when he was in London.

Ove Fundin receives the WRSA president's chain from outgoing president, Reg Fearman.

I eventually qualified for the World Final at Wembley but did not realise that I was obliged to have a mechanic with me in the pits on the night. Aub solved the problem by asking Reg's father to act as my mechanic.

Reg and I have stayed friends ever since 1954, the friendship continuing long after our speedway days ended. Being close to Reg over a period of sixty years, I guess I know him better than most.

After my wife, Ioana, and I had moved to the South of France to live, Reg and his late wife, Joan often used to visit us. Ioana and I also came over to England each year to see the Fearmans. When Reg met his present wife, Eileen, they decided to buy a house in Valcros, in Provence, and for several years we lived just half a mile apart, seeing each other most days, be it for dinner, golf or just to say hello.

Reg is one of those people that, the more you learn about them, the more you come to respect them. He is quite a legend among us in the speedway family. He has done everything concerned with our sport: been a rider, promoter, chairman of the Promoters' Association, a member of the Speedway Control Board and president of the World Speedway Riders' Association.

He has constantly tried to expand the borders of the sport, including taking speedway to the Middle East, and lately he has become active as a speedway historian.

Some of the things he has done over the years have brought him friends but, outspoken as he is, some things have made him unpopular.

I am sure a lot of us are looking forward to reading what he has written. I wish, Reg, that you had told us your story much earlier, as I know you have got much more to tell than what is contained in most of the speedway books we have seen in the last few years.

Reg is a fine writer, full of humour. He has given me lots of laughs over the years and I, for one, will read the book with enthusiasm and commend it to all speedway supporters.

FOREWORD BY JOHN BERRY

I'll bet I'm the only person in the world who is reminded of squid when he thinks of Reg Fearman. Sharp suits I can understand, or the trademark Rolls-Royce, or perhaps the large cigars, seemingly smoked for show rather than for deep enjoyment.

Yep, look for all the trimmings of an Arthur Daley lookalike and Reg was your man. He was the epitome of a working-class East End boy made good.

It is for Reg to take us through those early years, through his riding days, and on to his involvement in the promoting side of speedway. I came in after he had

John Berry and Reg Fearman.

made his pile – or at least a large portion of it. By then he had an enviable reputation in the sport, not least because he was one of the few who had taken on the hard-faced promoter Mike Parker and come out on the right side.

I've asked Reg about that situation and been given chapter and verse. I've also asked him about the disappointing ending to his speedway promoting life when things went pear-shaped at Poole and I have also been given full details there.

In telling me privately of those events, he did not have to worry about the laws of libel. I do hope he includes detailed explanations over what happened in the pages to follow, even if it might require carefully chosen words, balanced on the edge of legal nicety. His otherwise spotless reputation was damaged by the Poole affair and he is entitled to put forward his side of the sorry tale.

Reg has never turned his back on speedway even though many in it turned their backs on him. His speedway 'family' stretches around the world. He must be about the only person left anywhere who still writes thank-you letters to people for the most mundane of things.

Following in his footsteps around Australia as British Lions manager the year after he took the same tour was like being John the Baptist a year after the Lord had appeared. His was simply an impossible act to follow.

Reg has a massive circle of friends and apart from thank-you notes is a prolific letter writer (email these days). More importantly, he makes each of his correspondents believe he or she is the most important member of the circle. As age catches up with us all so do the accompanying illnesses and here again it is Reg who is quick with solicitations and good wishes.

Contrary to the popular belief of those who don't know him, he does care about people. That is not to say he didn't ruffle more than a few feathers on his way through life in general and speedway in particular. Speedway promoting, the second-hand car game, property development. They all have two things in common. First of all, you get nowhere unless you are trusted. Second, woe betide you if people see a weak spot. Making hard decisions is part of the job.

I don't do 'heroes'. Well, I do up to a point, but I don't get silly about it. Having said that, if I had a role model in the business of speedway promotion it was Reg. However, he always had one thing I never did. He had charisma. He was able to mix in any company and adjust his manner to suit. He was able to dominate situations but stop short of being a bully. He enjoys being in the limelight but does not try to put others down.

As a wet behind the ears (about life every bit as much as about speedway) new promoter I admired the way Reg stayed on top of situations. I also admired the fact that even though I did not go out of my way to make things easy for him when he was chairman of either league, he never appeared to hold it against me.

Towards the end of the 1973 season, I added a line on to the cover of the Ipswich programmes. In those days, part of the masthead of *The Times* newspaper included the words 'The paper the top people read'. I borrowed from this, changing it to 'The programme the top people read'.

Reg was the British Speedway Promoters' Association (BSPA) chairman then and I was well aware that the invariably less than gracious comments appearing each week in our programme were infuriating him and his management committee. I was receiving regular threats and warnings of likely dire consequences if I failed to tone down my rhetoric, which in retrospect might well have been somewhat over the top.

My programme always remained abrasive but Reg Fearman never retaliated, either privately or publicly. Matches between Reading and Ipswich were always close, full-bloodied affairs but, again, there was always a cordial welcome from the management whilst he was in charge.

I have always admired Reg Fearman. So many nouveau riche businessmen were shy about their success. Not Reg. He wanted to let people know he had done well for himself. The Rolls-Royce, the Saville Row suits, the Churchill cigars and the palatial pad in Henley-on-Thames' Fairmile were his badges of honour. They announced to the world that Reg Fearman had arrived! That such trappings were also sound business decisions was of secondary importance.

It was Reg Fearman who asked me if I would like to act as the British rider representative in the pits at the Wembley World Final of 1975, my first 'representative' position. It was Reg Fearman who asked me if I would like to manage the British Lions tour of Australia in 1975/6 and Reg Fearman who asked me if I would take over managing the full England team during the following European season. I believe it was also Reg who orchestrated my elevation to the BSPA management committee.

He and I don't always see eye to eye. We sometimes see situations from different viewpoints. Even now he challenges my contributions in the retro speedway magazine, *Backtrack*, whenever he feels my memory is not as efficient as his. For somebody a few years older than me he really does have a huge recall and I doubt there will be many situations in this book where he will be caught out on matters of fact.

That recall, his straightforward writing style and his own particular opinions on a whole range of subjects within and without the sport of speedway will ensure this book will become required reading for a great range of age groups. It has only taken me about ten years of nagging to get him to put his knowledge and experience down on paper and I am delighted that he finally has.

The squid? Well, in the late sixties, I, a fishmonger in a previous life, had never tasted squid. Working-class erks like me had a limited culinary horizon. A meal out at that time meant almost certainly a Berni Inn. Prawn cocktail and steak, chips and peas, washed down with Blue Nun, Mateus Rosé or, to push the boat out, a half bottle of Nuits St Georges.

An early BSPA conference was taking place somewhere in Spain. Who knows where? All the airports, hotels and shops look the same whatever the resort. Somehow I became part of a group of promoters going to a local restaurant for a meal. It was my first social occasion with Reg and I enjoyed it very much. He held court and everyone had a great time.

The whole evening got off to a wonderful start. As we sat down and the head waiter came over with menus, Reg declared in his best booming voice, 'Calamari! Bring us several plates of calamari whilst we study the menu!'

Calamari? I kept my trap shut, not wanting to show my ignorance, but when it arrived I loved it to death. Still do. So whenever I enjoy those tasty fried rings I recall it was he who, apart from everything else, introduced me to the delicacy of squid!

•   •   •

Whilst this book was being compiled the speedway world was deeply shocked to learn of the death of John Berry at the age of just 67 years. John died at his home in Perth, Western Australia, on 3 August 2012.

JB and I exchanged copious emails in recent years about subjects other than speedway racing. He always 'shot straight from the shoulder'. I was delighted when he agreed to co-write the Foreword for this book. I knew it would be an honest and forthright piece. In his passing, I shall miss the friendship and banter we had built up.

ACKNOWLEDGEMENTS

This book would not have been possible without the help and encouragement of so many people and my sincere thanks go to the following:

My wife Eileen, for her patience, inspiration and devotion to the task of transcribing my long-hand and dictation; to Philip Dalling for additions; to Dr Brian Belton; and to the late John Berry for cajoling me into putting my thoughts into word and for his Foreword.

To my very good friend, Ove Fundin, for his Foreword, and to Cyril Hill, my old school pal, and David Weeks, my army buddy, for their Appreciations.

Many of the photographs are from my own collection but I have to thank the following for their contribution: Alf Weedon, Huston Spratt, Sue Edwards and David Doe, Wright Wood, Eric Marsh, Tom Bromley, United Artists, the Royal Automobile Club, John Simpson, Peter Morrish, Brian Roach, the *Reading Evening Post*, *Staffordshire Sentinel*, *Halifax Courier*, Perales, R.S. Oliver and to John Somerville for a number of photographs from his collection. I have endeavoured to include all contributors but my apologies to anyone who has been omitted.

To Janet Lubaczewska and her son, Marek, for the photographs and information on the late Richard Lubaczewski.

To Ninette Grey for the loan of the Fay Taylour papers; the late Jim Shepherd for allowing me to quote from his book *A History of Australian Speedway*; Peter Wills for writing first-hand on his father, Lionel; Garry Baker for his input on the Wills family; Tony McDonald for the quotes I used from *Backtrack* and *Michael Lee, Back from the Brink*; and Peter Oakes, John Chaplin, Tony Webb, Peter White, Allan Quinn, Ian Hoskins, Ray Chitty, Bob Andrews, Ronnie Moore,

Igor Kalashnik, Ivan Mauger, Sue Edwards and Rosemary Lawson-Quinn for providing me with relevant information.

For information gleaned from Wikipedia, the *Daily Mirror*, the *Evening Sentinel*, *Reading Evening Post*, and *Motor Cycle and Motor Cycling*.

To the Manx Museum, Isle of Man, for details of the internment camp at Port Erin; to Canon Boyling, late of Liverpool Anglican Cathedral, for permission to hold and his co-ordination of the Peter Craven Remembrance Service in 2003, and the Reverend Michael Whawell for his Address at the service.

To the late Peter Arnold, the founder of the Veteran Speedway Riders' Association.

To John Balfe of the RAAF, flight crew member of Lionel Van Praag and author of *Far From Home*; and Lynne Olson and Stanley Cloud, co-authors of *For Your Freedom and Ours* published by Arrow Books in 2004.

Finally, to my in-laws, the Eley family, for photographs and family history.

INTRODUCTION

'He makes no friends who never made a foe.' (Alfred Lord Tennyson)

THE BEGINNING

When the internal combustion engine was invented and placed in between two, three or four wheels, it was inevitable that men would compete against each other, whether it be on board, path, sand, grass or dirt tracks.

It was due to reports and photographs sent from Australia in 1926 and 1927 to motorcycle magazines in Britain by Percy Lionel Bethune Wills (he preferred to be known as Lionel) that tens of thousands of people in the country were introduced to speedway racing.

It was through his repeated attempts to bring to the notice of people in Britain just what was happening on dirt tracks in Australia that Lionel Wills was indirectly responsible for

Reg Fearman, 2013.

what is generally accepted as being the first true speedway meeting in the UK, which took place at High Beech in Epping Forest in February 1928, promoted by Jack Hill-Bailey, the club secretary, on behalf of the Ilford Motor Cycle & Light Car Club, affiliated to the Auto Cycle Union (ACU) Eastern Centre.

In fact, there had been two previous dirt track meetings in 1927, one at Camberley in Surrey, held on a sand track with the riders racing in a clockwise (as opposed to the accepted anti-clockwise) direction.

The second meeting was at Droylsden in Greater Manchester in June 1927. *Motor Cycling* magazine reported the event as follows:

> The South Manchester Motor Club inaugurated dirt track racing in the north of England on Saturday when a series of races were held at Droylsden. The circuit was one third of a mile around and consisted of two straights with banked bends.

Neither of these events gained official recognition. It was the High Beech meeting which was acclaimed by the public, with a reported attendance of 30,000. It was the proceedings at High Beech which made front page news in the *Daily Mirror*, were reported in other national newspapers, and set the scene for the rapid development of speedway racing in the UK.

Of course, with more and more people interested in the origins of speedway racing, claims will continue to be made for other 'first meetings'. There is evidence from 1903 of motorcycle racing at Canning Town, London E16, on a banked cycling track (not far from where West Ham Stadium was later to be built), and forms of motorcycle racing at Crystal Palace and elsewhere.

The sport enjoyed ups and downs throughout the late 1920s and the 1930s, survived six years of war through regular competition at Belle Vue in Manchester, and, in 1946, the first season after the end of the Second World War, was watched by more than 6 million people at venues throughout the nation.

It is generally accepted by most speedway historians and authors (although by no means all) that speedway racing, as we know it today, began at West Maitland Showground, New South Wales, Australia, in December 1923.

Johnnie S. Hoskins, born in Waitara, New Zealand, in April 1892, was, as secretary of the Maitland and District Agricultural and Horticultural Society, involved in organising motorcycle races on the loose-surfaced track around the main ring at the showground, as part of an event known as The Electric Light Carnival.

Hoskins had arrived in Maitland in 1921 and had first obtained a job as secretary to the Maitland Hospital Carnival Committee. He was successful in organising and running several fundraising promotions on behalf of the hospital, some of them utilising the Maitland Showground facility.

He later successfully applied for the job with the Agricultural and Horticultural Society, taking up this post in October 1921. In those days, Maitland was regarded as the capital of the entire Hunter Valley area of New South Wales, a vast and well-watered plain. The majority of the land was ideal for all forms of farming and grazing, while under the rich soil were almost unlimited deposits of coal.

Johnnie Hoskins was a born organiser and a man quick to sense business opportunities. In 1922, he was convinced that the Agricultural and Horticultural Society should jump aboard the new gambling rage of trotting, which was beginning to boom in Sydney, although an application for a licence to stage regular meetings, with full betting facilities, was rejected. Early in 1922, he married a local girl, Audrey Bradshaw, an attractive and musically talented young lady.

Prior to 1923, there were many motorcycle race meetings of some sort in Australia and, in particular, in the Hunter Valley, including an event in October 1909 at the Newcastle Showground. The first known motorcycle track racing was held at Cessnock Bicycle Club ground in November 1909.

It is recorded that the Newcastle Showground, on 21 October 1922, staged a motorcycle race meeting, including sidecar racing on a dirt track. The meeting was arranged and promoted by the Hamilton Motor Cycle Club and attracted no less than forty entries.

There is plenty of documentary evidence for the event that has long been suggested as providing the true origin of modern-day speedway racing. It is strongly argued that a straight line exists between the event promoted by Hoskins at Maitland Showground on 15 December 1923 and the Grand Prix and league racing seen today across many nations.

Johnnie placed an advertisement in the *Maitland Mercury* on 8 December which clearly mentions motorcycle racing as one of the attractions for the event on 15 December.

Hoskins was evidently not the only man promoting motorcycle racing in Maitland.

In the same edition of the *Mercury*, directly underneath the notice placed by Johnnie, is another advertisement headed 'Sensational Cycling and Motor Cycling Racing', scheduled for an event on 22 December, a week after Johnnie's own promotion on behalf of the Agricultural and Horticultural Society.

The advertisement for the 22 December event lists W. (Bill) Dart as manager and Messrs Campbell and Du Frocq of Sydney as promoters. Campbell and Du Frocq were well known in the sports promotion business. They had held the lease on the Sydney Sports Ground for some years and were recognised as the leading cycling promoters in that city.

The West Maitland Showground Committee, with Johnnie Hoskins still fully employed as secretary, issued a lease for the purposes of motorcycle sport at the West Maitland Showground to Campbell, Du Frocq and Bill Dart.

Campbell and Du Frocq's lease with the West Maitland Showground expired at the end of the 1923–24 summer. A flat dirt track was subsequently laid down for 1924–25 and a hardboard safety fence put in place, with Johnnie Hoskins involved in the motorcycle racing promotions at the showground as a full-time employee of the Agricultural and Horticultural Society.

Towards the end of July 1925, Johnnie Hoskins, ever the gambler, resigned his secure job with the Maitland Showground and took a job for a short period of time with the Royal Automobile Club of Australia as manager of its touring department. From there, the records tell us, in December 1925 he became the speedway company secretary at Newcastle where the emerging sport was promoted by a man called Bertram Light.

Forever restless and in search of an opportunity to be his own boss, rather than as an employed manager or secretary, Johnnie moved with his family (son Ian, later to be a famous speedway promoter in his own right, had been born in 1924), to Sydney to stage speedway racing at the Sydney Royal Agricultural Showground at Moore Park.

This venture proved unsuccessful for Johnnie because of the amount of rain which fell during the Australian summer. In 1927 he went to Perth where he promoted speedway at the Claremont Showground.

The craze soon mushroomed from that December 1923 meeting to other New South Wales areas. In 1926, A.J. Hunting quit his vast concrete 'Olympia Motor Speedway' track at Marouba and moved to Brisbane Exhibition Grounds to promote dirt track speedway racing.

He arrived in England before Hoskins in 1928, having formed a company to promote speedway racing at a number of stadia. He quit before the season was over, taking a hefty payout, and moved to Argentina to promote speedway racing there.

Early in 1928, Johnnie Hoskins arrived in England and helped Fred Mockford and Cecil Smith to promote speedway racing at Crystal Palace, also assisting promoters at other tracks.

In 1929, Lionel Wills introduced him to Arthur Elvin of Wembley, the entrepreneur who was managing director of the company running Wembley Stadium. Johnnie was subsequently appointed manager to promote speedway at Wembley.

JSH was, without doubt, the greatest showman the sport has ever known. He continued to promote speedway racing in Britain from 1928 for six decades. His last promotion was at Canterbury, which he opened in 1968, within the sound of the bells of the cathedral. He died in 1987, a few days short of his 95th birthday, and Canterbury speedway ceased the same year.

In his autobiography, Johnnie explained how, soon after his arrival in London in 1928, he had been invited to a meeting with the secretary of the Auto Cycle Union, the governing body for motorcycle racing in the UK.

On behalf of the Auto Cycle Union, a gentleman by the name of T.W. (Tom) Loughborough was given the task of knocking together a set of rules for the conduct of speedway racing in Britain.

Loughborough, after interrogating Hoskins, listened intently as Johnnie explained that there were no written rules in Australia. 'We just made them up as we went along and any differences between promoters were quickly sorted out,' was the Hoskins explanation.

As Johnnie later remarked, the British, by their very nature, needed rules for governance. 'The fellow from the ACU,' as he described Loughborough, smartly compiled some as a result of the conversation. In seeking to codify rules, the ACU was effectively declaring that it was dealing with a new form of motorcycle sport.

●   ●   ●

The background of Lionel Wills, whose part in the birth of British speedway cannot be overstated, is of great interest.

For more than eighty years from 1928, Lionel was linked to the WD & HO Wills tobacco family. This has subsequently been shown to be incorrect.

In chapter seventeen I examine the true story of Lionel Wills (definitely a hero!), drawing (with his consent) upon the work of Melbourne-based speedway researcher Garry Baker, and Peter Wills, Lionel's son.

This brief history of the origins of speedway racing as we know it today will, I hope, sharpen the reader's appetite for this account of the part I have played personally in the sport over a period of more than sixty years – as a schoolboy fan, as a teenage rider, as a promoter, administrator and England team manager.

Given that the introduction has concentrated so heavily on Australia, it is fitting that some of my finest memories of the sport concern 'down under' and that my mentor, the great Aub Lawson, wore the kangaroo race-jacket of that country with such distinction for so many years.

Had it not been for what happened in Australia so many years ago, I would not have enjoyed my career in speedway racing, from West Ham in my native East End of London, right through to my involvement with introducing the sport to the Middle East many years later.

Reg Fearman, 2014

CHAPTER ONE

EARLY DAYS

The East End of London in the 1930s was a colourful and volatile place, already home to a mix of races and communities virtually unmatched in any other part of the British Isles.

Sport was one of the factors which helped cement together this cultural diversity, not only at West Ham United's Boleyn Ground but also at another iconic local sporting venue that played host to a team nicknamed the Hammers.

This venue, the massive West Ham Stadium at Custom House, was to provide me with the first experiences of speedway racing, the sport that has shaped my entire life and which remains, sixty-five years after I first drank in its intoxicating sights and sounds, a key part of my very existence.

My parents were among the tens of thousands of East Enders who flocked to Custom House in the 1930s, to be thrilled by the exploits of the world's greatest riders and to be entertained by the showmanship of the man who promoted at the track for most of that era, the flamboyant New Zealander Johnnie Hoskins.

The Second World War put a temporary end to speedway. When the sport returned on a regular basis in 1946, both my elder sister and I were old enough to join our parents on the terraces at Custom House. So began my lifetime love of a sport which has brought me a share of fame, some fortune, some hard knocks and, most important of all, the friendship of countless speedway people in every continent of the world.

My East End roots run deep. My father, Arthur Victor Fearman, was born to Henry and Catherine in Hoxton, just around the corner from Moorfields Eye Hospital, on 27 September 1897. He never moved very far away up until his death in Ilford in February 1972. My mother, Emma Sarah Aves, was born in the Salmon Road/ Burdett Road area, again in the East End, on 23 March 1903, achieving the great age of 95 until she died in September 1998, also in Ilford.

East Enders knew how to enjoy life but they also knew how to endure troubled times and keep their families together. My mother and her younger sister, Rosemarie, suffered the shock of the death of their mother when they were quite young, but they were kept together by the kindness of an aunt and uncle in Wapping.

These relatives had a large young family of their own and one of their children was also called Emma, with a birthday on 10 March. Because of this, it was decided to use my mother's second name and to celebrate her birthday on the same day. This was an arrangement which continued throughout her life.

My parents were married on 29 September 1928 at the Church of Holy Trinity, Mile End, in the Parish of Stepney. Both worked for the major grocery and provisions firm Patrick and Granger, which specialised in deliveries in the pre-Second World War era, with my father employed as a driver during his early married life.

Motorbikes were an integral part of the life of the Fearman family. Reg's mother, Sarah, is pictured before her marriage with husband-to-be Arthur's motorcycle combination in the background.

Arthur and Sarah Fearman, Reg's parents, married in September 1928 at Holy Trinity church, Mile End, in the Parish of Stepney.

My sister, Doreen Rosemarie, was born on 20 September 1929 and also spent most of her life in London until her death in St Thomas's Hospital in June 1988. I followed on 26 April 1933 and was christened Reginald Arthur Victor Fearman.

Our family then lived at 1 Maritime Street, Bow, E3, in the Borough of Stepney, but when I was 3 months old we moved to 137 New City Road, Plaistow, E13, in the Borough of West Ham and remained there until October 1954.

Our house was not big but was typical of so many homes of the era. It was terraced, and comprised a parlour with bay window, living room and scullery/ kitchen, with outside toilet. Eventually, my father found a second-hand, cast-iron bath which he fitted under the kitchen window, adjacent to the sink, and a gas geyser was installed which served the sink and bath.

Reg in his mother's arms with sister Doreen completing the family group.

The copper was in another corner where my mum did the washing, using dolly pegs and rinsing the white clothes in Reckitts' Blue Bags. Upstairs, there were bedrooms on each side of the staircase. A left turn took you into the second bedroom which you had to pass through to get to the third bedroom, which was shared by Doreen and me.

As children, we slept in two single beds, feet to feet, and I remember going to bed with candles and a cheese sandwich. When Doreen got older, she and my mother shared the middle bedroom and my dad and I shared the back bedroom.

The young Reg was a terror on four wheels.

Most people retain special memories of their early lives. My father was very clever with his hands and made many of my toys, including a pedal car. I remember when I was about 3 years of age pedalling along the pavement in New City Road when a lady stopped in front of me and said, 'That looks very nice – you wouldn't run over me, would you?' I ran straight over her toes.

My childhood in the 1930s was very happy and our home was always open to our extended family. Weekends often saw a singsong around the piano with my father 'tickling the ivories'. Our neighbours were good, in the fine East End tradition, and when my mum had to go into St Mary's Hospital, Plaistow, to have an ulcer removed from her stomach, Doreen and I were looked after by Mrs Hanns until Dad came home from work. Mrs Hanns' husband was a railwayman and I remember that he had lost a part of one arm in an accident at work.

Our holidays were usually spent with other members of the family, sometimes under canvas, at resorts like Margate, Maldon and Ramsgate, or sometimes at Clacton. My dad had an old late-1920s/early '30s Royal Enfield motorcycle, with cow horn handlebars and a sidecar, to carry Doreen and me. I can vividly remember my father's long, belted, leather coat, his flat cap and goggles. My mother's brother, Phil, would come at the same time with his girlfriend, who he eventually married. She used to lie outside the tent sunbathing. The rest of my mother's family, my cousins, the Aves family, also came along.

Every good East Ender knew the value of a trip to Southend and the famous, but now sadly closed, Kursaal amusement park. I have great memories of being there as a young boy with my parents. My favourite Kursaal character was Tornado Smith who rode the Wall of Death. My mother and I made frequent trips to Southend, almost up to her death. Our treat centred on one of the cafes under the arches at Westcliff. The fish and chips were always superb. On the way

Fearman family holidays were usually spent with other family members at resorts like Ramsgate, with Reg enjoying a traditional donkey ride.

back to East London, we would stop off at the Leigh cockle sheds and take some shellfish home with us.

Family links were (and are) particularly important in such a close-knit community as the traditional East End of London and I am still in touch with some of my cousins, one of whom, Billy Aves, has compiled an Aves family tree. In 2006, I received an email message from a Debbie Naylor asking if I was related to her mother, Kate Peck, *née* Fearman. I was delighted to reply to the effect that we were indeed related.

Kate was the daughter of my father's brother, which made us first cousins. We arranged to meet at Kate's house in Basildon, Essex. Kate and I had not met for some fifty years. I learned that Kate had eight children and her two sisters, Amy and Jessie, had another eight between them. All the children had married and had children of their own, which meant that overnight my blood relatives had increased beyond comprehension.

In a further twist, it transpired that Debbie's son, Rhys Naylor, was the mascot at Arena Essex Speedway. What a coincidence! From being the mascot, Rhys graduated to full-time speedway. The parallels with my own experience included the fact that, like me, Rhys signed a contract to ride for Kings Lynn Stars on his 16th birthday.

A real treat as a child was being taken to the East Ham Palace to see the old vaudeville stars like Burlington Bertie and the old-timer who did monologues – George Robey. At Christmas time, my parents would take in two boys from Dr Barnardo's for several days.

Family links were all-important in the East End of London. Reg, on the left, is pictured with his father, Arthur, sister Doreen and grandmother Fearman.

Doreen and I were brought up to share what we had with those less fortunate – including my toys – and, by our parents' deeds, we were taught not to be racist. I remember in either 1944 or 1945 my father bringing home for an evening meal a young man called Ali, who I believe was a Lascar, from Whitefields, Father's place of work in Plaistow. This was the first of many meals Ali had at our home. He lived on his own in digs and my father obviously thought he wasn't getting enough to eat.

For somewhat different reasons, I also recall Sylvia Dosad, a mixed-race girl who was really beautiful-looking. I can see her now, with her dark hair, large inviting lips and big boobs. The attention she received from the boys at school was akin to flies around a honey pot.

My early childhood memories also include an Italian who stood outside the school playground gate with a barrel organ and performing monkey. He used to draw a large crowd of schoolchildren, particularly to watch the antics of the monkey.

Life inevitably changed after 3 September 1939 when Britain declared war on Germany after Hitler ordered the invasion of Poland. Although I was only 6 years old at the time, I have distinct memories of the day, particularly of seeing an air-raid warden (preparations had been in motion for hostilities for some time) cycling along New City Road with a placard on his back saying 'War is Declared'.

The Second World War brought evacuation for Reg and Doreen to St Ives in Cornwall. At first, no host family wanted to take the siblings as a pair.

Both Doreen, 10 years old, and I were evacuated to St Ives in Cornwall in late 1939. Doreen was told that we must stick together. It was about a 14-hour journey by train from London Paddington to St Ives in the conditions that prevailed at the time, with other evacuee children being dropped off at various towns along the Great Western Railway route in Devon and Cornwall.

Old newsreels may show children with broad grins and talk of typically British stiff upper lips. For me it was certainly not a big adventure but a bad experience. We did not know when we would see our parents again. When we arrived at the end of the line at St Ives, the remaining children were lined up on the station platform where the local people were invited to choose which evacuees they wanted to take home. Nobody wanted to take Doreen and me as a pair.

The best we could get was accommodation on Draycott Terrace, overlooking Porthminster Beach. Doreen went to live with 'Aunty' Jane Uren, a spinster, who doted on her. I was not so lucky. I was two houses away with an elderly couple, Mr and Mrs Bunny, who treated me as a servant. At weekends, I had to polish the silver and clean and polish the stairs.

Doreen stayed at her St Ives home for the duration of the war. In my case, troubled and troublesome, it was a case of returning to Plaistow and then back again to St Ives on a number of occasions. One lady I stayed with, Miss Perkins, was really nice. Her house overlooked Clodgy View and the Atlantic.

Miss Perkins had a large map pinned on a wall, showing all the ships of the Royal Navy. If one was sunk, we would cross it off. Unfortunately, she was taken ill and I found myself back in Plaistow again. I had another trip down with my mother, who stayed in Cornwall for some time. At one stage my father got a weekend job, driving a coach down to Cornwall on a Saturday and dropping people off for their holidays, then staying overnight and seeing Doreen and me. Then he would take some people back on the Sunday or go back empty.

He saved my life on Porthminster Beach in an incident involving a pedallo. As a big wave hit, a couple of people jumped on the rear float. I fell off and went under the seat, with nobody missing me. Luckily my father, from the beach, saw it happen and, although he was wearing a suit, he came roaring into the water and carried me out. The next thing I remember is lying on the beach having the sea water pumped out of me. I was very afraid of the water after that for a long time. I still like to feel at least one foot on the sand when I'm swimming in the sea.

Overall, I think I blotted out a lot of the wartime period as they were traumatic years for me. Doreen fared somewhat better, staying as I said before with Aunty Janie for the duration and obtaining a scholarship to a local grammar school. She came home to Plaistow in 1945 and continued her education at Plaistow Grammar.

As far as we were concerned, Cornwall at that time was a very foreign part of England. The Cornish people were very different to us, almost like another race – a Celtic race really. I found it very difficult and disturbing and I didn't want to be treated the way in which I was treated. I'd been used to a warm, loving home and family. There were just the four of us at home, we were close and together with all our aunts and uncles formed a typical East London community family. In St Ives, all I had was a little room at the top of the house – the attic.

Of course, there were brighter spots to the experience. One of these was my meeting with a local farmer, George Bryant, who let me help milk the cows and ride his ponies from their field to the stables. At haymaking time, his sister Lily would walk up to the field at lunchtime and give us the biggest and the best Cornish pasties which she had baked that morning.

We stayed friends for many, many years and I had happy holidays at George's farm much later. The other good point was that Doreen got an evening/weekend job as a waitress at the Harbour Café, near the lifeboat slipway.

I was encouraged by Doreen and the staff to enter the kitchen and staff quarters by the back stairs and that's where I got my first and ever-lasting taste for lobster and shellfish. The Stenneck was my school but I don't remember very much about attending lessons. I do remember the fights in the playground with the locals. They would line up at one end of the playground, with us London boys at the other, then it was charge!

Venton Vision Farm. Reg's mother Sarah, farmer George Bryant, and Reg.

My experiences were obviously shared by a great many others who were children during the Second World War. In 1996, I joined the Evacuees Association which is run from Nottingham and issues a monthly newsletter. Michael Aspel OBE is a patron. On 3 September 1999, I went to Westminster Abbey for the Service of Thanksgiving to commemorate the 60th anniversary of the evacuation. Ironically, given that evacuation was supposed to safeguard the children, many evacuees were killed in raids and some were lost at sea on their way to Canada.

My schooling was seriously interfered with due to the coming and going between the East End and St Ives. I think that I actually spent most of those wartime years in Plaistow. I was certainly there for the Blitz and later for the V1 and V2 attacks launched by the Nazis. I used to go up onto a man-made landmark which gave a grandstand view of the action in the skies.

In the late 1800s, a very large sewer pipe was laid on the surface from North London, crossing many boroughs until it reached its outfall below Woolwich. It was then covered with earth and eventually grassed over. Known as The Greenway, it formed a good play area and an interesting walk.

As the highest ground in the locality, it was a great vantage point from which to watch the German bombers coming over with their escorts to bomb London's dockland – the King George, Royal Albert and other docks – and the City of London and also, of course, to see the Spitfires roaring into the attackers.

My dad was by then on war work and sometimes at night during the Blitz we would walk up to the sewer bank to watch. I remember the glow of the fires as London and the docks burned night after night, with the City of London itself on fire. There were so many bombs, it was horrendous.

At home, we had a wonderful Anderson shelter dugout in the back garden, with electricity, a couple of bunks and a store cupboard with emergency rations and torches. It was my job, every day, to fill up flagons with fresh water. Our Welsh collie, Bobby, could sense the imminent air-raid siren and later the V1 rockets before they arrived. He would sit in the garden, facing towards the river, sniffing the air. When we saw him do this, we knew it would not be long before the siren would sound and we would see the 'doodlebugs' coming over.

A 'doodlebug' was in fact a type of aeroplane packed with high explosive and powered by a rocket which was attached to the rear of the aircraft. It was powered by kerosene, with enough fuel to enable it to travel from northern France into the London area. When it ran out of fuel, it crashed to the ground, causing a great explosion.

We had a mobile ack-ack gun that would sometimes run up and down New City Road – I don't think it ever hit anything! I had a crystal set with headphones and an aerial which went outside the bedroom window. The 'cat's whisker' could be placed on different parts of the crystal and pick up different radio stations and signals. It was not uncommon to hear Lord Haw-Haw, the English traitor who broadcast from Germany in a bid to undermine the morale of his fellow countrymen. Following the end of the war and the collapse of the Third Reich he was hanged for treason.

I have mentioned already that my education was inevitably disrupted by wartime events and at one period there was no schooling available at New City Road School. My schooling had begun here at the age of 4, in the Infants department, where I remember getting half a pint of milk in the morning and half a pint again in the afternoon, before we had a nap on camp beds.

When the school was forced to close, small classes were held in private homes and indeed my parents had one of their rooms set aside for teaching purposes. As it did not involve my class, I didn't have the experience of attending school in my own home.

I was actually at New City Road School on the occasion in 1944, just before nine in the morning, when a V2 dropped in nearby Boundary Road. A small group of us in the playground were about to go across to a baker's shop, Dilliways, when the rocket exploded. There were no air-raid warnings for the V2 as it was faster than sound. The rocket, full of explosive, was again fired from northern France and reached a high altitude before descending on London and causing great loss of life.

I remember there was a tremendous explosion and the whole playground was covered in bricks and dust. A couple of the boys were hit by debris and I received burns to my legs from vitrol, the fuel used to power the rocket. This incident resulted in a trip to St Mary's Hospital in Plaistow for treatment.

Another vivid wartime memory is of the convoys of troops, mainly American (they would throw us sweets and gum), and armoured vehicles travelling down High Street North and High Street South to the docks, ready for embarkation for the invasion and liberation of France in 1944.

My father had seen service in the First World War, in Mesopotamia (now Iraq) as a whole and Baghdad in particular, but was too old to serve in the Second World War. Both my parents were hardworking all their lives and wartime made particular demands on those serving on the home front.

During one part of the war, my father worked in London for a firm making bomb carriers, spraying them with red oxide. My mother had a job at Pearks Grocery and Provisions in High Street North, East Ham. This helped to ensure we never went short of food as there was always some lady who didn't eat something and who would give her rations to my mum.

When the war ended, my horizons began to broaden. On many Sundays in that period, I would take a sixpenny (two and a half pence) all-day tram ticket with a friend named Cliff Short. The ticket allowed us to change trams as often as we wished. We would travel up to London and visit museums, which still had sandbags stacked against their doors and windows for protection against bomb blast.

I also joined the Odeon Club at the Boleyn which showed films on Saturday mornings. I made the club's football team as goalkeeper but after letting in too many goals at matches played at Dagenham and Romford I was replaced. At this time I also used to go to watch West Ham Football Club, where my particular favourites were the goalkeeper, Harry Medhurst, and the Corbett brothers. Harry Corbett could throw the ball from the touchline straight into the goal mouth ready for it to be nodded into the net.

There were responsibilities at home after school finished at 3.30 p.m. My mother, who was working, would leave me a list of what to do when I got home. Turn the oven on at 5 p.m. on regulo 5, at 5.45 put the pie in the oven and so on, so that by the time she got home, my father and I could have a hot meal.

It's surprising how much detail your memory retains after so many years!

Whilst I was still at school, I had a paper round based at a shop on the corner of Upton Road and Tunmarsh Lane. The titles on my list of deliveries included the *Daily Express*, *Daily Mirror* and, on Sundays, *The People* and the now vanished *News of the World*. Occasionally there was a horrendous mix-up. If I delivered the wrong paper at the first house I visited, it meant that everyone else got the wrong paper too.

This happened to me more than once, as I was always in a rush to finish my round and get off to school. The paper round earned me the sum of £35 which before too long would play a vital role in helping me to fulfil an ambition and set me on the road to my life in speedway.

Another friend, Cyril Hill, and I went on a week's holiday, cycling to Brighton, where we slept on the beach. We then cycled to Portsmouth and took the ferry over to the Isle of Wight. We cycled around the island and then all the way home to West Ham. Much later in life, when Cyril told his son about our holiday, the boy demanded to know how we got back home. When his son goes for a 30-mile cycle ride with friends, they have a van to pick them up from their destination. In addition, Cyril and I used to cycle to Southend and back, almost a 50-mile round trip, most weekends in the summer, travelling by way of the very steep Bread and Cheese Hill on the A13 at Benfleet.

In 1945, it was time for me to leave elementary school and make the step up to Burke Secondary Modern, formerly known as Balaam Street School. Here again there were distractions from the daily routine of lessons. One of the masters, a Mr Jenkins and Miss Haswell, the music teacher, were having an affair. We knew they were up to something because the curtains in the classroom were drawn at break time and lunchtime and some of us would creep back to do what we could to see what was going on.

Miss Waring was the headmistress and Mr Mitchell the headmaster. Burke was very hot on the three Ps as opposed to the three Rs – Pride in Personal Presentation. We would be inspected, with our hands and fingernails examined. We had to roll up our shirt sleeves to expose our elbows to check if there was any sign of a tidemark, and our posture was also assessed.

The three Ps was something I could excel in. I couldn't do all the paperwork involved in the lessons and I was very average academically. Sport did interest me and I represented the school in high jump, long jump and hop, step and jump.

Life at this period was full of new and sometimes baffling experiences. Opposite the newsagents where I worked was Harry Brooks' barber shop. I used to visit this establishment for a haircut and listen to Harry ask the adults if they required 'anything for the weekend, Sir?' I was very young at the time because I didn't know what he meant. The signs on the walls advertising Durex and Ona meant nothing to me.

In 1947, I started my first 'business' with a pal, Charlie Oates (not the speedway rider from Liverpool). We saw an advertisement in the *Sunday People* for plastic watch straps, which needed putting together before being sold. We sent off for a few hundred of them, made ourselves a tray each with a strap around our necks (like the cinema usherette selling ice cream) and set off for Petticoat Lane, where we walked up and down shouting 'watch straps, watch straps'.

We did sell a few but by the time we had had a mug of tea, ham roll and our bus fare home, we were well out of pocket on the first day's take. I think we very soon realised there was a very, very limited market.

Charlie, a few of the other local boys and I had an excursion one evening up to Soho, looking at the prostitutes. After asking how much it was, we decided that we could raise £1 between us and one of us could have a bunk up. We pooled the money and tossed the coin.

I was the winner but declined to go because I had on my best suit and it was a stand-up job against the church wall in Brewer Street. I passed my good fortune on to one of the boys and the rest of us watched while he had the knee-trembler.

I did a couple of years at Burke Secondary Modern, leaving in 1948 at the age of 15. When I said a final goodbye to Miss Waring and Mr Mitchell they may have regretted that I had not done better at lessons but they wished me well all the same.

On leaving school I started what was to prove both my first and just about my only job. I started work in the garage of Scruttons, Stevedores and Dockers, just off Humberstone Road in Plaistow. The firm had a fleet of shiny black Austin 16s, all chauffeur-driven, to take the bosses from the City offices down to the docks.

The foreman, Bill Bentall, would let me shunt the cars around and fill them up with

Two smart young fellas; the red-haired Charlie Oates (left) and Reg Fearman with Charlie carrying the tray from which the duo sold watchstraps in Petticoat Lane.

Mr Mitchell and Miss Waring, headmaster and headmistress at Burke Secondary Modern.

petrol from their own pump. He used to strut across the yard in his blue overalls that always seemed to be about six inches short of his shoes. He would push his horn-rimmed glasses up his nose and, giving it a twitch, say, 'Reg, you'd better do that again.' A really good fellow at the firm was a chauffeur named Jack who used to chase me around the premises.

COUNTY BOROUGH OF WEST HAM

EDUCATION DEPARTMENT.

✻

TESTIMONIAL

Burke County Modern School
Balaam St. E. 13
July 31ˢᵗ 1948

Reginald Fearman has been a pupil at this school since it opened in September 1945.

He is intelligent, and his school work is of a good standard. He is capable of expressing himself well and clearly, and can work well when his interest is aroused. He is very enthusiastic about sport, particularly speedway racing for which he is already training.

In manner he is courteous and polite. He is usually willing to help when he recognises the need. He is quite capable of taking a lead and acting on his own initiative.

He has always been truthful and obedient at school.

A. G. Waring

S. H. Mitchell
Headmaster

Sch. 2209. T8/L. 11/44.

Reg's school leaving report from Burke Secondary Modern.

My wages at Scruttons were about £1 15s a week, or £1.75p in new money. When the son of the owner, Philip Scrutton, took over the business he treated me very well. But after I had been at work for a short time or so, my life took a major step forward and being a wage slave was about to become a thing of the past.

My final school report had mentioned, more or less in passing, that I had a great interest in speedway racing. The teachers who wrote that report could hardly have realised at the time they put pen to paper what a huge impact the sport was to have on my life only a relatively short time after I had walked through the gates of the school for the last time.

Growing up. Sister Doreen and Reg pictured with their mother during the late 1940s.

CHAPTER TWO

THE LURE
OF SPEEDWAY

Apart from a return to a normal life and the greater independence that comes naturally as you grow up, the end of the Second World War brought another major factor into my life.

I mentioned in the previous chapter how my parents had watched speedway racing at West Ham Stadium in the 1930s and how, when league racing resumed at Custom House in 1946, both Doreen and myself were given our introduction to a sport which, from hearing so many stories about the pre-war exploits, was already in my blood.

Speedway has always been a family pastime and that was certainly true as far as the Fearmans were concerned. I would go along to the stadium straight from school and, at a time when the Hammers attracted regular crowds of at least 40,000 people, would take my place in a queue that was already substantial at 3.45 in the afternoon, hours before the tapes were due to go up for the first race.

It was my job to save places in the queue for Mum, Dad and Doreen. No one seemed to mind about the children saving places for the rest of the family. You might start off being in a queue of seventy people and end up, when the families arrived, being 270. I would then nip off round the back of the stadium and bunk in under the boundary fence with a lot of other boys.

The event that perhaps more than any other changed my life occurred just before the start of the 1947 speedway season, the second of the post-war era. In 1946, when league racing resumed on a limited basis, travel difficulties meant that both the pre-war overseas stars, eager to return, and the young newcomers from the dominions who were keen to break into the game in Britain, had been unable to take their places.

West Ham's Custom House Stadium where Reg Fearman's love of speedway began.

The arrival of Aub Lawson (left) and Cliff Watson to live at the Fearman family home changed Reg's life for ever.

That was all due to change in 1947 and I was to find myself excitingly close to the action and to the men who thrilled the vast crowds at Custom House and elsewhere.

Betty Clifford, a friend of Doreen who worked in the speedway office at West Ham, arrived on my parents' doorstep to ask if we could put up a young Australian speedway rider called Cliff Watson who had just arrived to race for West Ham. They readily agreed.

A few weeks later, Cliff said that a friend of his, Aub Lawson, was also coming from Australia to ride for the Hammers. Could Aub share his room? The answer again was yes. Cliff and Aub were to stay with the Fearman family for three English seasons, going home to Australia each October.

Aub had made his speedway debut in Britain in 1939, riding for the Wembley Lions. He took a great interest in me and in the late 1940s became my mentor when he realised that I was determined to become a speedway rider myself. Aub had a great interest in helping people and among those who benefited from his knowledge were fellow Australians like Jackie Gates, Ted Argall, Allan Quinn and his foster brother, Don Lawson.

He also tried to help young British talent, such as Frank Bettis and Wally Green. Both enjoyed success in speedway, particularly Wally, who, as a West Ham rider, finished second in the 1950 World Final. Although Wally was as old as Aub, he was just starting out in the game. Aub was there at Wednesday morning practise sessions, helping Wally find some extra speed out of the starting gate.

By the time Aub and Cliff Watson came into my life, I was a 'skid-kid', competing in the post-war craze of cycle speedway which, over the years, was to produce so many riders for the motorised version. I would come home from a meeting filthy dirty in my dad's old overalls which had been cut down to size.

In October 1947, at the end of the speedway season and before he returned down under, Aub obtained on loan from his pre-war track at Wembley two 1928 Douglas dirt-track racing machines which ran on petrol.

'Here you are, Junior, practise on these during the winter and see how you go,' was Aub's instruction. Although I was only 14½ years old, I needed no further encouragement. I rode those machines mainly on the Beckton cycle speedway track, opposite the Beckton Gasworks on the A13.

Reg, a fully fledged member of the West Ham Speedway Team in 1949.

Sometimes a man would stop in his tipper lorry and siphon a gallon of petrol from his truck and give it to me. I found out much later that the man was Sid Clarke who had raced for Harringay. Much later in life, he and I would reminisce about those days at Veteran Speedway Riders' Association (now World Speedway Riders' Association) lunches.

When the new speedway season opened at West Ham in March 1948, a track was constructed in the stadium car park and a training school introduced. I rode the Douglas machines around the new track and then, in May of the same year, my parents bought a JAP machine from Cliff Watson for £150.

This meant that on Wednesday mornings, before going to school, I was able to practise on the real thing – the big, 440 yards, silver sand Custom House track – at the regular practise sessions which followed the Tuesday night Hammers' meetings.

I also had a run out at the Rye House training track in Hertfordshire, riding both the Douglas and the JAP. These sessions took place before the Rye House Sunday afternoon meetings, a timing chosen so as not to interfere with local church services. At 4 p.m. the local vicar would give a sermon from the centre green, which I guess was all part of the deal.

Cliff Watson introduces Reg to the JAP machine in 1948.

The meetings were staged by Australian international, Dickie Case, who owned the track and the famous local pub, partnered by George Kaye, who also was the promoter/manager at Harringay.

I had my first competitive race in public at Rye House on 1 August 1948, aged 15 years and 3 months. The meeting was for the Holiday Cup. I scored 11 points and remember feeling very confident. Looking back, I believed for a long time that I was then immediately banned by the speedway authorities for riding under the minimum age of 16. I have since seen a reference to the fact that I raced for Rye House v The Rest in October that year, again scoring a few points.

Now mounted on a more modern JAP machine, Reg (right) practises with Cliff Watson in 1948.

A cartoonist captured the moment when Reg, on his 16th birthday, received his racing licence from injured Hammers' skipper Eric Chitty on the centre green at West Ham.

My legal speedway career began at West Ham in 1949. On my 16th birthday, 26 April, Eric Chitty, the captain of the Hammers, presented me with my racing licence in front of 40,000 West Ham fans. What a thrill!

Eric had returned in March from Australia on crutches. He had suffered a badly broken leg at the Brisbane Exhibition Ground just before he was due to leave for England.

I have had the pleasure in later life of meeting Eric's son Ray and his wife Traudl, something to be covered in a subsequent chapter.

Shortly after receiving my licence, Amy, the wife of Tommy Croombs (the family was devoutly Roman Catholic) had a St Christopher blessed by the local priest and, without my knowing, my mother sewed it into my leathers – I suffered no serious injuries whilst racing. I still have the St Christopher.

When I joined West Ham, I was quite shy and didn't have an awful lot to say for myself. At this time, the great Custom House track was dominated by the likes of Eric Chitty, Malcolm Craven, Aub Lawson, Cliff Watson and Kid Curtis. Except for Cliff, all had raced before the war.

They had all seen service during the war years in Asia or Europe and were tough guys, men of the world. I was just a youngster of 16 years of age, sitting in the corner of the dressing rooms. I would look at these riders and think to myself, 'I'm after one of their jobs.'

I don't think they took a lot of notice of me at first. Before I even got my licence, I had already tried to learn as much as possible by going around the

The Chitty family at home in 1950. From left to right: Eric, Raymond, Carol Anne and Eugenie (Jeanie).

other London speedways. A Division One track operated every week night in the capital city at that time. Monday was Wimbledon, Tuesday West Ham, Wednesday New Cross, Thursday Wembley and Friday Harringay.

Fred 'Kid' Curtis was the West Ham reserve at the time I started out as a rider at Custom House and he knew it was his job I was after initially. He was very protective of his position.

West Ham and speedway in general was full of the most unlikely characters in the late 1940s. In many ways the sport had a 'romantic' air about it. Certainly for me, the great stadium at Custom House, which had a nominal capacity of 100,000 people and attracted speedway crowds of up to 80,000, always had the feeling of walking into the Roman Coliseum. The sheer vastness of the stadium and the tens of thousands of spectators made you feel like a Roman gladiator, with your speedway machine as the modern-day equivalent of a chariot.

One personality of the time, who practised and raced at Rye House and at High Beech, was Johnny Fry, who lived at the top of East Ham High St North where he and his wife Doreen had a pet shop. His real name was Ronald Wright and in addition to changing his name to Fry for speedway purposes he also called himself 'The Laughing Count' and 'The Frisco Kid'.

West Ham 1949. From left to right: Stan Greatrex (co-promoter), Wally Green, Malcolm Craven, Howdy Byford, Eric Chitty (on crutches), Trevor Davies, Cliff Watson, Kid Curtis, George Wilks, Frank Bettis, Reg Fearman. Aub Lawson is on the machine.

In 1949 petrol, like many other things, was still on ration. There was red petrol for trucks and white for cars. Johnny Fry put red petrol in the tank of his car, something which was against the law. One day, he came up East Ham High St South to Barking Road traffic lights where he was stopped by the police who proceeded to carry out a litmus test.

Johnny (or Ron) attempted to brazen it out by telling the policemen, 'I don't know how that got in there. I was on tow and the rope broke.' The officers felt the bonnet of his car and it was red hot. Johnny got three months in Pentonville Prison where I visited him during his stay.

My first taste of league racing came as a member of West Ham's Junior League side, along with Frank Bettis and a rider called Trevor Davis. During my first year of racing, I won the Conran Junior Trophy at the same one-off meeting which saw my hero and mentor, Aub Lawson, win the Conran Senior Trophy.

I was quite proud of sharing success with Aub and felt that, after all the encouragement he had given me, I had not let him down. He always called me 'Junior' and once said to me: 'You can have my money, you can have my car and you can have my motorbike – but leave my women alone.'

In 1949 Reg won the Junior Conran Trophy while mentor Aub Lawson lifted the Senior award. The trophies were presented by Mrs Conran.

One of the boys. Gathering around the pits brazier on a cold evening are Harringay
and West Ham riders (from left to right) Lloyd Goffe, Arthur Bush and Nobby Stock of the
Racers, Reg Fearman, Wally Green and Malcolm Craven of the Hammers.

He used to give me tips and I remember particularly one piece of advice: Aub
told me to make sure people remembered me after a meeting – 'Either score a
maximum or knock off their best rider.'

The West Ham fans knew Aub and Cliff lived at No. 137 New City Road
with my family and it was not unusual to find a small crowd standing outside the
house. Sometimes there might be as many as a dozen girls, known in that era as
Bobby Soxers. Mum and Dad would sometimes invite them in for a cup of tea.
Often, following a Tuesday evening speedway meeting at West Ham, a crowd
of riders and friends would make their way to our home for tea. We would arrive
home about 10.30 p.m. and Mum would make countless pots of tea and rounds
of cheese on toast while that evening's race meeting was discussed.

Aussie Jackie Gates from Sydney came to race in the UK in 1949. We became
good pals during that time and were never out of contact for more than sixty
years, right up until his sad death on 14 May 2012. Jack would stay with us in
West Ham whenever he could and we would visit speedway tracks in London
and take the odd trip to Rayleigh in Essex. We had heaps of fun.

At the time, Malcolm Craven had a beautiful cream Buick convertible,
a 1938/39 model, with a red interior. It attracted much attention, with even

Sister Doreen was Reg's biggest fan.

grown men drooling over it. Malcolm had a special parking place next to the main gate at West Ham and would arrive at the stadium with a lady named Vi, who lived near The Spotted Dog pub in Forest Gate.

Malcolm was married and lived at Hornchurch. He later obtained a divorce and married Vi. The couple eventually emigrated to Canada where they lived until their deaths. Malcolm had served in the Royal Navy during the Second World War and after the war took flying lessons and qualified as a pilot. He would sometimes fly himself and other riders from Southend Airport to Holland for weekend speedway meetings.

The West Ham manager during the immediate post-war years was the legendary former rider, Tiger Stevenson. I got on very well with him. He had captained the Hammers in their first-ever league match on 2 May 1929, at home to Coventry, and was still the skipper of the side in 1937 when West Ham won the National League Championship.

He was a nice man, a lovely chap, a gentleman. You listened to him about racing and how to look after the machine and about being focused. But I'd already learnt a lot and I always thought I could do better than the likes of Phil Bishop, Benny and Buddy King and Fred Curtis who were my chief rivals for a team place.

Although I was relatively tall for a speedway rider – 6ft 1in at my peak – I was never awkward or ungainly as can be seen from some of the action photographs of the time. I had good balance and a cultured racing style. One of my favourite photographs, of the many taken during my racing career, features me and Nobby Stock, the former Harringay rider.

In the shot Nobby is in front but I am lined up to pass him on the inside. Nobby is sitting down with

National League Division One action from the golden age of speedway. From left to right: Arthur Bush, Nobby Stock, Reg Fearman and, just behind, Howdy Byford.

his leg out, looking awkward. I am standing up and have positioned myself in an orthodox manner. It illustrates my riding style perfectly.

Having long legs never seemed to be a problem. My leg didn't get in the way as my handlebars were the right shape. On some occasions during my riding career I seemed to be able to see it all in slow motion in front of me. I could see where a rider was going to go in front of me and I knew exactly where I was going to pass him, long before we even got to the manoeuvre.

I worked things out. I now sit watching the Speedway Grand Prix on television shouting 'outside turn!' or 'get on the pendulum' or sometimes 'get in that bit of dirt – you have to pass the man in two laps'.

Two teenage stars with London Division One tracks. Reg (right) with Wimbledon's future World Champion Ronnie Moore.

It was whilst I was racing with West Ham in 1949 that I made my first visit to Wimbledon's Plough Lane track. As a 16 year old I looked quite young and prior to getting changed for racing, Ronnie Greene, the experienced and respected Dons promoter, personally ejected me from the pits into the car park, despite my protestations that I was a West Ham rider.

Fortunately, I got back in by courtesy of Aub Lawson. I can't remember how many points I got that night but I'm sure it wasn't many. Wimbledon was a small track, particularly compared to the wide open spaces of West Ham, and the safety fence used to come up and slap you in the face coming out of the pit corner.

I have fond memories of another of the classic London Division One tracks – New Cross. I think it was one of my favourites – small, banked and wide. I remember well in one race being in front of a very hard man, the New Cross rider Cyril Roger. When I looked over my shoulder I could see his eyes sticking out like organ stops and boy that made me go even quicker. I knew that if he caught me he would bundle me into the safety fence.

Joe Abbott was the first speedway rider I saw killed on the track. He was 48 years of age. West Ham was at Bradford Odsal on 1 July 1950. He crashed on the pit corner and suffered severe injuries. His death was instant. Joe Abbott was born in April 1902 at Burnley, Lancashire. He began his speedway career at Burnley in 1928. He was an England international between 1930 and 1939 and qualified for the World Final at Wembley in 1937. I was just 17 years of age and there were to be many more fatalities during my speedway career, both as a rider and a promoter.

Being a fully fledged member of the West Ham team served to broaden my horizons in other directions that simply enhanced my racing experience. During the 1949 season, a Speedway Riders' Association meeting took place on a Sunday at the Birmingham track at Perry Barr. The legendary Jack Parker, the top man at Belle Vue, was the SRA chairman and on that Sunday brought three girls down with him from Manchester and announced that they were 'available' in his vehicle in the car park.

A number of riders disappeared for short spells during the day. I believe one of the three was the girl who I was deemed responsible for making pregnant. I do remember going with the girl when West Ham were at Belle Vue on a Saturday evening in 1949, around the same time or perhaps a bit after the SRA meeting.

Her name was Margaret Joan Eyre and I did go to a corner of the Belle Vue Pleasure Grounds and lay down on the grass with her. However, I am not absolutely sure what actually took place. I was only 16 and, I think, still a virgin – I certainly can't remember anyone before. I had heard lots of sexual discussions in the changing rooms at various speedway tracks but my experience was zero. For all I know, I may have been having sex with her suspender belt!

Jack Parker.

It was in October 1949, when I was on holiday at Venton Vision Farm, Burthallen Lane, St Ives (owned by my friend from my evacuee days, George Bryant) that I received a telegram from my parents to say that I was wanted back home.

When I returned to London, I was told by my parents that they had had a visit from a Mr and Mrs Eyre and their daughter was saying that I had made her pregnant. What was I going to do about it? I believe her parents wanted a shotgun wedding.

The outcome was a paternity case in court at Ashton-under-Lyne in the summer of 1950. My parents had taken me to a London solicitor at the top of Queens Road, on the corner of Manor Park Road, where I made a statement. The solicitor subpoenaed Freddie Williams and Split Waterman, two of the riders who had disappeared during the course of that SRA meeting in Birmingham.

Of course, neither Freddie nor Split were going to own up to having had sex with anyone. Both were a good ten years older than me, had seen war service, and were far more worldly-wise.

The court decided, however, that I was the father of a child born to the local girl and duly awarded the paternity order against me.

Every week for sixteen years I had to send a postal order to Mr A. Platt, Clerk to the Justices, Ashton-under-Lyne, except when the army docked it out of my pay during my National Service.

There was an unexpected follow-up many years later. At the 1981 World Speedway Championship Final at Wembley my wife Joan, my son Gary and I were walking along the concourse towards the Royal Box when I was approached by a couple. It was no great surprise when the man said, 'Excuse me, Mr Fearman,' as it was not unusual for me to be stopped and asked a question or two.

I told Joan and Gary to go ahead and said that I would follow. It was then that the man said, 'I believe you are my father. I am David Eyre.'

My response was to tell him that this was not the place for a meeting and that I would meet him in London. He gave me a telephone number and I did arrange to meet him some time later. He told me that he was living in Essex and that he had been brought up believing his mother was his sister and his grandmother his mother.

This state of affairs had lasted for some thirty years until something happened which caused him to discover the truth about the arrangement. When we eventually met, I told him that I did not believe I was his father although the court in Ashton-under-Lyne had deemed it to be so. He told me he was working in the West End of London as a graphic designer. He phoned me once or twice after this meeting but there was no further contact.

In the late 1940s and early 1950s, speedway was a glamorous sport and was watched by crowds which were huge by today's standards. Riders were treated like pop stars and it was not surprising that incidents such as the one I have described should have occurred.

After the court appearance in 1950 it was back to the speedway tracks. And as the British season ended in the autumn of that year, the chance arose for me to spend the winter as part of an English international team in Australia under the guidance of Jack Parker.

The visit down under, with both happy and tragic memories, was to prove one of the most memorable of all my speedway experiences. It also gave me my first opportunity to visit Australia, the home of Aub Lawson, the man chiefly responsible for my start in speedway.

CHAPTER THREE

BROADENING
MY HORIZONS

Over the years since I first became aware of international sport, several new nations have been admitted to the Test cricket arena. Speedway also saw a major growth in international competition during my years in the sport as rider, promoter and administrator.

International sport really does broaden your horizons and I welcome the newcomers unreservedly. The emergence in speedway of the Russians and the Danes and the return of the United States as a major power undoubtedly raised standards and thrilled the fans.

Nevertheless, to someone of my generation, whether it be rugby, cricket or speedway, it is the international clashes between the Lion and the Kangaroo, between England and Australia, that really raises adrenalin levels.

Riding for the Lions in an international series in Australia in the English winter of 1950–51, at the tender age of 17, alongside teammates such as Jack Parker and in opposition to such legendary Aussies as Lionel Van Praag, Noel Watson and my mentor and hero Aub Lawson, to say nothing of the up-and-coming stars like Graham Warren and Ken Le Breton, was a great thrill and certainly one of the highlights of my career.

Even before setting out for Australia, Reg knew that the Sydney Showground, the stadium at the bottom corner of this photograph, was a daunting place to race. The top arena is the Sydney Sports Ground with the cricket ground in the centre.

It was to prove a controversial series in many ways and certainly an unsuccessful one on the track for the Lions.

I had my first taste of international competition at the end of the 1950 British season when my team, West Ham, and Wembley were invited to race at the Olympic Stadium in Stockholm, Sweden, and in the Norwegian capital of Oslo.

When I arrived back in London from the Scandinavia trip, I was thrilled and excited to learn that I had been chosen to race for the British Lions in the Test series down under that winter.

My mind was quickly focused on the job in hand as I had only a week or so to prepare myself and my equipment ready for departure. The Lions were due to race in seven Test matches and I knew that we would face conditions often very different to those we were used to at home in the National League.

Many of the Australian circuits had more than 500 or more yards to the lap whilst in Britain, West Ham was the largest track at 440 yards. I also knew that the Sydney Showground was a daunting place to race – more than 500 yards in length, narrow, banked and with a solid concrete wall as the safety barrier.

Belle Vue captain Jack Parker, who had raced in Australia on many previous occasions, was both captain and organiser of the touring team. I reported to Tilbury docks as instructed and boarded the SS *Strathnaver*, 28,000 tons displacement, which was quite large for a ship in those days.

Travel in the years immediately following the Second World War was difficult and, in real terms, not particularly cheap, unless you were a £10 emigrant to Australia on a one-way ticket. My cabin, shared with three others, was on the lowest deck, very close to the twin drive shafts. When we went through rough seas the propellers would come right out of the water and a terrific vibration would travel through the ship. Nevertheless, I later learnt that the cost of my return fare was £63.

It is important to remember that although the war had been over for five years, Britain was still suffering the consequences of the immense sacrifice its people had made to resist the Nazi/Japanese Axis.

Rationing of everyday items including food and fuel was not only in force during the war years but lasted to some degree up to 1954, nearly a decade after hostilities had ended. Ration books for food had been issued right from the start, in September 1939, and petrol rationing had also been introduced that year.

In many ways, things got worse as the war years progressed. Food allowances were very small, with each person being allowed 4 ounces of butter, 12 ounces of sugar, 4 ounces of bacon and ham, while the meat you could buy was limited to the value of 1s 10d – less than 10p in today's money.

The SS *Strathnaver* of the P&O Line which took Reg and the rest of the British Lions touring party to Australia in 1950.

Cheese began to be rationed in 1941 together with jam and marmalade (8 ounces per person per week and the essential British standby of tea eventually succumbed to rationing as well, in 1943). Agricultural workers, vital to the nation's survival, got a little extra.

In 1939, motorists had been allowed a basic petrol ration enough to take them 1,800 miles a year but in 1942 the basic ration ceased completely and the need to produce coupons as well as cash for fuel continued into the 1950s. I remember paying the huge sum of £1 a gallon for black-market petrol during my early speedway career, just to enable me to get from track to track.

Altogether, it could be pretty grim in Britain at the time and there was a mass exodus of people seeking a new life in Australia. Steamship berths to Australia were at a premium. Fortunately, the speedway fraternity had a friend, Harry Flack, who worked for Thomas Cook in London's Leadenhall Street.

Harry had the foresight each year to reserve a number of berths on ships of both the P&O and Orient Lines sailing in October from Tilbury to Sydney. For a crisp white fiver in a brown envelope, Harry could produce one of these berths for speedway people. When my first wife Joan and I went to New Zealand in 1954 the system was still in operation.

Harry Flack, as you might say, became attached to the speedway fraternity through marriage. In fact, it was his daughter Bridget who married Poole and Swindon rider, Ken Middleditch. The family link with speedway continues to this day through Bridget and Ken's son Neil, a former Poole and England rider, later team manager for the Dorset Pirates and England team manager.

With all the bustle of preparation behind me, I headed off with my teammates on the great adventure, sailing to the sun from the grey English weather and the sense of austerity everywhere.

We each had a cabin steward who made our bunks and cleaned our cabins daily and who, for a small fee, would also do one's washing. We were served three meals a day in the restaurant, although sometimes in rough weather all the food and crockery would slide across the tables and onto the floor. You can imagine the mess it made. The tables and chairs were chained to the floor – it was before stabilisers on the ships.

The *Strathnaver* sailed through the Bay of Biscay, well known as rough water, and called first at the Mediterranean ports of Marseilles in France and Naples in Italy. We were allowed ashore at both ports. In Marseilles, we had enough time to visit the shady parts around the dock area.

At Naples, we were allowed ashore for a few hours whilst the ship unloaded goods and took on water and provisions. Some of us took an excursion to the ruins of Pompeii which had been abandoned after being partially buried in ash and lava from the volcano, Mount Vesuvius, in the year AD 79.

The city, the playground of the Romans, was left forgotten until the mid-1700s when much excavation of the ruins commenced. Some aspects of the culture were distinctly erotic, including phallic worship, and a large collection of erotic objects and frescoes were found.

Some houses and bath houses had been preserved. At the entrance to one, our guide, for a few lira, showed us a fresco of a man with an extremely enlarged phallic organ. The fresco had been boxed in and was to be opened only by a guide. Priapus was the ancient god of sex and fertility. At Port Said, dozens of small boats carrying hawkers, loaded with carvings of animals, rugs, poofies and other items for sale, came out to the *Strathnaver* which was anchored in deep water.

A rope would be thrown up to the deck rail and be caught by a passenger. The bargaining would then start, with the item for sale being transported in a basket via the rope. Every lady was called Mrs Simpson and every man Mr McGregor.

It was great fun, not only to buy but to watch the antics of others. And there were often antics galore. Even at this time there had been a long tradition in speedway, dating back to the earliest days of the sport in the late 1920s and early 1930s, for the riders to enjoy themselves on board ship, occasionally to excess. There were regular dances on deck, with the ship's orchestra in attendance, and sometimes a fancy dress competition.

On my first voyage, Wembley's New Zealander Bruce Abernethy decided to take part dressed as an angel. He made a halo and, dressed in a white sheet and with a rope tied around his waist, arranged for me and other riders to lower him through a hatchway.

He was hovering some feet above the orchestra when he yelled to us to let him go as the rope was cutting into him. This we did, scattering the orchestra, much to their displeasure. Such were Abernethy's pranks that he was eventually banned from all shipping lines operating between Australia, New Zealand and Britain.

His family, from Wellington, New Zealand, was well-off as his father owned the Chukka shirts company, and although he enjoyed considerable success on the track, he seemed to enjoy the fun and the social side of being a rider just as much.

Our journey continued through the Suez Canal to the Red Sea and on to Aden. At each port we were allowed off the ship for a few hours to do some sightseeing. We then crossed the Arabian Sea to Bombay (known today as Mumbai). I had never seen such squalor – children were purposely maimed by their parents to become professional beggars, an example being an arm or leg tied to the upper arm or leg so as the baby grew, the deformity grew with it.

On the voyage to Australia Reg cemented a firm and lasting friendship with Jackie Gates, one of the Aussie riders who was to be an opponent in the Test series.

We sailed down the coast of India to Ceylon (now Sri Lanka), with one of the new Test cricket teams I mentioned at the start of this chapter, to the city of Colombo. Some of us travelled by taxi up into the hills to the Mount Lavinia Hotel and the nearby tea sheds where the tea leaves were sorted from the dust by women sitting on the floor, wafting large fans across the tea and blowing the dust into the corners of the building.

There were plenty of opportunities for us to keep fit aboard the *Strathnaver*. We would swim in the pool, play deck quoits and deck tennis. There was a greasy pole competition with a pole placed across the pool, competitors approaching each other from opposite sides. When they met in the middle, they would flail each other with pillows until one (or sometimes both) took a ducking.

The famous Harbour Bridge provided Reg with his first view of Sydney.

The ceremony of crossing the line was a great occasion for any traveller crossing the equator in the Indian Ocean for the first time. A crew member dressed as Neptune would introduce the traveller to the captain who would present him or her with a scroll certificate to mark the occasion.

There was a daily sweepstake to guess the number of nautical miles the ship had travelled in the previous 24 hours. I remember it was usually somewhere between 480 and 520.

We completed our crossing of the Indian Ocean and made our first landfall in Australia at Fremantle (the port for Perth). We just gawped at the shops which were full of food, with meat, fruit and vegetables galore. No rationing here! The sun was hot and all the shops had a protective solid awning coming out from the buildings covering the pavements.

That was my first impression of Australia – wonderful. We sailed on to Adelaide and Melbourne and then to Sydney, through the North and South Heads of Sydney Harbour, catching our first glimpse of the famous Harbour Bridge.

What a magnificent five weeks' experience at sea it was for a 17 year old from London's East End. Because I was only 17, my parents had arranged with Aub Lawson that I should stay with his mother and his foster brother Don at Willoughby on the North Shore, whereas the rest of the team were at the Olympic Hotel opposite Centennial Park, much nearer central Sydney.

Ambassadors for Britain. Reg, his sister Doreen (left) and Eric Williams' wife Helen pictured at Alan Gerrard's home in Sydney, gathered around the pianola played by Eric Williams.

On arrival in Sydney, the British Lions were guests of Lord Mayor O'Dea who invited us to the Town Hall for tea and presented us all with a beautiful photographic book depicting the sights of the city.

Many years later, I attempted to take my second wife Eileen inside the Town Hall. We discovered a much less decorous occasion than my 1950 tea party. It was Mardi Gras and we could only get as far as being able to look through the main door. We saw couples, man and man, woman and woman, dancing together. Not our scene.

Altogether, the Australian hospitality was wonderful as was the country – blue skies, sunshine, golden beaches and surf at Bondi and many other beaches. There seemed no shortage of anything and dreary England seemed so far away.

Not that the Australians had things easy in the war. Far from it. Apart from the fact that Australian troops, sailors and airmen had served with distinction in every theatre of war, along with their counterparts from the other dominions – Canada, New Zealand, South Africa, India and many other parts of what was then the British Empire – the country suffered actual attack.

The Japanese carried out air raids on Darwin in Australia's Northern Territory where some 250 people were killed. Australian and Allied forces were sent to reinforce the defence on that far northern coast and to repel the Japanese.

A bit different from the luxurious transport enjoyed by modern speedway riders.
Reg moved his machine around in a motorcycle sidecar while in Australia.

The Australian rider Jackie Gates and I became good pals despite the fact that we were on opposite sides on the track. It was in Sydney that I met Jack's mum, sister Vera and grandpa (Jack's father had been killed during a jailbreak – he was a warder – when Jack was quite young).

I would stay at Randwick, a suburb of Sydney, with Jack and his family when time permitted, and it was Jack who taught me to surf off Bondi Beach. He also introduced me to my first nudist beach, known as Lady Jane, which was in a secluded cove. The only access was down an iron rung ladder, which I think was a relic from the war years as an army camp was nearby.

We managed the ladder and picked our spot to lay out our towels – not too near other people. When I did look around, it would seem that the majority of those who had taken off their clothes should really have kept them on. We eventually disrobed and ran into the sea. Swimming nearby was a woman who had the most beautiful face and jet black hair. I said to Jack, 'Let's wait until she leaves the water and walks up the beach, I bet she's gorgeous.' What a disappointment! She definitely was one of those who should have kept her clothes on …

Lest it seem that the actual speedway has so far taken a back seat in this account of my first Australian trip, let me reassure you that there is plenty to come about the racing in the Aussie season of 1950/51.

The stories from the voyage and the accounts of the social life I experienced in Sydney and elsewhere are, nevertheless, of great importance. They serve to show how riders, in the days when travel took time and patience, worked and played together as a tight-knit group and how the speedway community worldwide has always extended the most generous hospitality to visitors – at least off the track.

It is still happily the case today, as both globe-trotting former riders and their wives and the many British riders who have chosen in later life to make their homes down under will gladly testify.

On the track, as I discovered both in 1950–51 and particularly on a later visit as manager of a British team, the hospitality was equally warm but in a rather different sense.

CHAPTER FOUR

CONTROVERSY DOWN UNDER

I have written a great deal already about the warmth of Australian hospitality. It is a subject to which I shall certainly return as this story of my life unfolds.

On the speedway track in 1950 and 1951, the Australian speedway team certainly made things hot, in a totally different sense, for me and the other members of the British Lions team.

I am sorry to say that the British Lions were defeated by the Aussies by seven matches to none. Looking back, I feel my own contribution and performance were a great let down to the side. I do believe that my young age and lack of experience, both on the track and where engine tuning was concerned, had a lot to do with it. In particular, the engine tuning let me down.

I can remember having the twist grip screwed round to the stop and still the opposition raced away from me. There were some very good Australian engine tuners but they were not prepared to tune a Pom's engine. It has often been said that some Australian riders used oversized engines, i.e more than the regulation 500cc. Some riders who could not perform very well on English tracks simply flew on the vast Australian circuits.

An ace tuner, Charlie Ogden, once said in an interview that he had made an oversized engine for Lionel Van Praag without Lionel knowing it. Lionel's form had dropped off so Charlie Ogden boosted Lionel's confidence with a number of race wins on that engine then put him back on a 500cc motor.

The 1950–51 Lions touring party, as originally selected, consisted of Jack Parker of Belle Vue, Eric Williams of Wembley, Eddie Rigg of Bradford, Tommy Miller from Glasgow, Bob Fletcher of Coventry, Derek Tailby (also Coventry), myself and Ron Mason from Belle Vue. There was at the time, and has been subsequently, criticism of the relative inexperience of a fair proportion of the English Lions side, with Australian commentators complaining that the British Board of Control was not attaching sufficient importance to its touring side.

I suppose that my initial winter in Australian speedway taught me quite a lot. I learnt about speedway politics, about how to keep up your morale when part of a losing side and, sadly, something about the darker and dangerous side of speedway racing.

The pattern for the series, and I suppose for my own contribution, was set in the first match on 16 December 1950 at the Speedway Royale in Sydney. An English rider visiting Australia as a freelance, Fred Yates, had to be drafted in as reserve after Belle Vue's Ron Mason decided at the last minute not to travel out from the UK. Fred Yates was attached to Coventry.

Australia won 63–45, with 18 points from Aub Lawson, 17 from Graham Warren and 11 from Ken Le Breton, supported by former World Champion Lionel Van Praag with 7. Jack Parker kept the Union Jack flying with 14 points, backed up by 10 apiece from Eddie Rigg and Eric Williams. I failed to score in my only race of the night while Fred Yates did not even get a ride.

We had to wait until after Christmas and the New Year to get another chance to twist the Kangaroo's tail. The venue on 3 January was Sydney's other track, at the Sports Ground. It proved to be another fairly comprehensive defeat for the Lions although the match result 65–42 to Australia was completely overwhelmed by the incident, in the final heat, that caused the death of Australian star Ken Le Breton.

Getting to grips with Australian tracks. Eddie Rigg, Eric Williams, Tommy Miller and Reg Fearman practise at Sydney Sports Ground prior to getting down to competitive racing.

The England team for the first Test in Sydney. From left to right: Jack Parker, Derek Tailby, Reg Fearman, Eric Williams, Eddie Rigg, Bob Fletcher and Tommy Miller.

Up to that point in the match the big story seemed to be the emergence as a Test star of my friend, Jackie Gates, a relative unknown, who scored 15 points, the same tally as Aub Lawson, who was unbeaten by an opponent. Parker, Rigg and Williams again proved the mainstays for England although I did score my first Ashes point.

The Le Breton crash was at the time and, even today, controversial. I was an eyewitness and, more than sixty years after the event, it is something people still want to question me about. It was the saddest episode of the tour without a doubt.

Sydney Sports Ground was a fast, banked track with a solid wooden safety fence. The fatal race was the last heat of the night and the crash occurred on the last bend of the last lap. Contemporary reports speak of Le Breton attempting to cut through on the inside of Eddie Rigg, who was attempting to shepherd teammate Bob Fletcher home: 'Le Breton seemed to hit his opponent's rear wheel,' wrote Frank Assenza, an Australian contributor to speedway's equivalent of *Wisden* at the time, the famous *Stenner's Speedway Annual*. 'Both were thrown into the fence. Le Breton died later in hospital from a fractured skull.'

Much has been written about the event, with the controversy fuelled by suggestions of a feud between Rigg and Le Breton, caused by an incident in the first Test match of the series in December 1950.

I have to say that feuds and even vendettas did take place between speedway riders, certainly between those who raced in the 1940s and '50s. We shall never know for certain whether or not the fateful incident between Rigg and Le Breton at the Sports Ground in Sydney was a pure accident.

The Australian team for the second Test of the series in January 1951. Back row, from left to right: Lionel Van Praag, Dick Seers, Aub Lawson, Cec Weatherley (manager), Jack Arnfield, Keith Ryan. Kneeling at the front are Lionel Levy, Ken le Breton and Jackie Gates.

My own memory of the race tells me that Jackie Gates flew from the tapes and led from start to finish, followed by Bob Fletcher. I was standing with Jack Parker on the centre green, opposite the pit gates, and had a good view of the track action.

Rigg was in front of Le Breton and was roughly centre track. Le Breton made a move to take Rigg on the outside and moved a little higher towards the fence. It was all over in a split second. Le Breton's front wheel collected Rigg's rear wheel and Ken was pitched into the solid wooden fence. The impact also caused Rigg to crash.

A well-known Australian journalist and historian, Jim Shepherd, contends that it was a simple error of judgement. Jackie Gates, Le Breton's racing partner, had his own take on the circumstances. Jackie said that before the race Le Breton said to him, 'Jack, you take the number one gate position, as it is the best this evening. I'm too tired to do any anything, I'm so tired.'

It has to be said that neither of my two very good friends whom I have quoted on the subject, Jim Shepherd nor Jackie Gates, knew of any feud between Rigg and Le Breton.

A crucial aspect of the affair is that neither man was present in the British camp at Sydney Royale during the first Test in December. A photograph taken at that meeting clearly shows Le Breton boring underneath Rigg and about to rub his front wheel against the English rider's left leg.

This was an act frequently performed to make a rider lift his leg and move out of the way. It could be painful and result in a friction burn. What better reason for a feud? I was there on the night and was a witness to the oath that Rigg uttered on returning to the pits: 'I'll have the bastard.'

Now, these are comments that surely hundreds of speedway riders have uttered in the past. Whilst I do not dispute Jim Shepherd's description of the collision in the last race of the second Test at the Show Ground, with Le Breton hitting Rigg's rear wheel, I wondered at the time and wonder still if Ken went for a gap that suddenly closed? Jim Shepherd was unable to explain it.

Let's face it, we have all closed the gap or ridden another rider out wide to protect our position, although I am sure no one has ever done so with intent to maim another rider. If Eddie Rigg did close the gap or pull down on Le Breton, it was certainly with no intent of such a drastic result.

Both Eddie Rigg and Jackie Gates were pallbearers at Ken Le Breton's funeral.

The verdict of the coroner when the inquest into the death was held was that it was an accident. That has been the usual verdict in such cases.

I stick to my belief that we shall never know for absolute certain what really occurred. The evidence from people who were there on the night and the coroner's verdict do not mean that a feud did not exist.

Was there an incident between Ken Le Breton and Eddie Rigg in the first Test match of the series? This is a picture from that match featuring both of the riders. Lionel Van Praag leads the field, with Rigg managing to hold off a challenge from Le Breton, in his trademark white leathers.

Ken Le Breton (second from right) with Australian teammates before the fatal crash in the second Test at Sydney. The other riders are, from left to right: Dick Seers, Lionel Van Praag, Keith Ryan and, talking to Le Breton, Jackie Gates.

I was involved as rider and promoter for almost forty years and I think I've seen it all. Hard riding, dirty riding, cheating, you name it. Knocking someone off or running them out of track is all part of the game. It has always happened, even today at the top level in the World Championship Grand Prix.

But, having said that, no one, including Eddie Rigg, would have desired fatal consequences. Fatalities are part of speedway, as is serious and even paralysing injury. In the 1930s, '40s and '50s, many speedway riders died as a result of track injuries, mainly to the head. There is a record of the names of those who have died – some 180 since 1928.

In the 1960s, a full-face crash helmet was introduced to replace the 'pudding-type helmet' that we all wore during my racing career. The result of this and other safety measures is that, happily, fatalities today are rare. Ironically, the safety measures and the improved quality of initial medical attention mean that although they do not die, very many speedway riders are left either paraplegic or quadriplegic. There are far too many former riders in wheelchairs today.

Incidents like the one that led to the death of Ken Le Breton before my eyes in Sydney will always prompt discussion and lead to varied opinions.

And so the 1950–51 series continued. The show, as they say, must go on.

Jack Parker boosted English hearts with a win in the Australian four-lap championship at Sydney Sports Ground on 12 January. The light-hearted side to this contest was due to the fact that the normal racing distance on the big Australian tracks is over three laps. Aub Lawson, who beat Parker in heat 20, and was just a point behind the Englishman at the end of the meeting, had eased up in an earlier race allowing Jackie Gates and Arthur Payne to pass him. Aub confessed after the meeting, when it was clear that the lapse had cost him the title, 'I must have been day-dreaming.'

Australian supremacy was restored in the third Test at the Sydney Royale, which finished 60–48 in favour of the home side. Derek Tailby had broken a thumb in the previous Test and was replaced by Ron Clarke, flown across Australia from a racing engagement in Perth, and Eric Williams missed the match, suffering from tonsillitis.

Happier times. Ken Le Breton and his Alsatian dog at his home in Sydney.

Keeping up morale when a team is struggling is vital. There was hardly a dull moment with the irrepressible Bruce Abernethy (centre) around. Eric Williams and Reg appreciate the joke.

The show moved on to Bathurst in New South Wales but there was no let-up for the English Lions, Australia winning 67–40. Jack Parker was unbeaten but Tommy Miller, Eddie Rigg and Eric Williams had to ride borrowed machines, their own having been damaged in a road accident on the way to the track. To add to the team's troubles, Rigg had badly gashed a leg in the incident when thrown against the windscreen of the vehicle in which they were travelling and retired after one race. I had my best performance of the series, scoring 5 points from reserve.

The fifth Test was in Adelaide and England, still without Eddie Rigg, put up a stern fight in losing 58.5 points to 49.5, with just a six-man team. It goes without saying that Jack Parker was yet again England's spearhead.

The penultimate Test was in Brisbane and England again had selection problems. Rigg was still missing and Clarke had been recalled to Perth. This time, Jack Parker was riding a borrowed machine. He scored 16 of England's points but was beaten by Charlie Spinks and local star Keith Gurtner.

The series ended in Sydney, at the Royale, on 10 February. Australia completed the whitewash with a 60–48 victory. After the meeting, Sydney promoter Frank Arthur, himself a former Test star for Australia, revealed that just 4,000 people had watched the final meeting. He blamed the low attendance on daylight racing, caused by a ban on the use of electricity for overnight sport.

Apart from the controversy, the death of Le Breton, and the accidents and injuries along the way, the tour provided some memorable moments, quite apart from the racing.

For the Test matches at Adelaide and Brisbane, we flew from Mascot Airport in Sydney. Lionel Van Praag was contracted by the promoters to take the Lions team and some of the Aussies. In addition to being a still-active rider in 1951, Lionel, the first-ever World Speedway Champion – he won the title at Wembley in 1936 – ran his own air cargo business, using an ex-wartime aeroplane, a Lockheed Hudson, as transport. The gun turrets had been removed and the inside stripped out to make way for the cargo that Lionel was transporting around the country.

On the day, we duly arrived at Mascot for our flight with Lionel to Adelaide, complete with speedway machines, spare wheels, racing leathers and toolboxes. Lionel did a headcount – there were fifteen of us all told – looked at all of the equipment and said some of the toolboxes would have to be left behind as we would be too heavy with some twelve speedway machines on board.

The machines went on board, with the agreed toolboxes and spares, with the bikes loaded down one side of the aeroplane, strapped to each other and to the side of the aircraft. On the opposite side were two wooden benches for us, the riders, 'valuable cargo', to sit. No seat belts, nothing. I thought all aeroplanes were like this, especially in Australia.

Worse was to come. When we taxied to the end of the runway and Lionel had clearance from the Control Tower, above the noise of the engines he shouted and beckoned us all to join him just behind the cockpit and hold on to each other tightly. This action was necessary so that when the plane was hurtling down the runway Lionel, by moving the control column backwards and forwards, could get the tail wheel off the ground.

The old plane seemed to lumber down the runway and bounced several times, just managing to get airborne before the end of the runway. I swear to this day that, as we passed over the water in Botany Bay, some fishermen in their boats actually ducked. The old plane staggered up to about 10,000ft and when we were on course for Adelaide, Lionel asked his female co-pilot and navigator to vacate her seat. He called us up, one at a time, to take control of the plane.

I thought what a great thrill it was, me sitting there behind the controls, responsible, if just for a few minutes, for the valuable cargo behind me. Of course, as a 17 year old, I had no idea about flying or navigation and just sat there with the control column in my hand.

The noise in the cockpit was just as horrendous from the two engines as it was at the back of the plane. After a minute or so, Lionel tapped me on the shoulder and pointed to the compass. We should have been flying in a westerly direction and I had now veered northwards towards Alice Springs in the Northern Territory, which is some 1,500 miles north of Adelaide.

Lionel put the aircraft back on course and explained how I should keep it there, with one eye on the compass. We eventually arrived in Adelaide for the Test only to discover that not only was Lionel the pilot but he was also racing in the match.

I hate to think what might have happened had he got injured that evening. Perhaps we would have been in the hands of his female co-pilot and navigator for the return journey? Looking back, of course, the whole episode was hilarious.

It should be recorded here that Lionel Van Praag was a war hero. On 26 January 1942, Sergeant Van Praag was the co-pilot of RAAF DC-2 A30-8 when it was attacked by a Japanese aircraft and forced to ditch in the Sumba Strait while on a flight from Surabaya to Koepang.

Although some, including Lionel, were wounded, the entire crew survived the ditching to endure 30 hours in the ocean while fending off shark attacks. For their bravery in securing the survival of their crew, the aircraft captain, Flying Officer Noel Webster, and Sergeant Van Praag were both awarded the George Medal. A full account of the incident appears in the book *And Far from Home* by John Balfe, who flew with Lionel.

After recuperating from the ditching, Lionel returned to flying C-47s with No.36 Squadron RAAF out of Townsville.

As far as the racing performances of both the team and me as an individual were concerned, it took many years before I got my revenge. I was the British team manager for tours in 1973–74 and again in 1977–78 and I am extremely pleased to say that we won both series convincingly in typically rough, tough encounters.

On the first occasion, we defeated the Aussies by six matches to one and on the second we were outright winners by five matches to two. The results of the 1973–74 series for the Test matches in Perth: the Lions 55 points to 53, the second match in Perth by 75 points to 33; Adelaide 64 points to 44; Brisbane 62 points to 46; the second match in Brisbane we lost by 60 points to 47; Sydney we won 55 points to 53 and the second match in Sydney by 58 points to 50. The Lions' point scorers for the series were Reg Wilson 86, Peter Collins 84, Nigel Boocock 62, George Hunter 59, Eric Broadbelt 51, Jim McMillan 50, and Doug Wyer 24.

The results of the second series of which I was team manager in 1977–78 were: at Newcastle, the Lions 70 points to 38; Brisbane 57 to 51; the second match in Brisbane we lost 61 to 47; Sydney we won 55 to 53; the second match in Sydney we won 61 to 47; Adelaide we lost by 56 to 52 and in Perth we won by 70 points to 38.

The victorious British Lions of 1973–74 in Australia. From left to right: Reg Wilson, Reg Fearman, George Hunter, Nigel Boocock, Doug Wyer, Eric Broadbelt. Kneeling are Peter Collins and Jim McMillan.

The Lions' point scorers for the series were Peter Collins 108, John Davies 75, Gordon Kennett 72, Doug Wyer 59, Alan Wilkinson 52, Keith White 36 and Neil Middleditch 10.

The racing was always tough in Australia and sometimes got very rough. The crowd was usually hostile against the Brits when we were winning. At Brisbane, at one stage, some of the crowd invaded the track and I called the boys to the dressing rooms in the pits, which were up a flight of wooden stairs.

We all piled in there and I told them they could only come through the door one at a time and we would be ready. Nothing happened.

The referee had come to the pits to tell me to get my boys to calm down. I said, 'Sure, providing the Aussies calm down, otherwise we are ready as well as them to do battle.' We did have a few hard riders who could hand it out as well as take it. I told my boys not to ride near the fence on the way to the starting gate and not to ride near the fence after the race – beer cans had been thrown.

The very next race, Eric Broadbelt was on his way to the start when an idiot jumped the fence to lunge at him. Eric hit him full on and the fibreglass front mudguard – they were long in those days – pierced the chap's thigh, broke off and severed an artery. Eric fell off and banged his head but was all right after a little while – the time it took to attend to the wounded chap and transport him from the track to hospital.

Eric was dazed but not bad enough to prevent him asking, 'Who's going to pay for my mudguard?' Generally, the refereeing was abysmal, with the referees always home-biased, and many tracks had only an elastic cord stretched across the track for the starting gate.

POSTSCRIPT

Another of my many connections with Aub Lawson concerned his long association with Claremont Speedway in Perth, Western Australia, speedway's longest-running venue down under which opened its doors for racing in 1927 and closed in April 2000 – after seventy-three continuous years.

Claremont was what is known in modern times as a multifunctional venue, like others in Australia, operating as an agricultural showground as well as a racetrack. The pledge was simple: 'Our mission is to provide high quality and good value entertainment, recreation and service to Western Australia motorsport, the general public and business communities.'

Eventually the racing lease expired at the Agricultural Showground and was not renewed. A new site was found some miles south of the city and after protracted negotiations with the usual authorities, permission was granted to build a new, purpose-built stadium at Kwinana.

The driving force behind this operation was Con Migro and it is he whom the people have to thank for his sterling efforts to save speedway in the area.

Aub Lawson was Con's mentor and it was he who took on Con full time at the Claremont Speedway office in 1973. It was a labour of love that Con carried out for twenty-seven years. You will find no one in the whole wide world more enthusiastic about all forms of speedway racing than Con Migro.

Having started his speedway career in Sydney in the late 1930s and raced for Middlesbrough and Wembley prior to the outbreak of war, Aub joined West Ham in 1947, with such far-reaching consequences for me personally, and then, after five seasons at Custom House, was transferred to Norwich in 1953 where he stayed until 1960 when he retired from British speedway. Aub missed the 1952 season in Britain when he decided to stay in Australia having bought a farm in New South Wales.

He had always been interested in farming and it was while with Norwich that he gained much farming experience from Jack Norton, a keen speedway supporter with a large farm in Norfolk.

Aub Lawson on his tractor at Speedway Farm pictured with Jack Norton (left), his farmer friend from Norfolk.

He had a very good relationship with the Claremont speedway directors, Mick Tilby and George Milne, who also owned the Brisbane Hotel in a Perth suburb. It was in 1960 that Aub was asked to 'come on board' with the promotion at Claremont and it was he who managed and developed both the speedway and Speedway Farm in Western Australia.

The Swedish team at practice at Claremont, Perth, Western Australia.

The profits from the speedway operation were ploughed into the farm, which proved a great success. Many speedway riders from around the world who were racing at Claremont or passing through were entertained at Speedway Farm which, like most in Australia, covered many square miles.

Aub, having made such a success of Speedway Farm, decided to buy another farm for himself at Northam, some 50 miles from Perth.

The Swedish team at Speedway Farm, Perth, Western Australia prior to going hunting.

CHAPTER FIVE

THE ARMY YEARS

I returned from the Australian speedway tour in March 1951 to find an envelope awaiting me from the Ministry of Defence. I was being summoned to report to the YMCA in Greengate Street, Plaistow, to be assessed for my fitness for a two-year stint of National Service in the armed forces.

It was not a very welcome prospect. British forces were spread all over the world at this time (including Korea, fighting a full-scale war), and conscription was at the very least likely to bring a temporary halt to my racing career.

A family friend had told me that if sugar was found in the bloodstream at the medical, one would be rejected. I almost ate Tate & Lyle out of lump sugar but of course I was naïve and had not at that time connected sugar in the blood with being diabetic. At the medical I passed A1.

I had one further trick up my sleeve but this too proved unsuccessful. I knew some England cricketers had been granted a deferment of National Service to pursue their sporting careers. I duly applied for a deferment but my application was rejected.

In due course, I received my calling-up papers, directing me to report in June 1951 to the Royal Artillery Training Unit at Oswestry. It was with a sad heart that I said my farewells to the West Ham Speedway Team and supporters on my last Tuesday night of racing when I was presented with a signet ring engraved 'West Ham Speedway 1951'.

On reporting, I was given a number (22496767 – National Servicemen will tell you that you never forget it) and kitted out in the most ill-fitting khaki uniform you could imagine. It was a bit different to my gaberdine suits. I was no longer Reg Fearman, West Ham and England speedway rider, but Bombardier Fearman of the Royal Artillery.

After six weeks' initiation and training, I was transferred with the rest of my intake to the Royal Artillery 31st Training Regiment, 80/81 Battery at Kinmel Park Camp, Rhyl, in North Wales. This was designed to be a six-week further training period before a posting to Woolwich and then on to Korea.

The 80/81 Battery was a field battery with Morris Commercial Quads (four-wheel drive) carrying eight personnel and towing a limber containing 25-pounder shells and behind that the 25-pounder field gun. The object of the course was to train the new intake to drive and use this equipment. The battery was also a learner driver unit, with trucks ranging from 15cwt to 3 tons.

'Stand by your beds!' soon became the familiar cry of Sergeant Cox, whose quarters were at the end of a

Reg ready to take on all comers – weapons training in North Wales.

barrack room that contained thirty-two soldiers and their beds. We would stand at the end of our bed by the blankets, which were folded with the same precision as biscuits in a packet. Another display was our webbing, carefully blancoed, with any brasses made to shine.

Horror of horrors – our face had to be seen gleaming in the toe caps of the polished boots (my shoe cleaning thereafter has been something to be seen). Sergeant Cox would put his cane into the blankets and toss them on the floor, even if they were folded correctly.

The punishment was cookhouse duty for early morning breakfast. There was always a fully cooked, English-style breakfast, with the tea full of bromide to suppress sexual appetite. The tea tasted filthy on the one and only occasion I sampled it. Who wanted to be suppressed! Sometimes dances were arranged in the NAAFI when the local girls would be invited up to the camp. Most of them were safe with so much bromide swilling around.

As it turned out, I was not destined to experience the delights or otherwise of Korea. I was taken off the draft and given a permanent posting at Kinmel Park due to being responsible for exposing the unit's postmaster as a thief.

I had become suspicious after a registered letter from my parents had gone missing and I set a trap. The postmaster was discovered to be opening some of the mail and stealing money and postal orders. I was required to give evidence at his court martial.

Whilst I was happy not to be going to Korea, I was still concerned about the fact that my career as a speedway rider was being seriously interrupted.

The end result was that I was given a stripe as lance bombardier and given an administration job in the MT Office (motor transport). As such, I was in charge of the work tickets for all the vehicles which went out on daily learner driver missions.

Mum and Dad travelled up to North Wales to celebrate Reg's permanent posting in the UK and the award of a stripe.

With each intake that came in for their six weeks' training during that period, there was always a convoy of the aforementioned Quad 25-pounder gun and limber from Kinmel Park to Sennybridge Firing Range near Brecon in South Wales, for a week's training with live ammunition in the field.

It was a god-forsaken place as there were almost no fixed personnel. I travelled on a number of these missions, which could be quite hair-raising with the learner drivers towing this lot of gear through the Welsh villages and small towns. There was many a traffic hold-up whilst the Quad or gun and limber were extricated from a perilous situation, having run off the road.

One of the despatch riders who would go ahead was a good pal. Sergeant David Weeks, who was in charge of the MT Administration Office, was also a good trials rider. We got on extremely well and for nearly sixty years have kept in touch. I have made many visits to him and his wife, Amber, a local girl who David married at the well-known Marble Church at Bodelwyddan, near Rhyl.

After David finished his time in the army (he had been a regular soldier), he obtained a job with Pilkington Glass in St Asaph. We have discussed, on a number of occasions, the loyalty that has been shown by Pilkingtons to their former employees who reach retirement age and particularly to those who are not in the best of health.

David and Amber are guests at the Pilkington Retreat in Lancashire, usually twice a year for a couple of weeks at a time, free of charge. I wonder how many firms have shown that sort of concern for their former employees? They also have a week each year at a Llandudno hotel, again courtesy of Pilkingtons.

Despite my concerns about the interruption to my speedway career, I decided to make the best of my time in the Royal Artillery. With that in mind, I decided to have my own personal transport and bought a 350cc Matchless motorcycle.

This didn't last too long as I was run off the road by a truck turning right off the A5 at Fazeley, a town famous for manufacturing the Reliant Robin three-wheeler. I quickly learned how to lay the bike down the 'wrong way' – I had only ever been taught on the speedway to lay down my machine on left-hand bends.

Motorcycle and I ended up in the hedge. I then rode into Birmingham, put the motorcycle and myself on the train for London and that was it as far as road motorbikes were concerned. When the 1951 speedway season closed I had the use of a 1938 Austin 12 van. This had been driven during the season by Don Lawson, Aub's foster brother. I inherited it when Don went back to Australia for the 1951/52 racing season down under.

National Service had both its brighter side and the capacity to produce some hair-raising incidents. As a member of permanent staff at Kinmel Park, I made quite a few pals. Our favourite jaunts were into Rhyl to Green's Café for a delicious meal of ham, egg and chips and then on to the Queen's Hotel on the promenade which had a large room upstairs for dancing.

On one occasion, four of us climbed into the Austin 12 van and set off on one of these jaunts. Travelling back to the camp between 11 p.m. and midnight along a country lane, I ran off the road and put the Austin in a ditch. It stopped rather quickly (no seat belts in those days) and everybody was catapulted into the front. We all had various injuries.

Army life was not all square-bashing and kit inspections. Reg is pictured with Lieutenant 'Dickie' Bird, Bill Bartlett and Taffy Roberts.

As we clambered out of the stricken vehicle, the regimental ambulance pulled up. I thought the driver had stopped to help us but it turned out he was looking for his pal to give him a lift back to camp after a date with a local girl. The ambulance driver duly found his friend and then came back for us, put a tow rope around the axle of the Austin and pulled us out of the ditch. We were able to make it back to camp and reported, as was the norm, to the guardhouse.

The duty guard called up the medical officer and told him that he had four permanent staff requiring treatment. We went to the camp medical centre where the MO put the odd arm in a sling and inserted stitches in head wounds. In my case, I had a nasty gash over the eyebrow which had bled rather profusely and dripped down the front of my gaberdine suit (permanent staff were allowed to wear civilian clothes on evenings out).

The next task would be to explain the incident to the powers-that-be. Every day there was an 8 a.m. parade of permanent staff which Sergeant Major Fisher would inspect and detail. The four of us, standing close together, presented a sorry sight for his eyes and he guessed that I was the culprit.

We were told to fall out. The rest of the parade was dismissed after inspection then the sergeant major demanded to know the details of our accident. I told him I had been blinded by the headlights of an oncoming vehicle and had taken evasive action. He congratulated me and asked if there was any damage to the vehicle, which there was – a bent axle and bodywork damage.

He told me to get the vehicle into the MT shed so that the mechanics could straighten it out, and a good job they made of it too. Sergeant Major Fisher could be a very hard man but could also show compassion. He had a typical sergeant major's foghorn voice which could be heard way beyond the barrack square.

The incident, which I thought was closed, had a very interesting sequel. I took my beautiful gaberdine suit into Rhyl for dry-cleaning and some time later I was requested to leave the MT Office and report to the brigadier's office. Here I was introduced to Detective Inspector Williams and his sergeant. They asked me a number of questions, including whether I had travelled to South Wales and in particular to the Brecon Beacons, near Sennybridge. I had to admit that I had visited the locality.

They told me they were involved in an enquiry into the murder of a woman in the Brecon area and had information that I had deposited a bloodstained suit at a dry-cleaner's in Rhyl. I quickly assured them that it was my own blood on the suit and that details of how it got there were available from the medical officer.

There was no reason for me to hear from them again and I didn't.

Meanwhile, military life continued. There were two batteries in the 31st Training Regiment, 80/81 and 89, which only taught truck driving. The regiment had built up quite a successful trials team from regular soldiers and conscripts. Two of the conscripts in 89 were scrambles/motocross experts. Geoff Ward built up a large property portfolio in the Thames Valley after army life and Graham Beamish was the man behind what became Beamish Motor Cycles of Brighton.

Both were drafted into the unit trials team. This was headed by Captain David Miles, who had been successful in the Scottish 6-Days Trial and included my friend, Sergeant David Weeks. It fell to me on a number of occasions to test out a new trials course which had been set out by the officers.

On one occasion, riding an old BSA with girder forks, I didn't quite make the top of the climb and fell. The clutch lever went straight through my left boot and I could feel it in my foot. The officers rushed to see if I was OK and I said no, I was not. Would they please lift the motorcycle gently so that my foot could be separated from the lever.

They lifted the BSA very gingerly then took off my left boot to find the clutch lever had actually passed under the arch of my foot. The only damage was to the boot where the lever went in and came out of the other side.

Their subsequent actions and the tone they used to say 'Come on bombadier, let's try again', confirmed my belief that they were not best pleased!

Just along the coast from Rhyl, towards Colwyn Bay, was Gwrych Castle where the British boxing champion Randolph Turpin trained for his fights. A call came into the camp for volunteers to spar with Randy. I went along with several of the boys but my weight precluded me from taking part! I think I had had enough of boxing having been made to go along to PC Craddock's house in Lonsdale Avenue, East Ham, every Saturday morning in 1944/45 for boxing lessons. PC Craddock had a full-size ring and taught boys how to take care of themselves.

Randolph Turpin, in addition to being British Champion, was also World Middleweight Champion and a Lonsdale Belt holder, having beaten the legendary Sugar Ray Robinson for the title in July 1951. Turpin committed suicide by shooting himself in his home town of Leamington Spa in May 1966.

Life in the army continued to have its share of laughter and pranks and in general I was having a pretty good time as a soldier. One prank involved a good pal, Lance-Bombardier Bill Bartlett, who, after being demobbed, built up a chain of pubs, the main one being The Eagle and Child at Brentwood in Essex.

Bill, a driving instructor in army life, came from North London and was an Arsenal football fan. At the end of the day's activities, all the vehicles would be garaged in the MT shed I mentioned earlier, a massive corrugated-iron construction with a highly polished red concrete floor.

During the day, when all the vehicles were out on learner driver missions, Sergeant Major Fisher would climb into his 15cwt Ford V8 truck and seek out on the road any instructor who was skiving or having a crafty one in the Ty Fry Inn. On his

Firing a 21-gun salute in honour of the Coronation of Queen Elizabeth II in 1953 – one of Reg's last details of his army career.

return to the MT shed, he would scream into the centre and very expertly perform a handbrake turn, leaving black tyre marks on the floor, parking the vehicle up against the corrugated-iron sheeting wall, having completed a 180 degree turn.

One day Bill said to me, 'Let's wipe some oil over the floor and wait for the sergeant major to arrive back and see what happens.' We did. He came roaring into the MT shed as usual, applied the handbrake and did several 360 degree turns before slamming through the corrugated-iron sheeting into the next building, the gymnasium operated by the PT instructors.

After a minute or two, a flap opened between the corrugated sheets and the sergeant major appeared. Bill said, 'Sir, I don't think the PTIs are going to be very pleased with you.' No action was taken other than to recover the vehicle from inside the gym.

Life had also taken a major turn for the better when I realised that my permanent posting at Kinmel Camp offered an opportunity to get back into speedway racing. Just how I managed to achieve this I will describe in full in the next chapter.

With my army duties, a return to speedway and developments in my private life, there was certainly plenty to keep me busy in those hectic years.

Although National Service was, for many people, a question of counting the days to demob, everything comes to an eventual end. As 1953 progressed and my own freedom got closer, there was still one army highlight. Her Majesty Queen Elizabeth II's Coronation took place in June and 80/81 Battery was detailed to fire a 21-gun salute from Conwy out to sea. It was one of the last details that I attended.

In a way, I was sad to leave the Royal Artillery and Kinmel Park Camp as I had made a lot of friends there.

CHAPTER SIX

A RETURN TO SPEEDWAY

My period of National Service, from June 1951 to June 1953, coincided with a sea of change in the fortunes of speedway racing although neither I nor most other people were really aware of it at the time.

My racing debut for West Ham in 1949 had come at what was to prove the high-water mark of the sport's history in the UK. The post-war revival was in full swing and crowds for that season soared way past the 10 million mark. Even the usually sceptical national media was unable to ignore speedway's impact.

Although there were some commentators who believed the boom could not last, the vast majority of promoters, riders and fans undoubtedly believed that speedway was now a well-established and permanent part of British sporting life, light years away from its early circus image.

On my return from England duty in Australia in the spring of 1951, my impending call-up to the army occupied most of my thoughts. For a year or so it was military and other matters that took priority.

I don't imagine I gave a huge amount of time and thought during 1951 to the long-term future of speedway. The sport, on the surface, was still thriving and during that season the number of tracks in the three divisions reached a post-war high. Nevertheless, crowds were down and there were signs that all was not well.

As the 1952 season dawned, I realised that my permanent posting status would allow me to return to active racing, as long as I could find a track within sensible travelling distance of my camp in North Wales.

West Ham was willing to loan me to another track. Liverpool and Stoke, members of the National League Division Two, were each about 50 miles from camp.

Stoke raced on a Saturday evening when I could be free and by taking my leave in single days I could manage away trips.

I made an application to my commanding officer, Lieutenant Dickie Bird (not the cricket umpire), and he passed on the request to his immediate superiors who gave the necessary permission.

So it was that in March 1952 I got my first sight of Sun Street Stadium at Hanley, the largest of the Five Towns immortalised by the novelist Arnold Bennett. There were (and are) actually six towns making up the City of Stoke-on-Trent, but Bennett left one of them out of his novels and short stories for reasons of his own.

Arnold Bennett was not alone in adopting a confusing attitude to names and places in the locality that most people know as The Potteries, after the centuries-old craft industry that, along with coal mining, steel-making and engineering, made the district a smoky, and often noisy, industrial hothouse.

Sun Street had opened for greyhound racing in March 1928 and just over a year later, speedway made its debut at the venue. The sport's history in The Potteries pre-war was not impressive, with just a handful of meetings contested in the rather chaotic English Dirt-Track League.

Midget cars raced at Sun Street in 1938 and, in 1939, it was decided to have another attempt at speedway racing. The first team to ride at Sun Street a decade earlier had been called Hanley but the new side rode under the name of Stoke.

Back in the groove. Reg leads his aptly named teammate Don Potter and Dennis Parker of Leicester in a match at Sun Street.

Sun Street, Stoke, before demolition after the 1963 speedway season.

When the former West Ham star Harold 'Tiger' Stevenson re-opened Sun Street for National League Division Three racing in 1947, he reverted to the name Hanley. Then, for my first season in the side in 1952, it was back to the Stoke branding.

I met 'Tiger' several times after he retired from his association with speedway and I was saddened when he died from Alzheimer's disease.

There is still a speedway team operating in The Potteries today, I am glad to say, but along the way there was one further complication. After the closure of Sun Street, a new site was eventually found for the sport. This stadium was in the district known as Chesterton and for a while this was the name that figured in the fixture lists and league tables for Potteries' speedway.

Throughout all the changes, the nickname of the team – naturally it was the Potters – remained the same.

Stoke and its speedway has played a major part in my sporting and personal life, although I have to admit that my initial impressions of Sun Street were not particularly favourable.

My experiences of speedway up to this point had been as a spectator and later as a rider at West Ham. The Custom House Stadium in the East End of London held more than 80,000 people. Its two-tier main grandstand had been designed by Archibald Leitch, the man responsible for some of the most famous football grounds in the UK, including Ibrox, the home of Glasgow Rangers, Everton's Goodison Park and Villa Park in Aston.

Leitch's trademark was the criss-crossed steel balustrades at the front of the upper tier of his two-tier grandstands, visible in many old pictures taken of speedway at West Ham.

Custom House was well cared for and the riders enjoyed first-class facilities. There were home and away dressing rooms under the main stand, with a massive bath in each, plus showers, complete with an attendant to hand out the soap and towels. Most of my away matches with the Hammers in Division One had been to equally well-equipped tracks such as Wembley and Harringay.

Sun Street could not have been more different. West Ham's quarter-of-a-mile track (440 yards to a lap) had a surface of gleaming silver sand from Cornwall. At Sun Street, the racing strip was much shorter (350 yards to the lap), cigar-shaped and surfaced with the dust from crushed bricks.

The Stoke dressing rooms were in a corrugated-iron shed inside the pits enclosure. Although the Potters team of the time was successful (Division Three champions in 1948 and competitive members of the sixteen-team Division Two in 1951), the stadium had seen much better days and was displaying the lack of maintenance for all to see.

Reg is in the centre of a group of riders and fans at a Stoke Supporters Club dance at Cheadle in the early 1950s. Also included are Stoke manager Les Gregory (front left), Ken Adams (fourth from the left), the 1953 Stoke Speedway Queen, Vera Gregory, wife of Les, and Australian Joe Peck.

Signing autographs for some of the younger supporters at Sun Street.

What more than made up for the lack of facilities for both riders and the public was the friendly attitude of the Potters' fans who were so loyal, supportive and encouraging. The Supporters Club was very active and ran social events which included dances at Stoke Town Hall, Cheadle near Alton Towers, Trentham Gardens and other venues. They also organised day trips to Alton Towers and Southport beach and pleasure gardens among other places and, of course, there were always coaches to our away matches.

Stoke was a good team to race for – the fans appreciated our efforts and the riders had a great camaraderie, although there was much rivalry when it came to the second half of the meeting. This would be an individual event, usually four scratch races and a final, with more often than not silverware for the winner.

The full-time manager and promoter at Sun Street when I joined the Potters in 1952 was pre-war rider Les Gregory, a Londoner who lived locally at Trentham. He looked after the presentation, publicity, the team and everything to do with the running of a speedway track.

The actual 'bosses' – the men where the buck stopped – were three gentlemen, and I mean *real* gentlemen. Harold 'Tiger' Stevenson himself was a pre-war rider of international status and repute. His two co-directors were Mr Miles and Mr Galloway. I never did learn their Christian names, as the riders and members of staff always addressed them as 'Mr'.

Tiger Stevenson and his partners had a big tyre business in London named Kensington Tyre Services. Tiger was almost single-handedly responsible for speedway's quick post-war expansion. He founded and ran famous training schools during that era, creating Stoke and British speedway legends such as Ken Adams and Les Jenkins to name but two.

I have no hesitation in saying that this was perhaps the best part of my racing career. I was able to score points freely, both at home and away, which I guess helped a lot. I enjoyed travelling to Stoke and revelled in the racing and the sheer friendliness of the whole set-up.

Although I had not raced for a year, I soon found my mark and formed a formidable relationship with the captain, Ken Adams. Ken was a great help to me. He would prepare my machine for the next race meeting. In 1954, we were to act as 'best man' at our respective weddings.

One of my most memorable races was in a National Trophy match against Liverpool Chads in 1952, at Sun Street. For heat 12, I was partnered with Derek Braithwaite for what turned out to be the race of my life. The Potters' opponents in that race were Chads' captain Peter Robinson, and 'Tich' Read.

I flashed out of the starting gate into the lead and around the first bend. I tore down the back straight into the pit corner and made a bad mistake. I hit the safety fence, coming to a complete stop but with my engine still running. This was after leading the race for the first three-quarters of a lap. The other three riders passed me but miraculously I stayed on my machine and got going again.

I chased after them down the home straight and narrowed the gap. On the third lap, I passed Braithwaite and then charged by Read. Peter Robinson, no slouch, stayed ahead of me. In the final lap, on the last bend, he left me just enough room and I drove inside, diving under him and edging in front to win the race with the 15,000 crowd shouting and waving their programmes.

We won the match 55–52 but lost on aggregate. I had earned the nickname 'Fearless' a long time before this incident but it stuck a little more after that. It brought the house down as you can imagine. I had really got used to the tight bends at Sun Street.

The team during my 1952–53 stay at Sun Street consisted mainly of Ken Adams, Les Jenkins, John Fitzpatrick, Ray Harris, Don Potter and me. Two good riders came from Bradford in the form of Jackie Hughes and Ron Peace. I was sad to learn some years later that Ron had taken his own life.

Speedway has something of a history of such tragedies. George Smith of Belle Vue and Benny King of West Ham, from the 1940s and 1950s, also died in these circumstances and in later years the same fate awaited Alan Cowland, who first made his name at Exeter, Les Owen, a loyal member of the Coventry

Stoke Potters, 1953. Standing, from left to right: John Fitzpatrick, Don Potter, Ken Adams, Reg Fearman and Jack Hughes. Kneeling, from left to right: Les Jenkins, Ron Peace and Ray Harris. Both Hughes and Peace joined Stoke from Bradford.

team for many years, Kenny Carter, the Halifax No.1 who murdered his wife, Pam, and then killed himself in 1986, the Australian star Billy Sanders of Ipswich, and many more.

Stoke finished fairly low down in Division Two in 1952 and many speedway commentators felt the league performances did not fairly reflect the quality of the team. Les Gregory was quoted in the speedway press as saying that the tricky nature of the Sun Street track made it difficult for his riders to 'take a big handful' when riding on bigger and faster circuits.

For me, riding in nearly forty league matches in 1952 and finishing third in the Potters' averages, not that far behind Ken Adams and Ron Peace, was a matter for great satisfaction.

Stoke in the early 1950s proved to be a highly enjoyable experience both on and off the speedway track. I formed lots of lasting friendships and underwent some life-changing experiences.

When I had first turned up for practise at Sun Street in the spring of 1952, I was introduced to Rita Harborne (later Mrs Jones) who was Les Gregory's secretary.

Division One giants Belle Vue rode a challenge match at Sun Street in 1952. Skipper Jack Parker leads the Aces on parade. Behind Parker on the first row left to right are Willie Wilson, Ken Sharples and Ron Johnston (with helmet). On the second row left to right are Peter Craven, Bob Fletcher, Harry Edwards and Louis Lawson.

Reg Fearman leads Belle Vue legend Jack Parker during the Sun Street challenge match.

Les made it clear to me that she was spoken for and actually engaged. I can't remember all the details but we did see quite a lot of each other during that 1952 season.

I was very fond of Rita and I believe she was fond of me. She had an uncle and aunt who kept a very nice pub called The Windmill, just outside Stoke-on-Trent, at Meir Heath. Sometimes I would go there with her and she would spend an hour or so behind the bar washing glasses.

Then, in the winter of 1952/53, I met my future wife, Joan, through her brother-in-law who was serving in the army with me.

For transport from Kinmel Park Camp to Sun Street and the away tracks, I had bought a large and comfortable 1936 Ford V8 Saloon – the forerunner to the Ford V8 Pilot. It was also very thirsty on petrol. Being in charge of the MT transport and work tickets, it was not difficult for me to pick up the odd jerrycan or two from my driving instructor friends who had left them behind a hedge.

Reg and Rita met up again to reminisce about the old days at Stoke Speedway.

One of the first people to greet Reg when he arrived at Sun Street in 1952 was manager Les Gregory's secretary, Rita Harborne.

Reg with the Eley family, with future wife Joan standing next to him on the far right.

On Saturdays – race night at Stoke Speedway – I used to give a lift to three other squaddies. John Hodgson then took a bus on to Stafford while Sid Mellor and Frank Cartlidge caught the bus to Leek. I would go to Ken Adams' digs in Tunstall and have lunch with him and Bill and Mabel Smith, who were keen speedway supporters.

Bill, with his brother-in-law, ran a coach business and car repair business. I would stay with them overnight after the Sun Street meeting. Stoke Speedway sometimes used Bill and one of his coaches for the long trip to Scotland, carrying riders and machines. I well remember one night returning from Scotland when the coach became stuck on the steep incline at Shap Fell in icy conditions. We had to disembark from the coach and put our shoulders to the rear end and help push the coach until it got traction.

On a Sunday evening, I would pick up the same boys again in Hanley and get us all back to camp before midnight. Even after the speedway season ended, I would still go down to Stoke at the weekend and take the boys. I would have a night out with Ken Adams, sometimes at the Filly Brooks Inn at Stone on a Saturday night for dancing.

Ken was very shy, especially among the speedway supporters he would meet away from the track. Me, I was the other way. One time, Frank Cartlidge, who was married to Marjorie, invited me to Leek to his in-laws' house for a meal. When I knocked on the door it was opened by three young ladies (blimey! I thought). The first one said, 'I'm Kathy,' the second one said, 'I'm Doreen,' and the third one said, 'I'm Joan'. And that's how I met Joan.

Joan had never been to a speedway meeting and I took her to Stoke's first match of the 1953 season at Swindon. I had a very good night scoring a maximum 12 points and ran second in the second half scratch race final to Ian Williams, the local favourite and the younger brother of Wembley riders, Freddie (a double World Champion) and Eric.

As we travelled back to Stoke, I asked Joan what she thought of the racing. She said it was most thrilling and exciting but that she had not watched any of my races as she was frightened. After that, of course, she watched many and it became a way of life.

In September 1954, Joan and I married in her home town of Leek, 10 miles north-east of Stoke. Joan and I travelled a lot due to the world of speedway, not only in the UK but also abroad. She promoted with me in my speedway promoting career from 1960–86.

Rita herself had married in March 1953 and in October 1954 Joan and I went to live in New Zealand. It was, however, by no means the end of our contact. In March 1956, Joan and I returned to the Stoke area and about a year later I was driving through the town when I saw Rita waiting at a bus stop. We were both surprised to see each other. As it was her lunch break, we drove to the defunct Stoke Speedway and sat on a bench and talked. We met a few times after that, before losing contact.

Reg and Joan's wedding day in September 1954.

Over the years, I had often wondered what had happened to Rita. I now know that she had similar thoughts. Fifty-three years later, a supporter, Mick Mathers, wrote to me about something to do with Stoke Speedway. I noticed that his address was near The Windmill. I wrote and told him about Rita and me visiting The Windmill and asked him to pop into the pub and make some enquiries about Rita, her Uncle John and Aunt Nora.

No one had any idea but a few years later, out of the blue, Mick phoned me to tell me he had found Rita living in a retirement village at Bagnall, in the Staffordshire countryside, halfway between Stoke and Leek. He gave me her telephone number and I called her. She was so very surprised. We had several telephone conversations and I wrote to her and sent her some old Stoke Speedway photographs including one of her and me taken at Wigan Speedway in 1952.

Following Joan's untimely death, I had married Eileen and when we were visiting family and friends in the North West, we arranged to meet up with Rita for lunch at her local country pub, The Travellers' Rest. We intend to keep in touch and continue to exchange our life stories, which have spanned more than fifty years.

My first speedway links with Stoke came to an end in June 1953 when I was demobbed from the army. I was happy racing with the Potters and did not really want to leave but, in the end, I had no choice. I went back to West Ham but for only a short time as the management loaned me to sister track, Leicester.

It was in the winter of 1953–54 that the West Ham management decided to widen the track on the corners to improve the racing. They brought down from Coventry Speedway – a sister track – former rider and surveyor, Alf Elliott, as works manager and employed Pat Clarke, a West Ham rider, Jack Bibby, an Australian and former rider and me as the labourers.

When the ground had been excavated, the base was required to be filled with hardcore. The West Ham Stadium manager, Mr John Marlow, told Alf that the gigantic grass-covered mound in a section of the car park was in fact hardcore. It had been dumped there during the London Blitz when the streets had to be cleared. We used some of that hardcore for the base of the new corners of the speedway track.

Working on the Custom House track in the winter of 1953–54. From left to right: Jack Bibby, Reg Fearman, Alf Elliott and Pat Clarke.

In February 1954, the great floods came to the East Coast of Britain and the protective sea walls at many places were breached. Canvey Island was the last place to be hit by the great surge of water from the North Sea and its sea wall was breached. The first sea wall there was built in 1620 by the Dutch engineer, Cornelius Vernuyden.

The water surged up the Thames and lapped the top of the Embankment at Victoria and Chelsea. In 1953 the population of Canvey Island was 13,000 – the flood was disastrous and fifty-eight people lost their lives. (The population today is 37,000.) It took nine months to drain all the floodwater and make temporary repairs to the sea wall. Thirty years later the Thames Flood Barrier was built to protect London.

With the knowledge of the gigantic mound of hardcore in the West Ham Stadium car park and the need for hardcore to help remake the sea wall at Canvey Island, Alf Elliott and I approached John Marlow and offered to move the mound of hardcore (an eyesore) for £100. He in fact sold it to us for the sum of £100, borrowed from my parents.

Deal done, we placed an advert in the *Evening Standard*, saying 'Hardcore for sale at 2/6d a cubic yard at West Ham Stadium'. The next morning there was a queue of tipper trucks stretching a quarter of a mile from the main gate of the stadium.

We quickly hired a big Caterpillar loader and employed a friend of mine, Sid Mainwaring, as tally clerk. Sid had broken his leg while motorcycling and was off work. Within six weeks, the stadium car park was completely cleared and Alf Elliott and I had made a handsome profit after repaying my parents the £100 loan.

At the beginning of this chapter, I mentioned the major changes taking place in speedway racing in the UK. Crowds never again equalled the figure achieved in 1949. The sheer size of the crowds in the mid- to late 1940s and the early part of the '50s had helped to disguise the effect of the punitive 48 per cent entertainment tax levied by the government on speedway – a figure far higher than that paid by other sports such as football and cricket.

When the numbers paying at the turnstiles started to decline, promoters began to feel the pinch. The 1953 season was a real turning point. Wet weather and the increasing popularity and availability of television – thousands of families bought sets to watch the Coronation of Her Majesty Queen Elizabeth II in June that year – began to pose a real threat to the sport.

When I was released from the army, West Ham would, I believe, have agreed to my staying at Sun Street. They would, however, have wanted a transfer fee and Stoke, where crowds had begun to drop, were either unwilling or unable to raise the cash.

As it was, Stoke closed its doors to speedway at the end of the 1953 season so there would have been no long-term future for me at Sun Street. It is worth recalling that the Stoke promotion was unable to continue because the crowds had dipped to an average of 5,000 a meeting.

Today, that is a figure British promoters can only dream of as an attendance at ordinary league matches. It just shows the effect of the entertainment tax. Introduced by Attlee's Labour government just after the Second World War, it remained in place when Winston Churchill's Conservatives returned to power in 1951 and actually stayed in force until 1957, by which time it had virtually decimated speedway racing, at least in the North of England and in Scotland.

My Potteries speedway connection was later to be revived and my racing return to Sun Street will be covered in a subsequent chapter of this book.

My personal links with the area continued and Joan and I lived locally from the time of our return from New Zealand in 1956 right up until 1968. I have always had a great affinity with The Potteries and although my first visit to Sun Street had been in March 1952, even then I was no stranger to the Five Towns as a whole.

My grandmother Fearman was evacuated to Tunstall after being bombed out in London in 1942. She decided to stay there after the war and is buried in Tunstall churchyard. I travelled with my father from London to visit Gran on several occasions in the years 1945–47.

Stoke reunion in 1997. Back row, from left to right: Arthur Rowe, Eric Hockaday, Jimmy Heard and Tiny Small. Front row: Ken Adams, Dave Anderson and Reg Fearman showing Ken photographs of former glory days.

It is, in so many ways, a small world.

It was Paddy Heath, the then secretary of the Stoke Speedway Supporters' Club, who arranged the Stoke Speedway Reunion for 7 July 1997. A lovely day was organised for us with a visit to the Spode Pottery Factory Museum and to watch, in action, the various stages of manufacture.

We then moved on to what was the main entrance to Hanley Stadium in Robson Street. Amazingly, the white lettering proclaiming 'Hanley Stadium Speedway Racing, 7.45 pm' was still quite visible on the wall after nearly fifty years. We were taken for a tour of Chatfields, the Ford Agent, who had bought and built on the stadium site in 1964, and we all travelled to Loomer Road, Chesterton, for a look at the present Stoke Speedway track.

We had a light tea at the Friendly Hotel in Newcastle before travelling to The Hempstalls pub to meet the supporters, who gave us a wonderful reception. It was most satisfying to meet up with old friends.

Shortly after that reunion, Ken Adams, Dave Anderson and Arthur Rowe all died. All had been ill for some time – Ken with Parkinson's disease, Dave with heart problems and Arthur with cancer.

CHAPTER SEVEN

LEICESTER TO NEW ZEALAND AND BACK

Having said farewell to my Stoke teammates, I found myself back on the payroll at West Ham's Custom House Stadium in the middle of the 1953 season.

West Ham had undergone a rocky period in the winter of 1951–52 and the track could no longer rely on the support of 40,000 East Enders on a weekly basis. At one stage the management at Walthamstow, London's only Division Two track, had been agitating to take the place of the Hammers in Division One.

The husband and wife team of Arthur and 'Tippy' Atkinson who, with Stan Greatrex, had beaten Johnnie Hoskins to the racing rights at Custom House in 1946 and were the promoters when I made my racing debut, had called it a day and for a while the outlook was bleak for West Ham.

The saviour at Custom House in 1952 was the millionaire Alan D. Sanderson, who also had a controlling interest in the Midland Sports Stadiums organisation which owned Coventry's Brandon Stadium, that city's greyhound track at Lythalls Lane and Blackbird Road at Leicester.

The dynamic force behind speedway at Coventry and Leicester, Charles Ochiltree, suggested that Sanderson should acquire the promoting rights for speedway at West Ham for the 1952 season where the powerful Greyhound Racing Association (GRA) continued to own the venue and run the dogs. This effectively kept the Hammers alive for a further four seasons until closure at the end of 1955.

Johnnie Hoskins, 'Mr West Ham' in the 1930s but squeezed out of Custom House post-war, returned to East London. Johnnie was installed as speedway manager by Sanderson and Ochiltree but his second spell with the Hammers was not to last for too long. When Miss Alice Hart retired, Johnnie took over the

Reg was recalled to parent track West Ham in 1953 before being loaned out to the Hammers' sister track, Leicester.

managerial reins at Belle Vue. He was succeeded at West Ham by pre-war rider Ken Brett, who also ran the speedway workshops at the track.

Alan D. Sanderson was truly a larger-than-life character. He was the owner of the 365-bedroom (not all en suite in those days, of course) Selsdon Park Hotel in Surrey, which had an 18-hole golf course with Harry Weetman as the pro. Harry won no less than nine European tournaments and was seven times in the British Ryder Cup team between 1951 and 1963. He was captain in 1965. He died in a car accident in July 1972 aged 51 years.

In pre-war days, Indian maharajahs would stay at the hotel which, in later years, carved out a niche in British political history. In January 1970, Edward Heath held a brainstorming session of his shadow cabinet at Selsdon Park to formulate policies for the 1970 General Election, which Heath rather surprisingly won.

The Conservatives' radical free-market agenda that emerged from the meeting was condemned by outgoing Labour Prime Minister, Harold Wilson, as the work of 'Selsdon Man'.

Mrs Sanderson owned a large number of greyhounds which raced at Leicester, Coventry Lythalls Lane and West Ham.

Reg in Leicester colours for the 1953 season, on loan from West Ham. He finished second in the averages.

After the failure of the managements of Stoke and West Ham to agree my permanent transfer to Sun Street, I was temporarily back in the reckoning at Custom House. I made a few appearances in the West Ham team but I had been away for two years and the Hammers had a full complement of riders.

My immediate speedway future was to be at Leicester, on loan from West Ham. The Hunters were still flourishing and the move worked very well from the point of view of my individual performances as I finished in second place in Leicester's overall team averages for the 1953 season.

Alan D. Sanderson was a frequent spectator at all of his three speedway venues and would place himself in the most strategic viewing position in the restaurant or club room, right in front of the starting gate. At the end of the meeting, one was expected to approach his table and express the hope that he had had an enjoyable evening. If you had scored a maximum on the track that evening you would be in receipt of one of his Churchillian cigars!

At the end of each speedway season, Sanderson and his wife would invite the riders from West Ham, Coventry and Leicester, and their wives, to dinner at the Selsdon Park Hotel. I once witnessed Jack Young, twice World Champion, doing a dance on the snooker table.

After settling in with Leicester for the latter half of the 1953 season, I stayed at Blackbird Road throughout the 1954 campaign. A highlight came in August 1953 when, still something of a newcomer with the Hunters, I received a commendation from the then manager of the Speedway Board of Control, Major W.W. Fearnley. His letter read: 'On behalf of the Control Board, I want to congratulate you on a gallant action in the best traditions of our sport.'

The incident that led to the commendation occurred at Leicester on 14 August, which related to me laying down my machine to avoid Johnny Reason of Coventry who fell just in front of me. If I had run over Johnny, he may not have gone on to become a millionaire from the transport business he founded.

I had really enjoyed my time with Stoke, and Leicester wasn't too bad either. I was successful at Sun Street and I believe my best years in speedway were with the Potters in 1952 and 1953. This belief notwithstanding, I did well with the Hunters too in the 1953–54 period. My average for Leicester was probably about 7 points out of the possible 12 and I did record the odd maximum points here and there.

I dearly loved, for example, riding at Old Meadowbank, home of the Edinburgh Monarchs, and really flew around the track. Ironically, it was the decline and eventual complete shutdown of Scottish speedway, from the high point of four Division Two tracks in 1951 to zero by the end of 1954, which caused my retirement from British speedway and subsequent move to New Zealand.

I had worked my way up the rankings at Leicester to become the number two rider behind Len Williams. Then Glasgow White City followed the other track in that city, Ashfield, into oblivion and the Tigers' top man Ken McKinlay was signed by Leicester.

McKinlay quickly became number one at Blackbird Road, pushing me down to number three. Then the Hunters signed another rider from north of the border, Ron Phillips, and I went down another notch in the rankings. Gordon McGregor, another Scot, also joined the club from north of the border.

I could see the writing on the wall. As the tracks in Scotland and the North of England tumbled like dominoes, their top riders were emigrating to the venues still operating in the English Midlands and the South. The lesser lights at the Scottish and Northern venues were simply out of work and, in my mind, the end result was that I too could soon be out of a job at Leicester.

Reg found himself pushed down the Leicester order in 1954 when Ken McKinlay arrived at Blackbird Road from Glasgow Tigers. This was a Hunters' line-up after 'Hurri-Ken', who was to become a Leicester legend, arrived. Back row, from left to right: Cyril 'Squib' Burton (manager), Lionel Watling, Ken McKinlay, Don Potter, Reg Fearman, Alf Parker and Ted Flanaghan (assistant manager). Kneeling, Charlie Barsby and Bill Griffiths. On machine, Jock Grierson.

To a recently married man, that was just not acceptable. I decided I would do a little emigrating of my own.

During the 1954 Leicester season, I had been contacted by the management at the Western Springs speedway track in Auckland, New Zealand, to race there for the 1954/55 New Zealand season. After talking it over with Joan, I signed a contract. We both decided it was time to move on and we went to New Zealand with an open mind regarding how long we would stay there.

When Joan and I arrived in Auckland we were met by George Gair, the director of the City Public Relations Department, and the Western Springs speedway manager, Bill Sullivan. The Auckland City Council was actually promoting the speedway at that time.

George Gair, born in 1926, went on to become a politician and was at one stage deputy leader of the New Zealand National Party and later his country's High Commissioner in London. He is now Sir George Gair and holder of both The Order of St Michael and St George and The Queen's Service Order.

Joan and I were kindly accommodated at a hotel at the top of Queen's Street in Auckland, with the expense for the first week being met by the Western Springs speedway promotion. After that we were on our own. Accommodation in the mid-1950s was difficult to obtain, even with the help of speedway.

After a while, we were introduced to the mother of speedway rider Mick Holland, who was then based in Christchurch. Mrs Holland ran a boarding house for men-only in Grey Lynn, Auckland. The men would come in from the country to work in the city. Mick's mother agreed to take Joan and me in for a short period.

We had a bedroom to ourselves but shared the other facilities of the house with about sixteen men. Not really a suitable arrangement for a newly married young lady. Breakfast and dinner were served in the basement but one of the conditions of our being allowed to stay was that Joan should take her meals in the bedroom. In practice, I would take the food to her after eating my own meals with the men.

We had made good friends with former speedway rider George Mudgway, a former New Zealand champion, and his wife Ena, a friendship that lasted throughout their lives. They were exceptionally good to us and pointed us in the right directions. Ena's mother was a Macdonald who remembered, as a little girl, arriving in New Zealand from Scotland in the late 1800s when the immigrants' transport was a covered wagon train across New Zealand.

They introduced us to many other Kiwis and it was one of these, Danny Mason, a former midget car driver, who found a bedsit for Joan and me in Hakanoa Street

The open-air life in New Zealand. Fishing with the Mudgway family. George (pictured crouching with the snapper fish) was a former New Zealand speedway champion. Joan is on the far right with George's wife, Ena.

in Auckland. We were so happy to have even such a small place on our own, with our own little kitchen with a small table and a couple of chairs and a bedroom-cum-sitting room.

The old house, like so many others that had been constructed about 100 years before, was built from Kauri timber. I think there were some six bedsits in the house and a couple of shared bathrooms and toilets.

With just one race meeting a week, it was necessary for me to find other work. A great speedway fan, Roy Crawley was manager of the city's public works department and he arranged for me to have a job under his wing as a diesel fitter.

At that time, there were big road improvement schemes being undertaken. Most roads out of the city were simply composed of dirt. The Kiwis called it metal, which effectively meant crushed and hardened stone. The improvements meant a need for a lot of heavy earth-moving equipment, including caterpillar bulldozers, diggers and the like. There was always some piece of machinery that required repairing on site.

I acted as 'mate' to a great guy named Vic Brannen who was vastly experienced in this type of work. Through me, Vic became involved with the speedway and eventually became an official. We are still friends today. Joan, meanwhile, obtained a job with the Farmers Trading Company which entailed taking telephone orders from customers on their multi-line switchboard and transferring those orders to the delivery department. The delivery service was huge and covered a wide radius outside of Auckland.

Joan Fearman with the Ford Zephyr that Reg imported into New Zealand where, in the mid-1950s, cars were an expensive luxury item.

During the English summer of 1954, we had ordered a new Ford Zephyr from the export department of Fords in Regent Street, London. We eventually took delivery and wound a few miles on the clock in the UK – the more miles on the clock the cheaper the import duty in New Zealand.

The Ford was supposed to arrive at about the same time as ourselves in New Zealand but did not, due to a dock strike at Tilbury. When the car eventually did arrive it was collected by the handling agent in Auckland and made ready for the road. It had been waxed as a protection for the bodywork and chrome from saltwater. I had to sign a document at the Customs & Excise that I would not sell the car for two years.

Until the Zephyr arrived, we had relied on Vic Brannen to get Joan, me and my speedway machine (which was kept in the Mudgway's garage) to Western Springs in his 1926 Hupmobile which had wooden spoke wheels.

Motor cars in New Zealand were a luxury and very expensive. I soon learned that the Ford Zephyr, for which I had paid £365 in England, was worth more than £1,000 in Auckland.

At the same time as Joan and I had agreed to accept the contract offer from Western Springs, my parents decided that they would emigrate to New Zealand,

to Mount Maunganui, and they were followed by my sister Doreen. They had English friends there who had told them it would be good for my father's health – he suffered from emphysema – but it was not so.

By early 1955, they had become disillusioned with small-town life and wished to move to Auckland. The five of us rented a new-build three-bedroom bungalow until Joan and I decided to return to the UK in March 1956. My parents returned to London, which they had so dearly missed, in 1959, and my sister followed later.

I really could not blame Joan for wanting to return to England. It had been a tough start and now a newly married woman was sharing with the in-laws. It was not the right way to go and the way of life was so different to what we had experienced at home in the UK.

No shortages in mid-1950s New Zealand. Joan Fearman with an armful of grapefruit.

The women were not so 'matey' as the men. Everything closed at 5 or 6 p.m. on Friday evening until Monday morning. New Zealand is as far away from the UK as you can get – any further and you are on the way home!

Before the eventual decision to return to the UK, and having learned the new value of the Zephyr, I wrote to the Customs & Excise Department to ask permission to sell the car. The reason I gave was that we liked the country so much we wished to put the money towards buying a house.

Permission for the sale was duly given and I used the capital to source cars that were for sale and required some remedial work. So, in addition to my riding on the speedway, working for the Ministry of Works (Public Works Department), I was also buying and selling cars from home.

When stock car racing came to Western Springs, introduced by former Norwich speedway rider Merv Neil, I obtained a sponsor, Merv Hardy Car Wreckers, and drove stock cars too.

New Zealand, still a beautiful country, had in the mid-1950s a population of some 2 million people, a figure which has subsequently doubled. A million of the inhabitants live in the beautiful South Island, 2 million in Auckland itself, with the other million spread throughout the North Island. I have vivid memories of New Zealand in those summer days, now nearly sixty years ago, when the ladies, dressed in flower-print frocks, with white gloves and large sun hats, would wait for the tram to take them into the city of Auckland.

It was, as I suggested earlier, very much a man's world. Women were not allowed into the bars and pubs, which would close at 6 p.m. From 4 p.m. onwards, for the final 2 hours, it would be nothing less than a swill. The noise and babble of voices from inside the pub was unbelievable.

There were also dry areas where no intoxicating liquor could be sold. Strangely enough, when people went to a restaurant in the evening they would smuggle in their own alcohol, place it under the table, order some soft drinks, then it was a case of 'bums up, heads under' the table to top up the soft drink with one's favourite tipple.

When Joan and I motored to Christchurch in September 1955, down through the North Island, we were amazed at the lack of vehicles on the road. We would drive for miles and miles without seeing another car or truck and, all the time, there was this plume of dust from the unsealed road, billowing from the wheels of our Sunbeam Talbot 90 Convertible.

The scenery was magnificent and Rotorua was a mind-boggling place with the hot springs, the mud plopping and the everlasting smell of sulphur coming from the bowels of the earth. The North Island still has active volcanoes and in 1995 and 1996 Mount Ruapehu, which is over 9,000ft high, erupted and the ash carried far and wide, closing airports as far away as Auckland.

On the drive to the ferry at Wellington, we had at times to cross bridges which the road vehicles had to share with trains with no warning signals. One had to slow down, look carefully, straddle the rail lines and drive across. I have to say it was a bit scary but the shared bridges were always on a straight piece of road.

I had a fairly successful 1954/55 season at Western Springs and the Auckland promoter arranged for me to have two meetings at Aranui Speedway in Christchurch where I had my first encounters with a man who was to become six-times World Champion and one of the sport's all-time legends.

The first meeting at Aranui was scheduled for 8 October 1955. Being English and what they termed an 'import', I was given top billing. I had a very good meeting, winning a couple of races from the back mark in the handicap events and narrowly losing the scratch race to Brian McKeown. At the time, Brian was with Southampton in England and in later years was to race for my promotion at Middlesbrough.

That very first Aranui meeting of the season featured a 16 year old having his first speedway race in public. It was the very first race on the programme and he must have been quite nervous riding out of the pits in front of 10,000 speedway fans. His name, now famous throughout the speedway world, was Ivan Mauger (now Ivan Mauger MBE OBE).

The programme compiler had spelled his name incorrectly as 'Major', something which could hardly occur today and in fact it was swiftly corrected for the following week.

In that race, billed as the 7.45 p.m. novice race, with 10s for a start and prize money of £1 for first place and 10s for the runner-up, the finishing order was Alby Jordan, Ivan 'Major', Bill Blake and Cyril Lee.

That was the first of thousands of races that Ivan was to undertake. Ivan has told me that he had the cheque from that first race for £1 – 10s for the start and the same amount for coming second – framed. It is hanging on the wall at his

Runaway Bay home on the Gold Coast of Queensland, Australia.

It is worth noting that a 1954 Leicester teammate of mine, Bryan 'Chirpy' Elliott, also retained his first pay cheque from a second-half race at Coventry. This was for a much more meagre amount, one shilling, than Ivan's first earnings.

The teenage Ivan Mauger pictured at home in New Zealand before embarking on his first trip to Britain in the 1950s.

The local newspaper reported that first Aranui meeting in some detail and it is worth reproducing:

More than 10,000 spectators attended the opening of the speedway season at Aranui on Saturday night and the programme of 16 events was run without a hitch. The solo racing was of a very high standard, although some revisions in handicaps will have to be made. Riders included R Fearman of Britain, M Holland, B McKeown, A Thomas, W Rees and T Johnston, all with overseas experience.

The four BEST riders of the evening – Fearman, McKeown, Holland and Johnston – started in the scratch race for nominated riders. Fearman led the field round the first bend and down the back straight. Close behind was McKeown, slowly gaining. McKeown took the lead in the second lap and although Fearman made several attempts to catch McKeown the latter won. The race produced the fastest time of the night – 81.4.5 seconds.

Little did we know then the direction speedway racing would take us. In Ivan's case it was first as an inexperienced young rider to Wimbledon in the late 1950s, where success evaded him, then on a much more successful basis to Newcastle in the Provincial League in 1963 and subsequently to the first of many world titles in individual, pairs and team events.

In my case, I had little idea then that the future would lead to me playing a leading role in the formation of that same Provincial League which in 1960 revitalised British speedway.

In between my two speedway meetings in Christchurch, Joan and I spent a week touring the glaciated South Island, driving across the Canterbury Plains where thousands of sheep grazed. We saw in the far distance the famous Southern Alps and Mount Cook where Sir Edmund Hillary trained before tackling and conquering Mount Everest along with John Hunt (later Lord Hunt) and Sherpa Tensing in 1953, just in time for the Coronation. We were fortunate to see Invercargill and, in particular, Queenstown before it was spoilt by development and tourism. The beauty of the South Island lies in its mountains and many lakes.

Before leaving Auckland for our 1956 return to England, it was necessary to have an income tax clearance document. Without this, no ticket would be issued to travel abroad. Joan and I each obtained these without any problem. We requested our bank to transfer our money to a bank in the UK – we had of course much more than when we arrived.

We arrived by ship some four weeks later in England. It was March 1956 and I had intentions of racing again for Leicester, although I had my wrist in plaster as a result of a racing accident on Boxing Day.

Our destination was Joan's parents' home in Leek, Staffordshire. There, on our arrival, was a letter from our bank in New Zealand telling us that our bank account had been frozen by the Inland Revenue. We had to explain where the money had come from. We eventually satisfied the inquiry by sending a copy of the letter I had kept from the Customs & Excise Department giving me permission to sell the Ford Zephyr.

My return to British speedway proved somewhat problematical. By the time my wrist had healed, my racing equipment had still not arrived from New Zealand. However, the Leicester management said they would supply the track spare machine for me to ride, so I duly travelled to Blackbird Road for my first Friday evening booking, intending to stay over as the team was also racing at Swindon on the Saturday night.

In the meantime, I learnt that I was to be charged for using the track spare, the amount being my start money for each race. If I had been told this before travelling to Leicester, I would have refused the offer.

That Saturday morning saw a number of telephone calls from me in the Leicester Stadium office to the management at Coventry and to Lutterworth, the home of the Hunters' team manager and pre-war star rider Cyril 'Squib' Burton.

The management would not budge so I told them that I was now retired from speedway racing and would not be at Swindon that evening. In actual fact, Squib offered to pay me from his own pocket the money I had been stopped but I said, 'No thank you, it is a matter of principle.'

Joan and her family were most surprised when I walked into the house at some time after 3 p.m. that Saturday afternoon. They were all sitting around the black and white rented television set watching the Cup Final from Wembley Stadium. I joined them and witnessed Manchester City beat Birmingham City 3–1. The match was played on 5 May 1956. Bert Trautmann, the Manchester City goalkeeper, broke his neck in that match but played on.

That was more or less that as far as speedway was concerned for the next four years although I did ride in a handful of Britannia Cup matches for Leicester at the start of the 1957 season. But my heart was no longer in racing as I had gone into business with Bill Smith, the friend with whom I had stayed when racing for Stoke in 1952–53. We started a small metal fabrication business and were also involved in car refurbishing, repairs and car sales.

One reminder of speedway came when Bill and I travelled to Rolls-Royce in Scotland to bid for some work. On arrival at Rolls-Royce I unexpectedly met up with Ian Hoskins, who was a welfare officer with the firm. He was as surprised to see me as I was him.

Ian had previously been involved with promoting speedway racing in Scotland and was the West Ham mascot in the 1930s when his father, Johnnie Hoskins, was the promoter. When speedway folded completely in Scotland during the mid-1950s crash, Ian was forced to look for work outside the sport although, like myself, he was soon to bounce back.

I missed one trick when in the metal fabrication business. I had noticed when in New Zealand that almost every home in Auckland had a revolving clothes line, something unknown at the time in the UK.

When Joan and I left New Zealand for England in February 1956, I took with me all the dimensions for the revolving clothes line. When I was settled in my business, I made a prototype line and took it to the big stores in Manchester but no one was interested. Today, of course, the revolving clothes line is common-place in the UK. I missed that boat!

CHAPTER EIGHT

HAPPY TIMES AT STOKE SPEEDWAY

My decision to make an active return to the world of speedway in 1960 heralded some happy times, the well-documented conflicts with Mike Parker notwithstanding.

The first year of the decade which saw the sport's revival was also a very important milestone for Joan and me with the birth of our son, Gary, on 11 June 1960. At the time, it made our family complete and Gary was to grow up to be a tower of strength for both of us.

Reg and Joan with son Gary, just hours old, in June 1960.

Educated at Moulsford Preparatory School, near Oxford, at The Divine Mercy College in Henley-on-Thames, Henley College and Reading Technical College, his help in the administration and promotion of our speedway interests was invaluable.

He had learnt a certain amount of the Polish language at The Divine Mercy College, which was run by the Marian Fathers from Poland, and in later years there were occasions when he was able to act as interpreter for official British racing commitments in Poland.

All of that, needless to say, was some way in the future as I began to prepare, in the early months of the year, for the return of speedway to Sun Street, Hanley.

As a rider, I had always taken a certain interest in the broader aspects of speedway, never being content to simply turn up and race. Nevertheless, actually being pitched into the promotion business was something quite different and meant a considerable amount of learning on my feet.

It is easy to look back over the half century or so since the birth of the Provincial League and see it as an almost instant rebirth for a sport that had struggled badly for several years.

The Provincial League was an undoubted success but it was not achieved without considerable struggles and an awful lot of hard work. I still regard it as astonishing that two of the promoters who were involved in our initial meetings, John Pilblad at Aldershot and Charlie Dugard at Arlington (Eastbourne), were refused licences for a place in the new competition.

Although at the time they were both what you might call 'Cinderella' tracks, operating either on open licences or in the Southern Area League, the subsequent history of Eastbourne has shown the potential that exists for 'minnows' to grow and prosper.

Since the 1960s, glamour tracks such as West Ham, New Cross and even the original Belle Vue have fallen prey to development together with many other well-supported venues such as Norwich and Cradley Heath. Due to the hard work of the Dugard family, Eastbourne now operates in British speedway's Elite League, in a well-developed stadium that has the huge advantage of being set deep in the countryside with little likelihood of damaging complaints about noise.

Eastbourne certainly lived to fight another day despite the initial Provincial League rejection by the Speedway Control Board (SCB) although, sadly, Aldershot is now just a name from the past as far as speedway is concerned.

An inspection of Sun Street, the venue that had become so familiar to me in the early 1950s, revealed that all the necessary equipment needed to run speedway racing – the safety fence, track lighting, starting gate and disqualification lights among other things – had long since disappeared.

A speedway promoter has to be able to turn his hand to a great many jobs if the promotion is to be financially viable. My own engineering background served me well as I was able to make the track lighting arms myself from scrap boiler tubing with a certain amount of necessary welding and the fitting of adapters.

It was not long before the fifty-two new pieces were mounted on the existing lamp standards used to illuminate the greyhound track at Sun Street. A good friend, Cliff Wood, who had an electrical business in Fenton, did all the wiring and soon it was all systems go for our reopening on Good Friday.

It should be remembered too that none of the original Provincial League promoters had any firm guarantees whatsoever that the public would support the revival at tracks like Stoke, Cradley Heath, Sheffield, and Edinburgh, where several years had elapsed since the end of league racing.

As it turned out, although crowd figures for Mike Parker's Cavalcade of Speed presentations at Liverpool and Bradford in 1959 had been encouraging, the fans did not give sufficient support to those two venues during the first Provincial League season and they dropped out of the sport, in Liverpool's case for ever.

So it was very much a case of venturing into the unknown as I waited for the turnstiles to open on that Good Friday evening in 1960. Some things were in our favour; although Stoke had two professional football teams, City and Port Vale, no matches were allowed in those days on Good Friday.

As it was, without any such opposition, we rang the bell in no uncertain manner, with more than 10,000 people packing into the stadium. Those people who turned up that evening were fans who had been starved of their speedway for a long time together with newcomers too young to remember the post-war Potters.

My records show that the cash takings at that first meeting, with admission prices set at 2s 6d (12½p in today's money) and 1s 3d (roughly 6p today), totalled £1,411 before deductions.

It may not seem a lot when viewed in the light of the fact that in the twenty-first century a crowd of 1,500 people (which is more or less today's norm, even for most tracks in the Elite League), paying the going admission rate of between £15 and £17, would bring in something in the region of £25,000.

There really is no comparison between the eras. Gate money in 1960 was more or less the only income speedway had, with no sponsorship and certainly no television money.

The sport today is relatively stable with most clubs re-emerging each spring and the spectators who do attend meetings are no doubt just as enthusiastic as ever. Sadly, the crowd atmosphere generated at most tracks – attendances at quite a few Premier League (and occasionally even Elite League) fixtures are counted in hundreds, not thousands – is only a pale shadow of the past.

At Stoke in 1960 Reg, for the first time in his career, was obliged to juggle the duties of rider, coach and promoter. The Potters team above is, from left to right, Les Jenkins, Pete Jarman, Reg Fearman, Arthur Rowe, Gordon Owen, and Peter Kelly. Ray Harris is on the machine with the team's mascot.

At the end of Stoke's first meeting for several years, I felt so very proud to have been able to bring speedway racing back to the Potteries, not only as promoter but also actively on the track, racing that first season as the team's rider coach.

Despite my lay-off from the sport, I enjoyed a fairly successful season, coming second in Stoke's Provincial League averages with 158 points from sixteen matches. Just ahead of me in first place, and behind me in second, were teammates from my earlier spell at Sun Street in the shape of Ray Harris and Les Jenkins.

I also won the Provincial League's match race championship, the Silver Sash, in May 1960, beating Bristol's Johnny Hole at Sun Street (I subsequently lost it to Ross Gilbertson of Poole). Another landmark of that season was my last World Individual Championship appearance when I scored 10 points in a qualifying round at Cradley Heath.

Late in the 1960 season, we were joined by another former Potters' star, Ken Adams, who had spent most of the season in the National League with Oxford. Ken gave notice of how effective he would be at the lower level by averaging nearly 11 points a match in his three appearances for Stoke.

The first season of the Provincial League saw the competition split between the top teams, eventual champions Rayleigh, runners-up Poole and third-placed Bristol

Reg's first season back at Stoke brought him success on the track as well as in the role of promoter. He was one of the Provincial League's top riders and held the individual match race championship, the Silver Sash, for a period of time.

who packed their sides with experience, and the lowly sides who had in their pre-season team-building strictly followed what had been the original idea of the league, to give rides to up-and-coming novices.

Given the circumstances, it was inevitable that there were some pretty uneven matches across the season. Stoke took a middle course, with the experience of myself, Harris and Jenkins, and later Adams, allied to northern novices like Ted Connor, Arthur Rowe, Gordon Owen, Johnny James and Keith Rylance, all of whom had team opportunities.

This was reflected in our comfortable mid-table position in the final league table.

We also helped in 1960 to launch the league careers of riders such as Peter Kelly and Pete Jarman, who were to go on to ride with success in the British League in later seasons.

Perhaps the biggest 'find' from the four years of Provincial League racing at Stoke was Colin Pratt who, I am happy to say, is still deeply involved in the sport in the second decade of the twenty-first century as a promoter at Coventry and a leading figure in the World Speedway Riders' Association, the veterans' body.

Perhaps before leaving the statistical side of those early years, I should also mention another rider who rode in more than half of Stoke's 1960 Provincial League fixtures, scoring more than 50 points at an average of 6 a match. At that stage, local boy Bill Bridgett was still part of my happy times in speedway.

The Five Towns' fans certainly enjoyed the comeback season and so did I. In 1960 and in the first few years of the Provincial League, there was so much fun and enjoyment involved in staging speedway racing at Sun Street.

A star Potter in action. Colin Pratt leads the field in an individual meeting, with Provincial League ace Ivor Brown of Cradley Heath unable to find a way past the Stoke man.

It was almost like one big family gathering on a Saturday evening. I have to admit that there had not been much improvement in the dressing room accommodation or the pits area since the early 1950s when I had compared Sun Street's facilities unfavourably to the palatial West Ham.

The speedway office was adjacent to the pits in a corrugated-iron sheet building. It was in there after the meeting that we would have a few beers and sandwiches laid out for the riders and staff.

There was a piano in the office and someone would always sit down and play, a great sing-song would ensue. Time would fly past but we always knew when it was time for us to go as a neighbour in the street on the outside of the office would get a stick and rattle it along the ridges of the corrugated iron, shouting, 'Are you never going home?' We would shout, 'Sorry!' and abandon our melodious voices until the following Saturday.

There was still an awful lot of fun in speedway in the early 1960s. I presented many interval attractions to entertain the crowd including Stan Lindbergh who set himself on fire and dived from a 50ft tower on the centre green into a tank of water just 6ft deep.

Marcel (he didn't use a surname) on the swaying pole was another centre green attraction and there was always a big name personality to open the season, including *Coronation Street* stars of the era Patricia Phoenix (Elsie Tanner) and Ken Cope (who played the character Jed Stone in the *Street*).

In 1962, we had the big joker 'Igor Baranov'. He came for after-match trials in the second-half scratch races. He was reputed to be a Russian and when the Stoke *Evening Sentinel* sports writer Bill Deakin telephoned me for news, I said he was either a student who had defected or a seaman who had swum ashore from a fishing boat.

Interval attractions and big name visitors such as actress Patricia Phoenix – Elsie Tanner in *Coronation Street* – helped to keep the fans happy. Reg introduces Pat Phoenix to Colin Pratt, watched by Bill Wainwright (left), Pete Jarman and Ken Adams (right).

When I met Igor in the café opposite Robson Street, near the stadium, he spoke not a word. His partner interpreted, speaking gibberish. It was his act to get rides at various speedway tracks. I must say we had many column inches of publicity out of it. I met him many years later as a spectator at Wimbledon. He said, 'Remember me, Igor Baranov?' It transpired he was a Scot, John Jones, and by the time of our later meeting he was in the world of wrestling.

In 1963, we made an effigy of a Cradley Heath rider, erected a set of gallows by the starting gate, and had 'Tyburn Gallows' act as executioner and hang the effigy at the start of the meeting.

'Gallows' was a novice rider, real name Raymond Humphries, who changed his name by deed poll to overcome objections from a squeamish Control Board. He once claimed to be the assistant hangman to the Crown. Raymond, who died some years ago, was following in the footsteps of Igor Baranov and others before them, by inventing an exotic persona to try to get a step ahead of the many novices, all clamouring for a chance to make a breakthrough in speedway.

The Sunday after the starting gate 'execution', details of the 'act' were spread over two pages of the *Sunday People*, with a follow-up article the week after that. At that time, there was a great anti-capital punishment debate going on in Parliament.

Another unforgettable incident in the history of Stoke Speedway in that era concerned a real-life murder (although there was to be no execution). There are many reasons why crowds fall off at speedway tracks, but Stoke in the 1960s must be the only instance of a venue where attendance figures dropped because of a murder.

Perhaps our antics with the effigy of a Cradley rider and the gallows at the starting gate backfired …

The 1962 season had been quite successful for the Potters on the track and this was reflected in good crowd figures, good that is until Saturday, 29 September that year. A young girl named Joyce Bryan was murdered in a building adjacent to the speedway pits area, apparently during that evening's racing. Her body was discovered the next morning in a shed used for storing quartz which is used in the pottery manufacturing business.

Within a short time, Scotland Yard was called in by the Stoke-on-Trent police. The officers concerned were Detective Superintendent Bob Acott and his sergeant Kenneth Oxford, who was later to become famous nationally as the Chief Constable of Liverpool where he oversaw the policing of the Toxteth riots of 1981. He was knighted that year and died in Liverpool in November 1998.

In the 1960s, Ken Oxford was the investigating officer in two of the most notorious cases of the era. The first case was the Profumo affair, which concerned the War Minister John Profumo, a Soviet agent and the call girls Christine Keeler and Mandy Rice Davies who had slept with both the politician and the spy.

The second case was the trial for murder and the subsequent execution of James Hanratty. Bob Acott had overall charge of the Hanratty case, which was extremely controversial, with many people unsure that the convicted man was actually guilty. The case probably contributed to the abolition of capital punishment later in the decade.

As the speedway promoter at Sun Street, I was requested to attend some of the inquiries being made by Acott and Oxford. It had been quickly established by witnesses that Joyce Bryan had been to the speedway that Saturday evening with friends and had been seen talking to a boy. Her parents did not raise the alarm when she did not arrive home that Saturday evening as they understood Joyce was staying the night with a friend.

Timing seemed to be of great importance to the investigating team, who wanted to know exact details relating to the start time of the meeting, the time of the interval and the finishing time of the last race. My ACU timekeeper that evening was W.A. (Bill) Daff. He had recorded not only the time of each race but all of the other significant times. He was interviewed and his records of the meeting were noted by the investigating team.

As part of their enquiries, the investigating officers interviewed a man called Terence Peter Blunt who lived in Tunstall. They inspected the clothes he was wearing on the Saturday of the murder and when they looked closely at the turn-ups of his trousers they were clean with not even any fluff to be found.

When they examined a vacuum cleaner he had apparently used, they found pieces of quartz used in pottery manufacture. Blunt was charged with the murder of Joyce Bryan by inflicting blows with a blunt instrument. He was eventually convicted of 'Manslaughter on the Grounds of Diminished Responsibility'. The documents relating to the case are closed for ninety-five years under the Public Records Act.

Needless to say, the attendance figures at Sun Street for the remainder of the 1962 season plummeted and the fatal incident also had a knock-on effect on attendances for the 1963 season.

Sadly, 1963 was to bring about another death, this time of Sun Street itself.

The stadium had been built on a disused marl pit back in the early 1920s for the coming of greyhound racing. The first greyhound meeting took place in 1928 and the first speedway meeting in 1929.

I was never actually able to find any drainage around the track for rainwater. My answer to a flood was to take a 6ft-long spike from the workshop and plunge it into the lowest part of the floodwater, breaking the crust of the track surface.

Within minutes there would be a hole almost big enough to drop in a wheel-barrow. Problem solved. The base of the track was formed from house bricks and the racing surface was brick dust. It seemed to work OK.

All good things come to an end. Mr Reg Austerberry, the chairman of the company that owned the track, Northern Greyhound Racers (Hanley) Ltd, asked me into his office to tell me that the directors and shareholders had decided to sell Hanley Stadium, which stood in some 6 acres of land. Their decision was prompted by the fact that they were all ageing.

I was offered the first chance to buy the stadium for £36,000, which in today's money would be in excess of £600,000. There was little chance at that time that I could raise such a figure. Consequently, the local Ford agent, Albert Chatfield (who drove an American Ford Galaxy), bought the stadium and moved his business there from Marsh Street.

The decision of the greyhound racing company directors that they could no longer carry on promoting the sport and the running of Sun Street was a sad tale and, unfortunately, one that has been repeated far too often in subsequent decades.

In the 1950s, there were greyhound stadia all over Britain, ranging from the splendours of Wembley, the White City and West Ham. In all, there were once thirty-three greyhound tracks in Greater London alone, right down to extremely basic circuits

The closure of Sun Street brought heartache for the loyal fans of the Potters. In happier times, Potters stars enjoy an evening with the 1962 Stoke Speedway Queen and her attendants. The riders are, from left to right: Eric Hockaday, Colin Pratt, Ron Sharp, Peter Jarman, Reg Fearman, Pete Adams (behind Reg) and Kid Bodie (later known as Howard Cole).

operating outside the umbrella of the Greyhound Racing Association and known as 'flapping tracks'. Today, only Romford, Wimbledon and Crayford remain.

Speedway, over the decades since its introduction to Britain in 1928, has operated at around sixty venues originally designed for greyhound racing. The twin factors of a slump in popularity of 'a night at the dogs' and the fact that a great many of the stadia were in locations ripe for development, has meant that today there are fewer than thirty greyhound venues in operation.

Many promoters have shared my Stoke experience. Of the twenty-six venues currently staging speedway, just ten share their facilities with greyhound racing.

The dog tracks, especially London's 'big five' of Wembley, West Ham, Wimbledon, Harringay and New Cross, had big spectator capacities with excellent facilities and provided ready-made homes for speedway in the late 1920s, although some people have argued that their availability discouraged the sport from developing its own purpose-built venues.

The relationship often proved fraught and speedway promoters, usually only tenants, had the onerous task of covering the dog track before racing could take place with the same covers having to be removed once a meeting was over.

During 1964, with the closure of Sun Street, I looked at other venues in the Stoke-on-Trent area. One of these was Cobridge Stadium which had staged midget car racing in the 1930s and, at this time, was in the ownership of the Stoke-on-Trent Education Department and used as a sports stadium. My application was refused and enquiries at Trentham Gardens, a local pleasure grounds complex, also came to nothing.

It was not until 1968 that a promoting company with which I was involved, Allied Presentations Limited, made a satisfactory arrangement with British Railways to lease the Crewe Sports and Cricket Ground for speedway racing. We opened in 1969 and although it was some distance for the Stoke fans to travel, at least they had speedway back in their area.

It proved to be a black day for Crewe when a building company built the present Stoke Speedway venue at Loomer Road, in the Chesterton district. There was not enough support to allow both tracks to survive and Crewe eventually closed for good.

CHAPTER NINE

MIKE PARKER AND
THE PROVINCIAL LEAGUE

Speedway and controversy have often walked hand-in-hand. In fact, over the years, there have been many instances when promoters have 'talked-up' quite innocuous issues into full-scale rows simply for their publicity value.

In writing about my relationship with Mike Parker, it will be impossible to avoid controversy, in this instance of a completely genuine kind.

Parker was (he died in November 1987 at the age of 62) the sort of man about whom there is rarely any middle ground. Some people in speedway genuinely believe the role he played in the creation of the Provincial League merits the award of the title of saviour of speedway in the UK. Many of those who rode for his various promotions can find only positive things to say about his methods.

In my case (and my dealings with him were as close as any over a fair period of time), it is a case of speaking as you find. For my thoroughly candid appraisal of the man, you must wait until the end of this chapter.

Even though many years have passed since I last had any dealings with Parker, my anger at the way he treated not only myself but other figures in speedway whom I respected, has not cooled.

To begin at the beginning. It was in October 1959 when our paths first crossed. Dave Anderson, a pre-war rider at the Dagenham non-league track, captain of Hanley (Stoke) in the late 1940s and a resident of the area, called into my garage in The Potteries to ask if I was interested in racing again.

Dave told me that Parker, a midget car driver who had run some Cavalcade of Speed meetings in the North of England and the Midlands during the 1959 season, mixing solos, sidecars and the small but potent speedcars, was planning to revive speedway at Sun Street in Hanley, the scene of some of my own best racing memories.

I was interested in getting back into the sport and so I met Parker in the winter of 1959/60 at his office and flat which was situated above a hardware store he owned in the Moss Side area of Manchester. Moss Side even then was an extremely rundown area of the city. It later became notorious for gang warfare and was eventually completely demolished.

At our meeting, I told him about my background in speedway and, in particular, of my racing career at Stoke. The result was a deal for us to promote on a 50/50 basis through a company we formed named Northern Speedways Ltd.

I set about installing at Stoke all the equipment necessary to stage speedway racing including the track lighting system.

At this stage I knew very little about Parker, apart from the positive fact that he was seriously interested in reviving speedway in areas of the country where it had been defunct ever since the post-war boom turned to virtual bust.

I certainly did not know at the time that Parker was on the way to becoming the Rachman of the North*. As his business partner, I inevitably started to learn more and more as time went on.

Some of what I learnt about him was routine and blameless. Parker told me at our first meeting that he had spent some time in the Merchant Navy and that in addition to running the hardware store, he was doing property repairs as a jobbing builder.

His connection with short circuit racing centred around the midget cars that he drove in the second halves of speedway meetings at Belle Vue. I believe that Parker had managed to acquire most of the cars in Lancashire from their owner, giving him control over the racing.

Over the years, both before and after the Second World War, there were many attempts to establish midget car racing in the UK. Parker's cars in particular were very unreliable and hard to keep going for four laps.

The Belle Vue speedway riders apparently became fed-up with the Hyde Road track being badly cut up by the cars. Parker went off to Liverpool and Bradford to stage the pirate (unlicensed) Cavalcade of Speed meetings during the summer of 1959.

The meetings featured sidecar racing, organised by a grass track man called Harold Hill from the Birmingham area, Parker's midgets and pukka speedway racing. With the number of speedway tracks very restricted, and racing opportunities hard

*Peter Rachman (1919–1962) was a London landlord in the Notting Hill area in the 1950s and 1960s. He became so notorious for his exploitation of tenants that the word 'Rachmanism' entered the Oxford English Dictionary as a synonym for any greedy, unscrupulous landlord.

to come by, there were many junior speedway riders in the North who were willing to race in these meetings, despite the fact that they were unlicensed by the SCB and Auto Cycle Union.

All this knowledge merely supported his claim that he wanted to revive speedway on a bigger scale than simply reopening the odd track for non-league speedway.

The other side of his character was gradually revealed to me, ultimately by bitter personal experience.

My first experience of his methods came quite early in our relationship. In the late 1950s/early 1960s you could buy a whole street of rundown terrace houses in Moss Side for about £100 each. Parker would convert the ones he bought into bedsits.

I actually accompanied him one day (without knowing it when we set off) on one of his evictions. He broke down the door of the property, threw all the contents out into the street and put hasps and padlocks on the doors. This gave me a new insight into his character.

It was this ruthlessness that he carried forward into his speedway and stock car promoting career.

When Parker came into promoting the sport in 1960, his knowledge of speedway racing was just about zero. My belief was that, as far as he was concerned, it was simply business with no feel for the sport of speedway racing or its history.

I used to feed him all the information at promoters' meetings. Along the way, he also picked up a lot of knowledge from the other promoters in the game. I believe he saw, through speedway racing, a means of making money. Eventually his promoting interests were to expand into stock car racing, a sport which shared many circuits with speedway, usually to the detriment of the two-wheeled sport.

It was an advertisement in the speedway magazines of the time and the medium of word of mouth that brought interested parties to the inaugural Provincial League meetings. They were initially held during the winter of 1959/60 in Parker's flat above the shop and later at the Palm Court Restaurant (it was also a pub) at the main gate of Belle Vue Pleasure Gardens, the zoo and entertainment complex that was the brainchild of John Jennison and which opened in 1836. In 1969, it became Caesar's Palace. It housed a cabaret bar and restaurant which was converted into an amusement arcade in 1976 when it was once again renamed as Jennison's Ale House in honour of the Belle Vue founder.

Mildred, Parker's live-in girlfriend, made the tea during the time the meetings were held on his own premises. We later learned that Parker's wife and daughter lived in Blackpool. He visited them on Wednesdays and sometimes at weekends.

Most of the people attending these early Provincial League meetings had been involved in the past, often as riders, but had dropped out of the game for various reasons during speedway's 1950s downturn. All were keen to become involved once again.

New Zealander Trevor Redmond, a former Wembley Lions star, attended with the Jephcotts, Captain Fred and his son Morris, together with their associate Alan Martin, all from Cradley Heath in the Black Country where, as in many other instances, greyhound racing had kept the venue alive after speedway had closed.

Ian Hoskins who, as mentioned before, had been forced to work in industry after Glasgow Tigers' demise, was there with ambitions to reopen the Old Meadowbank Stadium in Edinburgh for speedway.

Pre-war Belle Vue and England star Frank Varey, who had dropped out of the promoting business when the bottom dropped out of speedway in the North in the early 1950s, represented Sheffield and Charles Foot and Charles Knott travelled up from Poole.

Also present were former riders Pete Lansdale and Wally Mawdsley, who had spoken to the owners of Rayleigh Greyhound Stadium with a view to reintroducing speedway racing at The Weir.

Other representatives from the South of England, where several tracks had continued to operate throughout the 1950s in the more or less semi-professional Southern Area League, included another former rider, Charlie Dugard, who owned the Sunday afternoon Arlington track near Eastbourne, enthusiast John Pilblad, a top BBC outside broadcast cameraman from Aldershot, and John La Trobe, essentially a stock car promoter from Brafield in Northamptonshire.

The first secretary (there were to be many) of the Provincial League was the journalist John Wick, editor of *Speedway World*.

A committee of the prospective speedway promoters for 1960 met the SCB which, to the surprise of some in the business, agreed to sanction the new Provincial League.

The inaugural season of 1960 saw the partnership between Parker and me get under way. Each of us had individual responsibilities under the overall Northern Speedways umbrella, something which was to continue for some time to come. In 1960 Parker ran the Stanley Stadium track in Liverpool and I ran Sun Street in Hanley.

Stoke was extremely successful but Liverpool, although having staged several Cavalcade of Speed meetings in 1959, failed to draw a paying crowd for Provincial League speedway.

Northern Speedways dropped Liverpool in 1961 and opened Newcastle, Wolverhampton and Middlesbrough, all tracks which had been closed for

Ultra-enthusiast John Pilblad, a top BBC outside broadcast cameraman, seen here with HRH The Prince of Wales, was one of the unsuccessful applicants for a place in the Provincial League. Pilblad had wanted to enter an Aldershot team in the new competition.

speedway for many years. Newcastle's Brough Park in the North East and Monmore Green in the Midlands were owned by the same dog-racing company, the Midland Greyhound Racing Company Ltd. Middlesbrough Greyhound Stadium was independent.

As Northern Speedways now had four tracks to manage, including the successful Stoke Speedway, I suggested to Mike Parker that we should take in Bill Bridgett for a third share in Wolverhampton, for which purpose we formed a separate company. I knew Bridgett as a rider at Stoke, an enthusiast and a businessman who had inherited a fish and game shop in Newcastle-under-Lyme. I thought he was honest and would do a good job.

The return of speedway to Newcastle and Wolverhampton was extremely successful (both operate today after experiencing various ups and downs over the years). Middlesbrough, while good initially, was never as successful as the other two. Cleveland Park is now closed but a new side, Redcar Bears, rides today at the South Tees Motor Park.

Continuing the policy of sharing responsibilities, I took over the day-to-day running of Middlesbrough in addition to my duties at Stoke whilst Parker did the same at Newcastle. I continued to ride in 1961 and although my appearances were less frequent due to a troublesome back injury, which was to be the cause of many hospital visits, I again averaged more than 9 points.

I have no memory of riding for Stoke against Middlesbrough or vice-versa when my two sides clashed, although I do not believe there was any rule forbidding it. In my view it just would not have been the done thing.

Speedway in the North of England has had rather a chequered existence over the years, with Belle Vue at times being almost the lone standard-bearer for the sport.

Middlesbrough, a large manufacturing centre on the River Tees, famous for its iron, steel, shipbuilding and chemical industries, tends to be associated, at least when it comes to football local derbies, with Newcastle and Sunderland, although the town is traditionally part of the North Riding of Yorkshire.

The town's speedway history goes back to the very beginning of the sport in this country in 1928. Racing at the Cleveland Park track, like at many other provincial centres, had an on and off existence during the 1930s, but when speedway began to test the waters immediately after the Second World War, Middlesbrough was quick to reopen.

Virtually a Who's Who of Provincial League stars, taken during a world championship round at Stoke, topped and tailed by promoters Reg Fearman and Mike Parker. The riders are as follows: back row from left to right: Brian Craven, Pete Jarman, John Fitzpatrick, Ron Bagley, Alan Jay. Middle row: Geoff Mudge, Ernie Baker, Kid Bodie (Howard Cole), Kevin Torpie, Cyril Francis and Cliff Cox, Front row: Colin Pratt, Roy Bowers, Eric Hockaday, Trevor Redmond and Ken Adams.

Stan Greatrex, soon to become part of the management at my old track, West Ham, ran some open meetings in September 1945 and when league racing resumed the following year the Bears, as the team was then known, was one of six tracks to enter the second-tier Northern League.

Middlesbrough were wildly successful, winning the 1946 Northern League title and repeating their success in 1947, when the section had become Division Two of the National League.

Speedway folklore has it that Middlesbrough closed its doors at the end of the 1947 campaign because the team's supremacy saw far too many runaway home wins. Crowds dipped spectacularly due to a surfeit of success (can you imagine that happening in any other sport?), and even a deliberate weakening of the side for 1947, by transferring top riders such as Wilf Plant elsewhere, had no effect on either the league table position or the support.

Racing of a sort took place again in the 1953–55 period, using local motorcycle club riders, but Bears' fans had to wait until the start of the Provincial League's second year of operation in 1961 to see league matches again.

The Provincial League is quite rightly seen as being a huge success that revitalised speedway at a time when the sport was at a low ebb. It was, nevertheless, a patchy success.

At the end of the first season in 1960, four of the inaugural ten tracks withdrew for one reason or another. The introduction of Middlesbrough, together with our other revivals at Newcastle and Wolverhampton, plus a West Country revival at Plymouth and Exeter, meant that despite the closures, the Provincial League was actually stronger for its second campaign.

On the track, our teams didn't enjoy a great deal of success, with Wolves, Middlesbrough and Newcastle, in that order, occupying the bottom three positions. Poole Pirates were champions and Stoke was third.

Results are not always the sole factor in ensuring the success of a speedway track. As I mentioned earlier, Middlesbrough had reportedly closed its doors more than a decade before when the fans got tired of one-sided matches.

In 1961, the performances of the Bears were enough to bring enough fans through the doors to make the promotion viable. The main riders in that first season at Cleveland Park were Rick France, a comparative novice on loan from Coventry who rode consistently in thirty-seven matches to score more than 200 points, and several others who would go on to play a major part in my future speedway life.

Former England Test rider, Eric Boothroyd, was allowed to step down from the National to the Provincial League. Both he and Tommy Roper, who had been a mainstay of the struggling Bradford side in 1960, scored consistently in that first season at Middlesbrough. Clive Hitch was both reliable and entertaining and the 1961 season also saw the league debut of one of the top discoveries of my promoting career in the form of Eric Boocock, whose elder brother Nigel was already an established star.

For most of August that year, the Silver Sash match title was in the hands of Bears' riders, with wins and successful defences for first Roper and then Boothroyd. Earlier in the season, Rick France had been the first 1961 winner of the Sash.

Middlesbrough rose only one place in the Provincial League table for 1962 but Eric Boothroyd made a huge impact in the league, finishing with an average of 10.5 points. His teammate Brian McKeown, a New Zealander formerly with Southampton, was not far behind. Eric Boocock confirmed his promise and the Bears unearthed another find in local boy, Dave Younghusband, who at the time was in the army with Rick France, both doing National Service at Caterick.

Cleveland Park continued to be a reasonably successful venue in 1963 although, once again, the Bears were closer to the bottom of the league table than the top. A respectable placing was achieved in 1964 but crowds were on the slide at Middlesbrough.

Major Middlesbrough discoveries. Dave Younghusband (left) and Eric Boocock (right).

The truth is that Cleveland Park was a 'cinderella' track. Compared to some other venues around the country, the attendance figures were OK but no more than that. No matter what I tried in terms of publicity, it proved impossible to improve the attendance figures on a regular basis.

If I introduced a personality such as Pat Phoenix, Elsie Tanner of *Coronation Street*, or her fellow cast member Kenneth Cope (Jed Stone), the attendance figures soared. Sabrina, the model who was perhaps a fore-runner of today's celebrity culture, also appeared at a meeting and generated much publicity. But on a day-to-day basis it was difficult to generate a big crowd.

Personality appearances caused attendance figures at Cleveland Park to soar. The cabaret artist and model Sabrina is interviewed by Reg on the centre green.

The 1962 season brought me yet more promoting responsibilities when Northern Speedways took up the reins at two venues. Leicester had a long pedigree in speedway, whilst Bradford's Greenfield Stadium was a much smaller and hopefully more manageable venue than the huge Odsal bowl.

Odsal had reopened for the inaugural Provincial League season in 1960. The team was weak, winning one and losing seventeen of its league matches, but might have surfaced again in 1961 had it not been for difficulties with the Rugby League club.

Promoter Jess Halliday, who was a stockbroker in Bradford and a speedway fan, now turned his attention to another local venue, the Greenfield Autodrome, a greyhound stadium which had staged a few dirt-track meetings in 1928 and coincidentally had been an earlier home of Bradford Northern Rugby League Football Club.

Halliday laid a new track at Greenfield and ran six open meetings in 1961. He successfully applied for membership of the Provincial League for 1962 but soon ran into financial trouble. Northern Speedways agreed to go in and run the track until the end of the season. Racing took place on Fridays and because Parker was occupied at Leicester on that evening, I took on the day-to-day respon-sibility for Greenfield. Bridgett was the front man at Wolverhampton, which was also a Friday race night.

It was not a particularly pleasant experience. Bradford's team was again very weak and there were problems with the track itself which had large lumps of clinker on the surface. No fewer than seventeen riders appeared in Bradford colours, with the most regular team members being the veteran duo of Geoff Pymar and Wal Morton.

Geoff and Wal rode in forty-three matches between them, scoring a total 212 points, which was not bad considering that their aggregate age was in excess of 100 years, no doubt a record for a speedway pairing.

The list of the other riders who appeared for Bradford that season looks quite impressive at first glance. It included Belle Vue loanees Jack Kitchen, Peter Kelly and Jim Yacobi, together with Tommy Roper, Ray Day and Reg Duval, who had a lot of National League experience. The problem was that they rarely, if ever, came together in the same line-up.

Bradford, predictably, finished bottom of the Provincial League again, although on this occasion the team won seven matches.

One of these Greenfield victories, right at the end of the 1962 season, was against the second team to come under the Northern Speedways umbrella for that year, Leicester. Again, it is not a particularly happy tale and once more serves to illustrate the up-and-down nature of Provincial League speedway.

Leicester was another track that operated off and on in the 1930s at the Blackbird Road greyhound stadium. At one stage in that decade it was joined by a second venue in the East Midland city, Leicester Super, with a 586-yard track.

Blackbird Road re-opened in 1949 under the control of Alan Sanderson of Midland Sports Stadiums. It was a well-appointed stadium with an impressive grandstand and concrete terracing all the way around. It was a favourite venue of former World Champion, Jack Young, who once wrote in a magazine article that going into the main entrance of the grandstand was like entering a picture palace!

Leicester was one of speedway's survivors during the sport's 1950s downturn, well managed by Charles Ochiltree, a director of Midland Sports Stadiums, and pre-war rider Cyril 'Squib' Burton. As speedway shrunk from three divisions to a single National League, Leicester eventually found itself in the top tier.

Despite the brilliance of the team's skipper, Ken McKinlay, and a succession of Polish stars allocated to Blackbird Road in the late 1950s, dark clouds began to appear on the Leicester horizon.

At the end of the 1961 season, Charles Ochiltree closed Leicester in the National League due to falling attendances and offered the speedway rights for Provincial League racing in 1962 to Mike Parker and me under the Northern Speedways Ltd umbrella.

The CO closed Leicester when the average attendance at Blackbird Road had been 3,000-plus. Despite the downturn in the sport, the surviving tracks in the National League in the late 1950s could still attract paying attendances that are unthinkable in the second decade of the twenty-first century.

Leicester's 3,000 loyal fans were not quite enough for Charles Ochiltree and Alan Sanderson but the CO thought the figure would not go lower if the track operated in the less costly to operate Provincial League.

Consequently, Parker and I took it on. Unfortunately for us, the attendance figures plummeted. The norm at Leicester in 1962 was a crowd of 1,200 or even less and the promotion haemorrhaged money.

At the end of the 1962 season, I made an unexpected return to racing. My last appearance had been for Stoke in a Provincial League match at Plymouth in 1961 and, troubled by my recurring back injury, I had hung up my leathers, as I thought, for good.

My return to the track could hardly have been in a more important match. Stoke had beaten Poole by just 2 points in the semi-final of the Provincial League Knock-out cup, raced over just one leg at Sun Street in September. A hero of that meeting, Jim Heard, who was joint top scorer with 11 points, was later to prove the villain of the piece.

The two-legged final, against Exeter, was not scheduled to be raced until more than a month later. The first leg was at Stoke on Saturday, 20 October. Jim Heard stunned me, his teammates and the Sun Street fans by retiring at what was reported as 'short notice'.

The Potters rose to the occasion and beat Exeter by 60–36. Colin Pratt scored a 15-point maximum and he was well backed up by Pete Jarman with 14 points and Ken Adams with 10. I scored a useful 6 points through what was described at the time as 'some hectic riding'.

The tables were to be turned when we travelled to Devon for the second leg on the following Monday evening. Things began well when Pete Jarman won the

Len Silver (with guitar) and vocalist Howdy Byford entertain the fans, although the Stoke supporters were not over impressed when Silver led his Exeter side to victory in the Provincial League Knock-Out Cup Final.

first heat but Exeter eventually triumphed 70–26, winning the cup on aggregate by 106–86.

Jarman was our top scorer with 10 points, Ray Harris got 6 and I managed 4. Colin Pratt, unbeatable in the first leg, failed to score. Unfortunately, the record books do not state whether he was injured or had machine trouble that evening.

At the end of the 1962 season, around October time, I went on holiday abroad. When I returned, Parker was very cool on the telephone so I went up from my Stoke-on-Trent base to Manchester where I learned that he 'did not want to do business with me'.

Parker informed me that he had negotiated a new lease for Newcastle and Wolverhampton in his own name and, thank you very much, I could have Stoke and Middlesbrough. We parted acrimoniously. That winter of 1962/63 saw the start of my litigation against Parker.

We both had new interests which would take up much of our time in the run-up to the Provincial League's 1963 season. Parker got involved with Hackney Wick in London, where speedway had operated in the mid- and late 1930s (the track is now buried somewhere below the London 2012 Olympic Stadium), and I prepared to re-launch speedway at Long Eaton, a track about midway between Nottingham and Derby which had last staged league racing in 1952.

Despite new and continuing responsibilities, the position was far too serious for me to fail to take any action. Parker had a substantial powerbase at this level of the sport, having been chairman of the Provincial League Promoters' Association in the league's first three seasons, from 1960–62 inclusive.

Consequently, when the promoters gathered for their pre-season meeting at the Harbour Heights Hotel in Poole in January 1963, I made my stand. I stood up at the beginning of that meeting and addressed the assembly, saying that I had a statement to make that Mike Parker was dishonest and a thief.

He had stolen the Wolverhampton and Newcastle speedway leases from our two companies, Babasbat Ltd and Northern Speedways Ltd, and had converted them into his own name and was not fit to be chairman of the Association.

As you can imagine, the balloon went up and Charles Foot proposed that, for the sake of the meeting, Parker should be removed from the chair for that conference.

During the meeting, Long Eaton and Hackney were accepted as members of the Provincial League which gave Parker and me three tracks each out of a total membership at the start of the 1963 season of fourteen. Few people outside the inner circles of the sport, and certainly not the supporters at Long Eaton and Hackney looking forward to seeing their teams revived, realised what was going on behind the scenes.

I read carefully the Memorandum and Articles of Association of Limited Companies and told my lawyers that a director of such a company was there to protect the company's interests, not to divert its assets to his or her own personal benefit, as Parker had clearly done.

In February, Major W.W. Fearnley, the secretary of the SCB, notified Parker, myself and the Provincial Promoters' Association, that it would not licence the six tracks we operated between us until the litigation was resolved.

I was suing Parker for a considerable amount of money and those words from the SCB brought the litigation to a swift conclusion, with the result agreed between our respective barristers at Lincolns Inn, London.

The outcome was a financial settlement to me which took Parker about two and a half years to pay in instalments. After that, I would not have p****d on him if he had been lying in the gutter and on fire.

The 1963 season eventually got under way, the licences were granted and I had time to concentrate on running my tracks at Stoke, Middlesbrough and Long Eaton.

Long Eaton supporters looking forward to the first league speedway at Station Road for eleven years had no idea that the venture was threatened by the Parker-Fearman legal dispute. When the meeting did take place the Archers team, pictured with Reg, was, back row from left to right, Gil Goldfinch, Jon Erskine, Vic White and Dennis Jenkins, who stood in for Charlie Monk, camera-shy as usual. Front row, Bluey Scott, Slant Payling and Ken Vale. Kenneth Cope, Jed Stone of *Coronation Street*, is on the right of the back row.

Long Eaton is a medium-sized former lace-making town almost midway between the big population centres of Nottingham and Derby. The greyhound stadium was opened in 1927 and a year later the venue staged its first dirt-track meeting.

It won an early if unflattering place in speedway history when the track entered the English Dirt Track League for 1929 and then failed to fulfil a single fixture. Nottingham was by then an established speedway centre and Long Eaton's Station Road circuit staged a Nottingham v Leicester challenge match in 1930, promoted by some of the Nottingham riders.

The track re-opened for a season of challenge matches in 1950, just as the speedway boom was starting to waver, and attendances never really came up to expectations. Nevertheless, the Archers entered the National League Division Three in 1951, finishing next to the bottom. The team's greatest achievement was perhaps its nurturing of future Australian Test star, Peter Moore.

Division Three became the Southern League in 1952 and Long Eaton pulled out mid-season. The attendance for the final meeting was not far off 4,000 but, in those days of high entertainment tax, that was not enough to sustain league racing.

The stadium staged some unlicensed meetings in 1954, run by former Norwich rider Paddy Mills and the stadium lessee, a Scot called Tom Beattie.

The arrival on the scene of the Provincial League sparked new interest around the country and in late 1962 two local chaps from The Potteries, Olly Oliver and Barry Norman, came to see me at my Stoke-on-Trent home and invited me to become interested in promoting speedway at Long Eaton.

They had already been to the Station Road Stadium and had met Tom Beattie whose family had interests in open-cast coal mining in their native Scotland. I readily agreed to go over to Long Eaton with them to meet Beattie, who was also a successful racehorse owner. His horse Purple Silk ran second in the Grand National in 1964 to Team Spirit at odds of 40–1.

Although the stadium was rundown, I could see the possibilities of speedway racing, which would have to share the track with the stock car promoters, something which was later to cause many problems.

Once an agreement was in place with Tom Beattie, we started work to transform the derelict track, pits and spectator areas into a venue fit for speedway racing. Costs soon mounted up and it became necessary for us to deposit a considerable sum of money into the bank if we were to proceed any further. Neither Olly nor Barry could come up with their share so, by agreement, I bought them out and continued alone.

Some time after racing got underway in the Provincial League in 1963, I invited Ron Wilson to become the Long Eaton team manager. A former Leicester rider, Ron had performed that role for Mike Parker and me at Blackbird Road in 1962 during that ill-fated, money-down-the-drain season.

In 1965, Ron decided he wanted to be a promoter. He went off to Peterborough and made an arrangement with the owners of the greyhound stadium there. His application to the local council for a change of use was rejected. It was after this that I offered Ron a half share, as co-promoter, in Long Eaton Speedway.

Long Eaton, like Middlesbrough, was a reasonable success from a crowd point of view without ever pulling up too many trees. On the track, the Archers were at least consistent, finishing next to bottom in both the 1963 and 1964 seasons.

Vic White, who had captained Leicester in 1962, moved over from Blackbird Road to Station Road and another Provincial League Young Hunter, Maurice 'Slant' Payling, joined him. The publicity-shy Australian, Charlie Monk, and Jon Erskine were recruited from Trevor Redmond's now defunct Welsh track at Neath and Gil Goldfinch, a former Wimbledon rider, joined from Newcastle.

Eric 'Bluey' Scott, who had ridden for Motherwell and Southampton in the early 1950s, came back to Britain with his Scots wife for an extended stay in 1963. There was no place for him at Edinburgh but I was delighted to add him to the Archers' line-up.

The Archers caused a bit of a stir when they won their first away match in the curtain-raising Midland League at Parker's Wolverhampton, but at home results went against them in the first few meetings. I talked Danny Dunton, a World Finalist in his Harringay days, into signing for the team and things eventually came right, with a side strong enough to win most of its home matches.

Team manager Ron Wilson, a former Leicester rider, became co-promoter at Station Road in 1965. Son Ray, left, became perhaps the greatest rider to be developed at Station Road.

One of Ray Wilson's greatest exploits at Station Road was to beat Barry Briggs in a Silver Sash contest.

Making a start at this time in second-half rides across the Midlands was Ron and Freda Wilson's 16-year-old son, Ray. He broke into the Archers' team at the end of the 1963 season and was going great guns in the Provincial League in 1964 when his career was interrupted by a broken thigh in a challenge match at Weymouth.

Long Eaton, like Middlesbrough, was to move on with me to new challenges in speedway and will figure again later in this story.

The Provincial League years as a whole were busy ones, in the main successful, but with the dark shadow of the dispute with Parker adding a sour taste. The vendetta continued for many years until his death at a comparatively young age. After finishing with speedway and stock car racing, he ran a restaurant business in Lancaster. He had lived most of his life in the Blackpool area and Manchester.

Although the vendetta continued, circumstances meant that Parker and myself were at least nominally on the same side when a new dispute arose, this time between the Provincial League Promoters' Association on the one hand and the long-established top tier of British speedway, the National League and the sport's governing body, in the shape of the Control Board, in the opposite corner.

Mike Parker's Wolverhampton won the Provincial League Championship in 1963. The Wolves' success coincided with the sale of Bannister Court Stadium in Southampton for development and the demise of the Saints speedway team.

The National League, which had operated in 1963 with just seven teams, half the number in the supposedly junior but obviously flourishing Provincial League set-up, now faced a situation in which its six member teams would not constitute a viable league.

Under the SCB rules as they were at the time, the Board had the right to elevate a team (or teams) from the lower league to the higher division. In the Control Board's 'wisdom', its members decided that Wolverhampton and one other (unnamed) Provincial League track should be so elevated to National League status.

We, the Provincial League promoters, held emergency meetings and decided that we did not want to lose any of our tracks. We told the Control Board and the National League promoters as much but they were insistent. We therefore decided that for the 1964 season we would go it alone, outside the SCB's jurisdiction and that of the Auto Cycle Union.

The response of the Control Board was that, should we decide to go down that route, everybody would be banned – promoters, riders and any officials who chose to accompany us.

There was a considerable degree of pressure exerted by the National League promoters and the authorities in those early months of 1964. Charles Ochiltree telephoned me and asked me to put my tracks at Middlesbrough and Long Eaton into the National League. Other National League promoters also phoned around to try and divide and rule but the Provincial League promoters stuck together.

When the 1964 season eventually began, with no one really knowing what would happen, it transpired that our riders in the main stuck by us. In most cases they did not really have a choice as they could not expect to get a contract and, in real terms, a job in the National League.

The Provincial League Promoters' Association rose to the challenge of running outside authority. We expanded our office, took on former riders, timekeepers and team managers as referees. A great coup was to obtain the services of Lieutenant Colonel Vernon Brooke, a former leading light in both the SCB and the RAC, as our disputes adjudicator.

At this time, there was a great camaraderie among the Provincial League promoters and there were very few rows, appeals or protests. The SCB thought we could never manage to run our own affairs, but we did so with great success.

Charles Foot from Poole drew up the new Provincial League rulebook and there was no shortage of volunteers to fill the 'official' positions. I think we were all a bit anxious at the start of the season and a number of promoters travelled to Exeter, the venue for the very first meeting under the Provincial banner, to give support to the promoters, Wally Mawdsley and Pete Lansdale.

The success of the 'black' Provincial League and the knowledge that yet another National League track, Norwich, was likely to close at the end of the 1964 season, again for development, concentrated minds in the Control Board and in the thinning ranks of the National League promoters.

During the course of 1964, the Royal Automobile Club, which was then the overall governing body of all motor sport in Great Britain, set up a formal inquiry into the running of speedway racing with Lord Shawcross, a former British Attorney General who made his name representing the UK at the Nuremburg war trials, as chairman.

The outcome of the inquiry was the crucial declaration that, 'in truth, speedway racing is a business'. Shawcross effectively ruled that the SCB had acted illegally in trying to coerce the individual businesses which made up the Provincial League tracks to agree to giving up two members to the National League.

Shawcross said the Control Board should be reconstituted and several heads rolled in the make-up of the Board following the verdict of the inquiry.

Common sense started to be the order of the day, reluctantly or otherwise, and meetings were held between the National League and Provincial League promoters during the winter of 1964–65.

During the same period of 1964–65, I decided to transfer the assets of Middlesbrough, which was no longer a paying proposition, to Halifax. With Stoke already gone, that had left me with just Middlesbrough and Long Eaton to run. I was ready for a new venture and eager to find a track that would be a real success, from both a financial and a speedway point of view.

The outcome of the meetings between the promoters from the rival leagues was the formation of the British Speedway Promoters' Association (BSPA) and the amalgamation of the two leagues into one large British League for the 1965 season.

Before telling the story of my part in making the British League the success it undoubtedly was, I have to relate the subsequent history of my relationship (and that of other promoters) with Mike Parker.

In 1965, Parker became chairman of the new BSPA. My point of view was that after my experiences with him in 1963, I would eventually have to have him removed from office.

The vastly experienced Charles Foot had, however, always said to me (and he proved to be right) that if we left Parker in office, at least we would know where he was. Despite this, in the late 1960s, with the British League proving a great success, I decided that a *coup d'état* should indeed take place.

Charles Ochiltree was, at this time, in conflict with Parker over the Stock Car World Final. (By this time, Parker had branched out, with Bill Bridgett, into promoting stock car racing.) Under the circumstances, the CO was the obvious choice to take the BSPA chair and he agreed to stand for the office.

Peace of a kind after the National and Provincial leagues combined for the 1965 season with Mike Parker as chairman of the new British League Promoters' Association. This meeting of the promoters at the Harbour Heights Hotel, Poole, features the men who ran the sport during one of its most popular periods. Front row, Trevor Redmond, Charles Ochiltree (arms folded), Johnnie Hoskins, Frank Varey (sitting on the floor), Dave Stevens (secretary), Mike Parker, Ronnie Greene. Back row, extreme left, Ian Hoskins, Reg Fearman, Alan Martin, Norman Parker, Wally Mawdsley, Charles Knott, Charles Foot, Bill Bridgett (with beard), Eddie Glennon, Pete Lansdale and Len Silver. Behind Wally Mawdsley are two guests.

I did the lobbying, which was all quite secret and, at the BSPA annual conference at Chesford Grange Hotel in Warwickshire, the bomb dropped. Parker's face was ashen as Charles Ochiltree was sworn in as chairman for 1970.

Charles carried through those duties to the end of 1972 and then I was appointed BSPA chairman in 1973. The inaugural Second Division of the British League had been launched in 1968 and I had chaired that division through to the end of 1972. In all, I was chairman of Division Two for five years and Division One for seven years.

My own experiences with Mike Parker had echoes elsewhere within the sport. He was in partnership with Len Silver at Hackney but there was soon a parting of the ways, with Len taking control of the East London track. A further relationship, this time between Parker, Charles Foot and the Knotts at Newport, which had opened to great success in 1964, lasted only a short period of time before they fell out, with Parker taking control.

Parker was a maverick and at times a law unto himself. At one time, he and Bill Bridgett signed Rick France for Wolverhampton without the consent of the Rider Control Committee. They were threatened with expulsion from the league.

The only person who remained with Parker throughout was Bill Bridgett (who must have been a yes man). Poor soul, I understand in the end Parker hijacked Bridgett's pension fund.

In 2002, I heard that Bridgett was not very well and offered him an olive branch via a phone call to his home during which I invited him to become a member of the Veteran Speedway Riders' Association to enjoy the fellowship of ex-riders together with regular news bulletins to keep him in touch.

He declined the offer, saying that his life was now spent within his own four walls, watching football (his first love) on television at every opportunity. He told me that he had blown up to a weight of 20 stone and could just about hobble across the room.

Harold (Bill) Bridgett died in Stoke-on-Trent in 2004, aged 76. He is buried at Barlaston Cemetery in Stoke.

Charles Foot proved to be correct in his view that Parker was best left in the chair of the Association. After he was removed from office, Parker, accompanied by Bill Bridgett, would waste as much time as possible at meetings of the promoters, concentrating on the smallest items on the agenda and filibustering.

Then, at 2 p.m. on the dot, he would leave the meeting to catch his train home to Manchester. The rest of us remained until 6 p.m. catching up on the outstanding business.

The vendetta continued, with further incidents, some of which turned really nasty.

In 1975, the Rider Control Committee allocated the Swedish rider, Bengt Jansson, to my track at Reading from Parker and Bridgett's Wolverhampton. The Rider Control Committee had five members, two of which were Len Silver and me.

Subsequently, the Wolverhampton Speedway Programme and Press Bulletin named Len Silver and me as being associated with the Mafia. Len and I took legal action against Mike Parker, Bill Bridgett and Michael Beale, the Wolverhampton Press Officer, resulting in an action in the High Court.

Len and I won and received unreserved apologies and a retraction in the Wolverhampton Speedway Programme and Press Bulletins.

I always remember Parker turning up for the first meeting of the new era at Stoke on Good Friday, 1960. That winter, I had written down all the things I could remember about the promotions at West Ham and Leicester during my days as a rider.

One thing that stood out in my mind was the fact that the promoters and managers I had ridden for were always well turned out. So, at Stoke that day, I was there in my Sunday best. To my embarrassment, Parker turned up in jeans and a blue shirt with his sleeves rolled up.

Parker became a tremendous thorn in the world of stock car racing, in particular to Charles Ochiltree. Charles was such a docile man but he was driven to swear a bad word to me in describing Parker, which is really saying something.

The CO actually kept a dossier on Parker with information gained through private investigators.

At the start of this chapter I promised to give my candid appraisal of Mike Parker as a man and as a businessman. Well, here it is: Parker was a pirate and a bandit if ever there was one.

It is time for me to move on, as speedway itself did with such success, to the brave new world of the British League.

It was a new era for the sport and, for me, it opened up one of the most successful chapters in my entire career.

CHAPTER TEN

HALIFAX AND THE BRITISH LEAGUE

The bare facts of the transfer of my Middlesbrough team to Halifax during the winter of 1964–65, amid the run-up to the birth of the British League, have been recorded elsewhere. What has not been told is how the change actually came about.

My captain at Middlesbrough throughout the Provincial League years at Cleveland Park had been Eric Boothroyd who was Halifax born-and-bred and the owner of a flourishing local greengrocery business.

Eric's 'spanner man', the chap who helped him in the pits on race nights, was Arthur Ambler, who worked for the Ford Motor Company agents on Skircoat Road in Halifax.

Arthur had on many occasions asked me to have a look at the ground of Halifax Town Football Club, perennial strugglers in the lower divisions of the Football League and a club which had to compete for support with the West Riding town's rugby league side, much more successful in that era than in later times.

I had never raced at the track when it had operated in Division Three and later Division Two of the National League in the late 1940s and early 1950s. In fact, I had never even seen it until I stopped off in the town to meet Arthur one day in 1963 when I was travelling up to Middlesbrough.

Arthur took me across Skircoat Road to the stadium which was known as The Shay. We peered through some cracks in the fencing and then climbed a small fence to get a better view. I liked what I saw, a football pitch in what can only be described as a bowl, similar to the famous Odsal Stadium in Bradford.

There was no track there of course as speedway had died in Halifax some ten years previously. The football club had built a pre-cast concrete fence up close to the football pitch but I could see the possibilities, especially as Halifax itself was surrounded by 'chimney pots' in the form of the densely populated centres of Huddersfield, Bradford and Leeds, all of which were within striking distance of The Shay.

Without delay, I wrote to the secretary of Halifax Town, outlining my interest and seeking a meeting with the football club's board of directors. The reply was swift and dismissive, with the directors stating firmly that they were not interested in sharing their stadium with speedway racing.

The Shay, Halifax, after returning the stadium into a speedway race track in the winter of 1964–65.

That could have been the end but, in 1964, Arthur Ambler told me that a new football club chairman had been appointed who was a speedway fan. That new chairman was Sydney Hitchen, a man who had won £75,000 on the football pools. Arthur Ambler said I should write to him. I did so and this time the response was very positive, with a meeting quickly arranged at the football club.

We came to an agreement that included the provision that I had to bear all the costs involved in making The Shay Stadium suitable for speedway racing. Speedway promoters rarely, if ever, have the luxury of being able to employ contractors to do construction work. It is usually left to the hard work and ingenuity of the promoter and his helpers.

I had a good pal in Bill Smith, an engineer, with whom I had previously been in business in The Potteries. Bill did the drawings and planning for the whole operation. We hired local labour from the Halifax Labour Exchange and machinery when required from the local plant hire firm. Maurice Morley, who had been team manager at Middlesbrough, oversaw the day-to-day work. Bill and I would travel from The Potteries to Halifax several times a week.

With Halifax being in the Pennines and quite a wet area, I decided at an early stage to dispense with the usually preferred red shale (which came from the spoil heaps of coal mines). I went instead for granite in the form of one eighth of an inch to dust for the Halifax track. It may not have been the prettiest to look at but it was extremely practical in that the surface still gave good grip to the rear tyre in wet conditions.

First of all, the pre-cast concrete fence had to be removed. A new track had to be shaped and laid, with drainage and a safety fence erected. The fence consisted of wooden planking along the straights with the material from steel Morrison air-raid shelters left over from the Second World War on the corners (shades of Exeter where the fence was of similar construction).

A control box for the speedway officials had to be constructed from steel and timber. This was craned up into the roof of the grandstand and bolted to the girders. That box held the referee, timekeeper and the announcer on race nights and once a month I would climb the shaky aluminium ladder to check on the nuts and bolts holding the structure, which were prone to work loose because of the vibration of the three people occupying the box.

It was a climb that I never enjoyed but it didn't seem to worry Mrs Boocock, Eric's mother. Eric moved with me from Middlesbrough, became an England international and much later the England team manager. If a referee excluded Eric and Mrs Boocock didn't agree with the verdict, she was off up the ladder like a shot to the cheers of the crowd, who shouted, 'You tell him Mrs Boocock!'

I have had my share of good luck during my career and lady luck certainly shone on me yet again as far as Halifax was concerned. The amalgamation of the two speedway leagues for the 1965 season meant, to use an expression, that all tracks started again on a level playing field. I was able to opt for Saturday night speedway racing at The Shay, something which was accepted by the promoters of the other seventeen British League tracks.

Saturday was obviously the best night to entice the public out but the option did not exist for many other speedway promotions. These were restricted as far as their race nights were concerned by the priority given to greyhound racing in shared stadiums controlled by the dog operators.

I transferred the rider assets from Middlesbrough to The Shay. In addition to Eric Boocock, the riders who moved with me to The Shay were Dave Younghusband and Clive Hitch whilst Eric Boothroyd, who had retired after being injured in 1964 during his spell with Long Eaton, could not resist the opportunity to ride for and captain his home town team.

There had been an attempt (not always very effective) to equalise team strengths for the start of the British League. This process failed to do a great deal for my new track. The one rider I was allocated was Bryan Elliott from Coventry who, despite being a useful performer and an England international, was not one of the big names in the sport.

Then, as now, in speedway there were plenty of young Australians looking for a break in Britain. I chose three of these hopefuls – Bert Kingston, Bob Jameson and later in the season, Dennis Gavros – to make up the side.

The speedway pundits probably did not rate Halifax's chances of competing with the glamorous former National League teams such as West Ham, Belle Vue, Wimbledon, Swindon and Coventry.

Initially, their estimate of Halifax's chances seemed to hold some water. After a couple of away matches, the new Dukes – the team's nickname comes from the fact that the Duke of Wellington's Regiment was stationed in the town, and the regiment's elephant symbol was used on the race jackets – made their home debut on Easter Saturday 1965 in front of a crowd of 10,000 people.

The opposition that night was provided by my other interest, the Long Eaton Archers, not exactly renowned for successes on away tracks. Ironically, the Archers proved to be the party poopers that evening at The Shay. Ray Wilson and Kid Bodie were in fine form and the visitors registered a 41–36 victory over the Dukes who were missing Bryan Elliott, injured at Newport the previous night.

Success was not long in coming for the Dukes, however. The pundits were right in as much as the first British League title was won by West Ham, followed in the league table by other former National League tracks in the shape of Wimbledon, Coventry and Oxford.

THE SHAY GROUNDS
HALIFAX

HALIFAX

SPEEDWAY

THE HOME OF THE 'DUKES'

1st MEETING   ∴   1st SEASON

BRITISH LEAGUE MATCH

HALIFAX 'Dukes' v.

LONG EATON 'Archers'

SATURDAY, 17th APRIL, 1965 at 7-30 p.m.

OFFICIAL PROGRAMME **9**d.

The programme cover for the first match under Reg at The Shay – against his other British League interest, Long Eaton.

Next in line, in a highly commendable fifth position, was Halifax, ahead of the much more fancied Belle Vue and Swindon ex-National League boys and also in front of Mike Parker's three tracks at Newcastle, Hackney and Wolverhampton, which had occupied the first three positions in 1964's last-ever Provincial League table.

Eric Boocock and Dave Younghusband showed that they could more than hold their own against both the former National League stars and the former Provincial League's top men.

Eric Boothroyd's comeback was a great success and Bryan Elliott scored solidly. Clive Hitch was not completely at home on the big, steeply banked Shay track and part way through the season he was replaced by Tommy Roper who proved an instant success. Young Australians Bert Kingston and Dennis Gavros, together with Bob Jameson and former Bradford and Middlesbrough man Ray Day when required, contributed useful points.

I was a pretty satisfied speedway promoter at the end of the 1965 season. And even better was to come in 1966.

The first practice sessions at Halifax in 1965. From left to right: Reg Fearman, riders Dave Younghusband and Eric Boothroyd, Maurice Morley and friend, Eric Boocock and Tommy Roper.

The second British League campaign saw the Dukes line-up with a virtually unchanged side from the previous year. The only rider missing from 1965 was Bryan Elliott. His retirement meant that Halifax entered the new season without a single rider in their ranks who had ridden in the 1964 National League.

The Dukes' lack of big-time experience, with the exception of Eric Boothroyd, now very much in the veteran stage, was more than compensated for by the solidity of the side and the wonderful team spirit. The team won the treble of the British League Championship, the Knock-Out Cup and the Northern League.

The 21-year-old Boocock, now an established international star, improved his average to over 10 points a match, putting him in fourth place in the national averages behind Barry Briggs (Swindon), his own brother Nigel at Coventry and Swedish star Gote Nordin who rode in 1966 for Newport.

Boothroyd scored nearly 300 league points at an average of more than 9, Younghusband joined him on the 9 point mark, Roper was not far behind and the Aussie trio of Kingston, Jameson and Gavros all gave effective support to the heat leaders.

The magnificent seven rode in the vast majority of matches, always a bonus for a team in any sport, and there was another young Australian, Greg Kentwell, waiting in the wings.

The Dukes slipped to seventh spot in 1967 after that scourge of all promoters, the Rider Control Committee, decided Halifax was too strong and allocated Tommy Roper across the Pennines to Belle Vue.

Polish team Gornik Rybnik visited The Shay during the 1965 season. Team managers Reg and Polish counterpart Jerzy Kubica are seen leading the riders onto the track for the parade. The Halifax rider with his hand to his head is Tommy Roper and Maurice Morley can be seen at the end of the home column. The first Rybnik rider is Andrej Wyglenda, second is Stanislaw Koc, third is Anton Woryna and the sixth man is Andrej Pogorzelski.

Eric Boothroyd joined me as co-promoter in 1969 after retiring from racing and was to become full promoter in 1980.

The Halifax years marked one of the happiest periods of my speedway life and I have some great, and in some instances highly amusing, memories of my time at The Shay. The speedway office, operated by Joan and her staff, was situated behind the racing pits and approached by a narrow path. At the end of each meeting, I would reverse my car as far as I could along the path to get as near as possible to the speedway office.

I would then use a wheelbarrow to carry the night's takings to the car where the cash was placed in the boot. It was mostly silver and coins in those days – half crowns, florins, shillings and sixpences were heavy.

When the cash had been loaded into the boot, the car would sit like a speed-boat with its rear end lowered by the weight of the coins and the front of the car raised up in the air. When the engine was started, the automatic suspension would come into play and the car would level out.

From that time onwards, it has been a standing joke with those who raced for me at Halifax that there was so much cash that Joan and I had to take it away in a wheelbarrow. Sometime later, the police suggested, for safety and security, that the takings should be left in a cell at the police station over the weekend. This practice continued for many years.

The track itself at The Shay was excellent for racing. After laying the drainage all around the inside perimeter of the circuit to take away the rainwater, we broke into a manhole in the car park which proved to be an underground culvert carrying water into the River Calder in the valley below.

Some three years later, we had a visit from the River Authority, looking for the source of 'contaminated water'. The speedway track was composed of grey granite dust and the drainage system meant this was washed first into the culvert and then into the river.

It turned out that a few miles downstream, water was taken out of the river for use in the local textile industry. This was being adversely affected by the contamination from The Shay. We solved the problem by moving our outlet to a 'foul' drainage manhole.

Halifax Dukes, British League champions in 1966, pictured at Wimbledon after beating the home side on aggregate for the Knock-Out Cup. From left to right: Eric Boocock, Maurice Morley (team manager), Bob Jameson, Maury Robinson, Eric Boothroyd (captain), Dave Younghusband, Reg (promoter) and Dennis Gavros.

In the late 1960s, my son Gary was at Moulsford Preparatory School, near Oxford. Joan, Gary and I would leave our home in Henley-on-Thames (we had moved there at the end of 1968) early on a Saturday morning for the long drive to Halifax for the staging of speedway racing that evening. Sometimes we drove back during the night and other times we stayed overnight at an hotel in Huddersfield.

Gary has always made friends quite easily and one boy at his school invited him on several occasions to spend a Saturday at his home and to meet his parents. Gary's response was always the same, saying, 'I'm sorry, Crispin, but I have to go to Halifax.'

After about the third negative response from Gary, the telephone rang at home and was answered by Joan. The voice on the other end said, 'You don't know me. My name is George Cole (Arthur Daley of *Minder*) and my son, Crispin, has asked Gary on several occasions to come to our home on a Saturday. Gary always replies that he can't because he has to go to Halifax. I'm perplexed and I am ringing to ask why Gary has to go to Halifax on a Saturday.'

When Joan explained the circumstances George replied, 'Ah, the penny has dropped.' We became good friends with George and his actress wife, Penny Morrell. Penny read a poem at Joan's funeral in August 1999. When I opened Reading Tilehurst Stadium for speedway in 1968, George was a frequent visitor, having previously seen the sport at Wimbledon.

During those Halifax years, I became the first speedway promoter to hold a testimonial meeting for a rider who had given

Reg Fearman's son Gary, pictured in the pits with Dukes skipper Eric Boothroyd, puzzled actor George Cole by constantly telling Cole's son (a schoolfriend) that he could not play on Saturdays because he had to go to Halifax with his parents!

Actor George Cole, who played the character Arthur Daley in *Minder*, could not at first understand why his son's schoolfriend Gary Fearman disappeared each Saturday to Halifax!

ten or more seasons' service to one track. The rider in question was Eric Boocock who had served both Middlesbrough and Halifax loyally by the time I arranged the testimonial in July 1974.

There had been benefit meetings in the past for severely injured riders, including one at West Ham in 1946 for Colin Watson, severely injured in a crash at Odsal while riding for the Hammers.

I had, of course, to apply to the BSPA for permission to hold the meeting. Many of the other promoters were adamantly against such recognition because if one of their riders qualified for a testimonial it would deprive them of one of their own race nights and takings.

I have been blessed with having persuasive powers (Eileen says, 'You can say that again!') and was able to convince my

The cover of Eric Boocock's ground-breaking testimonial meeting.

colleagues that it was a worthwhile recognition for a speedway rider who had given loyal service. I am pleased to say that since that time other promoters have followed my lead.

The event was planned over a period of time and blessed with good weather. The meeting drew more than 7,800 people and Eric was able to receive £5,000. An official Eric Boocock testimonial brochure, entitled Booey, was produced, sold and autographed, for 40p. For some time now it has been a collectors' item.

I was involved in the Halifax promotion for twenty-one years but all things eventually come to an end. In 1986, I sold my shares to the Hamm brothers of Bradford, Alan and Bobby, the latter a former Bradford footballer. In their wisdom, after a couple of seasons at The Shay, the brothers transferred the Halifax outfit to Odsal Stadium, Bradford, one of several occasions when the sport has been revived in that city.

The vastness of Odsal, which had once held more than 100,000 people and was later to attract tens of thousands to stagings of the World Championship Final, produced little atmosphere for ordinary team racing and closed after several seasons due to lack of support.

The problem with the hierarchy in professional sport is that most of these people have no first-hand practical experience of promoting or presenting the particular sport with which they become involved.

An interesting postscript to the Halifax story is the fact that former Dukes rider Ian Cartwright, his wife Anne and son Simon, who also went on to race speedway, here pictured with Reg Fearman at the New Forest Show, own the renowned furniture business in Kilburn, Yorkshire, known as Robert Thompson. They are famous for the distinguishing mark of a mouse carved into each piece of furniture.

There was at one time an agreement between promoters that another speedway track would not be licensed to open within a radius of 25 miles of an existing venue. When I opened Halifax in 1965, the nearest tracks were Belle Vue, Manchester, some 30 miles away and Sheffield, a similar distance.

There were thousands of chimney pots in the West Riding of Yorkshire area, in towns and cities such as Halifax, Huddersfield, Wakefield, Dewsbury, Leeds and Bradford.

In 1970, my old adversary Mike Parker and his partner, Les Whalley, applied for a licence to the SCB to open Bradford Odsal in the Second Division. I objected to the proposal due to the closeness of the two venues – there were just 9 miles between The Shay and Odsal.

The hierarchy (and old farts) of the SCB – and I name two, Norman Dixon MBE of the Auto Cycle Union and Dean Delamont OBE of the Royal Automobile Club – had no idea whatsoever about the business of speedway racing.

If a track was to be successful in attracting the crowds from the surrounding towns, as Halifax was, it certainly did not require opposition from another track in the vicinity. In its wisdom, the SCB granted a licence to Bradford which meant there was a split audience between the two speedways.

Halifax survived this decision by the SCB and it was Bradford that closed after a few seasons, not surfacing again until the decision by the Hamm brothers to switch from The Shay. The damage to the sport by the opening and closing of Bradford in the 1970s could have been avoided by the correct decision having been made originally.

At FIM meetings staged in Britain, particularly the World Final at Wembley, the likes of Dixon and Delamont would love to strut the hallowed turf wearing their FIM armbands. Looking back, what a lot of tossers!

CHAPTER ELEVEN

LONG EATON
TO LEICESTER

In the winter of 2013, I had the pleasure and privilege to be the guest of honour and main speaker at a social event organised by the Long Eaton Speedway Reunion Group.

Speedway fans in the East Midlands are a particularly tenacious bunch. When the original Long Eaton Archers closed down midway through the 1952 season, the fans kept an organisation, called the Midland Speedway Supporters Club, going for more than a decade.

When I moved into Station Road to promote Provincial League racing for the 1963 season, the organisation was still functioning, and provided a basis for reviving a new Long Eaton club to support the new Archers.

Speedway continued (with a few gap years) at Long Eaton long after I had vanished from the Derbyshire scene. First former Cradley star Ivor Brown, who had started his career as a novice at Station Road, and Vic White, and then a succession of promoters ran the sport in the Derbyshire town, and the Invaders, as they were then known, won the National League (Division Two) Championship in 1984.

Then, after the 1997 season, the Invaders, as the team had become, found themselves homeless, with the stadium sold for redevelopment.

The site, ravaged by fire and vandalism, remained derelict for many years. A group was formed to fight for its retention as a sports venue, and for a long time their efforts were encouraged by the local council.

Sadly, the inevitable came to pass and the former stadium site is now a housing development. But despite all the setbacks, the hard core of fans have remained loyal, holding twice-yearly reunions, well attended by both supporters and former riders.

There is even an Invaders team again; riding matches in the Midland Development League, staging home matches at neighbouring Leicester's new home at Beaumont Park. Leicester's fans proved equally as obstinate as Long Eaton's in refusing to accept that speedway was dead in the East Midlands, and I was delighted to be part of a crowd of 4,500 people who packed in to the new stadium to see the sport's return back in 2011.

I have to confess, however, despite the loyalty of so many of the Long Eaton fans, that my five years promoting at Station Road proved to be an horrendous experience. I will explain why my memories of the time are not particularly happy ones.

No matter how hard I tried to build up a successful team, injuries to riders were frequent, right from the start, and success on the track was never forthcoming.

In addition, the track itself required constant major attention, because of the frequency of the stock car meetings held at the stadium.

At one time the stock cars were running every two weeks on a Saturday evening, leaving myself and Ron Wilson, who was at first team manager and later my co-promoter, with no option but at one stage to run the stox ourselves, simply to get some control over the track conditions.

Leicester's Blackbird Road Stadium, less than 30 miles away from Station Road, had been a highly successful speedway venue for a decade or so after its post-war re-opening in 1949. Crowds began to fall as the 1960s dawned and at the end of

Long Eaton in 1966 with John Mills, Ray Wilson, Vic White and Ove Fundin on parade. Vic White was later to become my co-promoter and team manager at Leicester.

the 1961 season the management pulled the plug, declaring that an average crowd of 3,000 was not enough to show a profit at the top-tier National League level.

As I described in an earlier chapter, my then partner Mike Parker and myself considered there was a future for racing in the Provincial League at Leicester, and we acquired the promoting rights for 1962. This was a major error and we haemorrhaged money, with crowds sometimes falling below four figures.

In 1963, at the same time as I launched Long Eaton, Alan Sanderson, the millionaire behind Midland Sports Stadiums (Leicester, Coventry and West Ham) attempted to run a season of open meetings at Blackbird Road at National League level, mainly to give riders additional bookings in a division reduced to seven teams.

Again, the Leicester public failed to support speedway. Nevertheless, Blackbird Road was an excellent stadium, and there was a good chance that four seasons without speedway of any kind might encourage the old supporters and newcomers to the sport to turn out in numbers again, especially as the new British League was proving to be such a success.

With only modest (if loyal) crowds at Station Road, poor facilities, and the problem with the stock cars, as 1967 drew to a close Ron Wilson and I decided to approach Charles Ochiltree, the managing director of Midland Sports Stadiums.

We thought about the situation and came to some firm conclusions. We could reintroduce to Leicester racing in the top tier, the British League. We had three ready-made heat leaders in Anders Michanek, Ray Wilson and John Boulger, who had contributed to Long Eaton's best-ever season in league racing (the Archers finished third from the bottom!).

We had a stadium that was well-cared for and a track which had always produced good racing (both Ron and I had raced for Leicester Hunters in the 1950s).

Charles Ochiltree agreed to our proposal and we switched the British League licence from Station Road to Blackbird Road. The Long Eaton fans were naturally disappointed, although many of them followed us down the road.

We staged our first meeting of the new Leicester Lions in March 1968. The attendance was just short of 8,000, which was more than twice the average attendance at Long Eaton.

The takings grossed just under £2,000. Today's take for that many people would be in the region of £120,000. It is a fact that one has to do just as much work in promoting speedway racing for a couple of thousand people as for 10,000. It is rather like a theatre – a great atmosphere with a full house but dead when only a quarter full.

Leicester ran continuously for sixteen seasons and became a major force in the British League, producing riders of international quality. Ron Wilson promoted the day-to-day business until the winter of 1976–77.

During that winter, Ron approached me to buy his 50 per cent share in the company, as he wished to move on to other things. I bought his half, and this gave Joan and me 100 per cent of the company's shares.

I had discussions with Vic White who had raced for Leicester in 1962 and later for Long Eaton, and who had more recent experience of management. I appointed him co-promoter and team manager. He also took over the day-to-day running of speedway at Blackbird Road.

In December 1979, Martin and Lin Rogers approached us and asked if Joan and I would sell them a half share in the company and allow them to take over the running of Leicester Speedway. They had some good ideas they wished to put into practice.

They bought the half share and duly ran the speedway. All went well for four seasons but at the end of 1983, we received a letter from Midland Sports Stadiums to say that Leicester Stadium would no longer be available for speedway racing as it had been sold for development.

To say that it was a bombshell was an understatement. There had never been a rumour or hint that the stadium may be sold. The last speedway meeting to be staged was in October 1983, Leicester versus Belle Vue, with the Aces winning the match by 40 points to 38.

CHAPTER TWELVE

DIVISION TWO AND READING – DREAMS FULFILLED AND SHATTERED

By the end of the 1967 season, the third year of operation for the British League, it had become apparent that the new competition had ushered in a new era of stability for speedway in the UK.

The British League started off in 1965 with eighteen tracks, adding Kings Lynn for 1966 after the Norfolk venue had operated on a probationary non-league basis for a year and completed 1967 without a casualty.

The competition was to enjoy such an unprecedented level for many years. Fifteen years after the inaugural season there were still eighteen tracks competing. Few of the changes in the British League line-up in its early and middle years were due to tracks closing because of financial problems.

In some cases extremely successful tracks, such as Edinburgh's Old Meadowbank, were forced out because their venue disappeared. In other cases licences were transferred for commercial reasons. Long Eaton, for example, was a reasonably viable promotion but the continual expense of trying to patch up a circuit torn to shreds by too frequent stock car racing made Leicester, ripe for speedway again after a lay-off, a much better proposition.

Having established the British League, it was time to think about expanding the sport once again by re-opening former venues and introducing speedway to pastures new.

In the winter of 1967–68, the BSPA's annual conference was held in Manchester. During the meeting, it was suggested that some promoters were interested in starting a Second Division for the British League, mainly with the intention of encouraging the development of British talent.

There were, indeed, a number of promoters interested in such a scheme, including myself. After the business had been concluded on one of the days, several of us got together and decided to form a consortium with the aim of re-opening tracks which had lain dormant for several years, together with new venues.

The consortium, eventually to become known as Allied Presentations Limited, consisted of five promoters who already operated tracks in the British League. The men concerned, all to be equal directors and shareholders, were Maury Littlechild of Kings Lynn, Danny Dunton (Oxford), Ron Wilson (Long Eaton/Leicester), Len Silver (Hackney) and me (representing Halifax and Long Eaton/Leicester).

I recall vividly how we talked that evening with such great enthusiasm, discussing possible venues for a new division. We all shared a dream of how we could expand the boundaries of the sport we loved.

Of course, speedway is a business, or at least it was in those days when crowds were much higher than at present. But it is and always has been unpredictable, with no guarantees of financial success. There was money to be made in the 1960s and 1970s but no promoter could succeed, whatever his business acumen, without a genuine feeling for speedway racing.

Our discussions included consideration of Middlesbrough and Rayleigh as two examples of venues where league racing had taken place with some success at various times whilst Reading emerged from our talks as a potential new venture.

The initial suggestion to look at Reading came from Maury Littlechild. He knew the Luper brothers, Horace and Eddie, who had considerable shares in both Clapton and Reading greyhound stadiums. The Reading Stadium at Tilehurst had previously staged stock car racing but this had ceased to be staged at the venue some time previously.

When the conference finished, we forged ahead with negotiations and leases were agreed with the owners of the stadia at Rayleigh, Middlesbrough and Reading. Ron Wilson took on responsibility for Middlesbrough (under the new title of Teeside), Len Silver would be in charge at Rayleigh and I would be the director running Reading.

With these tracks in the bag, we turned out attention to other venues. Some proved to be viable whilst others quickly dropped out of the running. Older fans will probably remember how the speedway press of the time was full of suggestions for potential new tracks, some of which were never really likely to come to fruition.

In some cases, the stadia were simply unsuitable while in other instances the owners did not wish to share their facilities with speedway.

We looked at the Horton Road football stadium in Gloucester where there was ample space for a track around the pitch. We even got as far as staging a noise test for the local council, with four riders racing around the pitch perimeter. Unfortunately, the council turned us down on noise levels, with the fact that the stadium was close to a hospital not being a very helpful factor.

Two new venues did, however, meet the requirements of Allied Presentations Ltd. The first, and perhaps the most unlikely venue to surface since the pioneering days of the late 1920s, was Crewe where we inspected a cricket ground owned by the British Railways Staff Association.

Speedway racing had in fact been staged at the venue in the 1930s. By using a little imagination one could make out the outline of the old track. There was a lot of work to be done. We had to construct a new track, install a safety fence, boundary fence, turnstiles, pits, lighting for both the track and the public areas, together with all the other paraphernalia associated with speedway.

We were fortunate in that a young New Zealand rider, Colin Tucker, was a master carpenter/joiner and

Young New Zealander Colin Tucker, a master carpenter by trade, was the project manager for the new Crewe circuit, with the promise of a team place when the job was completed.

an absolute marvel with wood. He became the working project manager with a promise that he would be in the Crewe team when the project was up and running.

The other new venue was the East of England Showground near Peterborough. The Showground committee was agreeable for us to stage speedway racing but under very strict terms. The committee members insisted that they should at all times oversee the construction of speedway facilities.

Peterborough had tremendous potential. Opposite the main showjumping ring was a magnificent modern cantilever grandstand with 2,000 seats and boundary fences were also in places. As at Crewe, we still had to put in the track and all the other necessities for speedway racing.

In the end, both venues took time to bring up to the standard required. The new British League Second Division was in place for the 1968 season but Crewe was not ready until 1969 and Peterborough made its debut in 1970. Maury Littlechild became responsible for Crewe and Danny Dunton was in charge at Peterborough.

There were interesting parallels between the new Second Division and the Provincial League in its early days, both in the initial commitment to encourage new talent as opposed to established riders, and in the supply of replacement tracks for any who dropped out in the early days.

Ten teams lined up for 1968, including a Belle Vue Colts team full of promising youngsters discovered by manager Dent Oliver, a former star rider with the Manchester track. Weymouth dropped out at the end of the season but there were no fewer than seven newcomers to swell the size of the league to sixteen clubs for 1969.

Plymouth left the league at the end of that season and there were several more changes due to licence switches. Rochdale (formerly Belle Vue Colts), Doncaster and Workington saw speedway for the first time since pre-war days. Geographical outposts such as Boston in Lincolnshire and Canterbury in Kent, where Johnnie Hoskins enjoyed a successful Indian summer as a promoter, saw speedway for the first time.

In addition to the original tracks under the Allied Presentations banner, the consortium also took over the running of speedway racing at Newcastle and Sunderland for a limited time in the period between 1968 and 1974.

From my own point of view, Reading was a great success. Speedway in the Berkshire town was to play a huge part in my life from the initial negotiations for Tilehurst in the winter of 1967–68 to the day when I, with great sadness and in controversial circumstances, bowed out of Reading speedway a decade later.

Reading, of course, continued to operate into the new millennium. At the time of writing, there is no speedway in the town, something which arouses in me feelings of great anger. I will come to these feelings and the circumstances from which they arise later in this chapter.

The fact that speedway racing is almost always a tenant in the stadia in which it operates means that over the years many successful clubs have been forced at best to seek new venues or, at worst, cease to operate.

The majority of the greyhound stadia that also saw speedway in the post-war boom period were still there when the Provincial League and later the British League revived the sport in the early to mid-1950s. Major tracks, such as West Ham and New Cross which had closed in the '50s slump, had survived to enjoy revivals and even Harringay, closed at the end of the 1954 season, was able to stage a Provincial League Riders Championship final.

As the 1960s gathered pace and turned into the '70s, so the spectre of the sale of stadia for redevelopment into industrial, business and retail parks or into housing developments, accelerated alarmingly.

In 1968, I was given the remit for the promotion of speedway racing at Reading Greyhound Stadium, Tilehurst, on behalf of Allied Presentations Ltd from 1968–73 inclusive – the Reading Racers, the same nickname enjoyed by Harringay in the past. The lease was renewable on an annual basis.

After three enjoyable seasons in the Second Division, Reading acquired the licence for Division One speedway from Newcastle. The Racers finished sixth in the top tier in 1971 in a league that had exciting echoes of the sport's golden age, with great names such as Wembley, West Ham and Wimbledon competing, sadly, for the last time.

In 1972, Reading were runners-up to champions Belle Vue and all concerned at Tilehurst were looking forward with great enthusiasm to the next campaign.

The hopes of both management and fans were realised in 1973 with the Racers being crowned British League champions.

There was, however, a dark cloud on the horizon. At the beginning of the 1973 season, I was told by the owners of Tilehurst, the Greyhound Racing Association, that Reading Stadium had been sold for development. Both speedway and greyhound racing would cease at the end of that year.

This is a side of speedway racing that the media and the non-racing public must find hard to accept. Reading Racers were champions of a booming British League Division One at a time when speedway was in the midst of a new era of success, yet the club faced the prospect of homelessness and potential oblivion.

One of the early heroes of the Tilehurst crowd, Dickie May leads Geoff Maloney of Rayleigh Rockets and teammate Bernie Leigh.

A Reading Racers line-up from the Tilehurst years. Pictured left to right are Dickie May, Dag Lovaas, Mick Bell, Anders Michanek, Bernie Leigh, Geoff Curtis. On the machine are team manager Dick Bailey and Geoff Mudge.

Can you imagine Manchester United or Arsenal facing the prospect of being turfed out of their stadia immediately after being crowned champions of the Premiership?

Of course, the economics and indeed the whole structure of the two sports are entirely different. But bombshells such as the one that hit Reading speedway in 1973 must contribute to a public perception of speedway being somewhat unstable.

I was determined to save the sport in Reading. I immediately put into action a 'Save our Speedway' campaign, lobbied local councillors and applied for a new venue. The chairman of the Supporters Club, Mick Smith, and the Racers' fans as a whole, were a great help.

Not everyone was on board with the campaign. Many critics believed Reading speedway would never resurface, including the then team manager who defected to Oxford. I never lost faith in the project, being a super optimist.

The result, after much negotiation, was a new site for speedway in the shape of Smallmead, a former refuse tip. In 1974, on behalf of Allied Presentations Ltd, I signed a ninety-nine-year lease with Reading Borough Council for 25 acres of land. The length of that lease is something I want to emphasise.

As will be explained later in this chapter, it had a crucial bearing on the eventual future of Reading speedway. As you will learn later, it came as something of a surprise to me when, subsequently, it was announced that the lease had expired after only thirty-four years.

Smallmead really was constructed out of nothing. Here the turnstile block is seen being built.

Reading speedway was given a leave of absence for one year from the British League. There was no racing in the town during the 1974 season whilst construction work proceeded at the Smallmead site.

The drawings and plans for the new stadium had been drawn up by a close friend, John Spratley of John Spratley & Partners, architects of Abingdon, near Oxford.

The whole Smallmead area was a wilderness and bears no resemblance to the massive development you see in the area today. The relief road of Rose Kiln Lane was but a line on a map for the future and the only access to the stadium site was from Bennett Road, via Basingstoke Road.

I wish to dispel the myth that the speedway track at Smallmead was based on the old Bannister Court circuit at Southampton. It was not. Having the advantage of a virgin site, the first act of constructing the new stadium was pegging out the actual track, which was designed in excess of the FIM regulations for international meetings as they existed at that time.

Much time and effort was spent on the laying-out of the track by three ex-riders, Len Silver, myself and Eddie Lack, who was in our permanent employ. We marked out a perfect semi-circle for the bends and then, as the three of us walked down the straight against what would be the safety fence, we imagined throwing our machines into the corner we were approaching.

We then gradually moved the pegs, marking the white line inwards so that there was a good lead into the corner. We did the same for the exit.

Overall, a great deal of time was spent in perfecting the shape of the corners. Much comment has been made by riders and the media regarding the many racing lines that existed on the Smallmead track and the good racing that ensued.

I am pleased that so many riders and fans over the years enjoyed the fruits of our labour.

Apart from the hard work involved in designing and constructing the track and the spectator facilities, there were also the off-track aspects to consider and overcome. During that summer of 1974, a meeting of the directors of Allied Presentations Limited took place at which it was decided by the majority to abort the Smallmead project due to the economic climate at that time.

That was not acceptable to me. I told my co-directors that it was my dream and that I wished to continue with the operation. They agreed and things were settled amicably, including agreement that I took the company name with me.

Constructing the spectator terracing at Smallmead.

Track grading by a hands-on Reg as Smallmead nears completion.

I invited any of the directors who were willing to join me. Len Silver agreed to do so. We subsequently offered a third share in the project to Frank Higley who had sponsored several riders at Tilehurst and whose bulldozers and other equipment were shaping the Smallmead track. Frank also owned a sawmill in the area.

Towards the end of 1974, we received an approach, through an envoy, from a man named Bill Dore who was a greyhound owner, racing his dogs at Swindon and other venues. Dore visited the Smallmead site and then invited us (Len Silver, Frank Higley and me) to his place at Shipton-under-Wychwood in Oxfordshire.

Bill Dore told us that his interest was greyhound racing and that in the grounds of his property he had greyhound kennels and a training track. He also told us he would like to be involved in the Smallmead project and explained that he was a builder, trading under the name of W.H. Dore Construction. The firm had constructed a number of schools for the Oxfordshire Education Authority and had also carried out other large contracts.

I telephoned Ted Nelson, part of the speedway management at Swindon whom I had known for many years and who knew Bill Dore quite well as a greyhound owner. I wouldn't say that Ted gave Bill Dore a glowing reference but, by all accounts, he was not too harmful.

When Len, Frank and I visited Shipton, Dore showed us around his property, including the practise greyhound track. Our negotiations finally resulted in the four of us taking a 25 per cent stake each in the company.

The building of the Smallmead stadium was a mammoth undertaking which started in December 1974. Bill Dore brought in his work gang, machinery and equipment. He oversaw the construction on a daily basis.

It was necessary to build a bridge to motorway standards across Foudry Brook and install submersible pumps inside the stadium to dispose of water and effluent across to the Bennett Road main sewer. We also had to pay Reading Borough Council to alter the junction of Basingstoke Road and Bennett Road by widening and installing traffic lights at a cost of £35,000.

All of this was on top of normal new stadium requirements. It was a construction effort virtually unprecedented in the speedway world, at least since the pre-war era. It certainly captured the imagination of the public locally and of the national media.

Many fans will recall a substantial feature article that appeared in the *Daily Mail*, written by the well-known sports reporter and columnist, Ian Wooldridge. This was very supportive of the project and provided speedway with the sort of highly positive coverage that it could well do with today.

The great day when speedway bikes roared around Smallmead for the first time, captured on film by TV cameras.

A section of the packed crowd for the first meeting at Smallmead.

We opened for speedway racing at Smallmead at the beginning of the 1975 season with me as the promoter. Shortly afterwards greyhound racing began at the venue, which was Bill Dore's forte.

Those first few speedway meetings in 1975 saw the new stadium full to capacity. Traffic would be queued all the way along Basingstoke Road and down onto the M4 motorway, in both the east and west directions.

Police motorcyclists would travel up and down and relay to me the length of the queues waiting for access to the stadium. We often had to delay the start of the meeting. I had an excellent rapport with most of the riders who raced for Reading over the years, in particular with Anders Michanek who won the Individual World Championship title in 1974 but was also an excellent team member who led by example.

Although we had plenty of success in league racing and other competitions, I think my favourite meetings were the occasions when we would have a galaxy of individual talent chasing the Manpower Trophy.

I continued to promote Reading speedway on a day-to-day basis from the stadium offices during the 1975, '76, and '77 seasons. Len Silver had dropped out in the meantime, having decided in 1976 to sell his interest in Allied Presentations Limited to Higley, Dore and myself. Len declared that his position had been made untenable by Bill Dore.

My own position was soon to be challenged and my days at Smallmead would come to an end. In December 1977, I was manager of the England speedway team that visited Australia. We returned victorious to the UK in March 1978, having beaten the Aussies by five matches to two. Joan had accompanied me down under and we travelled secure in the knowledge that the trip had the blessing not only of our son Gary, but that I had the backing of Bill Dore and Frank Higley.

Consequently, on my return, I took up the reins again of promotional duties and set about preparing for the 1978 British League season. Soon afterwards, I faced a fait accompli. Bill Dore called a meeting of the directors, namely himself, Frank Higley and me, when it was stated that they (Dore and Higley) considered that, as directors and shareholders, we should not have to go into the stadium on a daily basis.

It was proposed that an employee of Bill Dore, a Swindon speedway supporter called Brian Constable, should be the promoter at Reading.

My response was that I was not willing to put my share of the business into the hands of an unknown manager. I thoroughly disagreed with their point of view as I had a substantial financial interest in the stadium (as indeed Dore and Higley had too) and felt that it needed 'hands on' promoting.

There were only two possible outcomes; either I bought them out or they bought me out. In the event, they bought me out and I left with bad feeling as I had put so much of myself into the venture.

Some of Reg's greatest memories of Reading revolve around the Manpower Trophy meetings. Here Reg is pictured presenting the coveted award to Ivan Mauger.

Memories of another great Manpower Trophy event. Pictured are, from left to right: Ann Sutton, secretary at Manpower, John Louis, Reg Fearman, Peter Collins, Anders Michanek, and Hugh van Zwanenberg, Managing Director of Manpower UK, Reading.

My actual departure came after promoting my final Reading meeting – the Jubilee Trophy – on 17 July 1978. Brian Constable's reign was short-lived (he lasted about a year) and shortly afterwards Bill Dore introduced his daughter, Pat Bliss, to do the day-to-day running of the business.

I am sure Bill Dore always had his eye on Smallmead Stadium becoming a family business. Now, he and Pat became co-promoters of speedway. His son, Martin, was drafted in as greyhound manager and handicapper. Frank Higley too was later bought out, although I know not the circumstances.

The final part of this chapter is nothing less than a lament for Reading speedway which, in my view, was eventually sold down the Swanee. Bill Dore and his daughter have a lot to answer for in this respect.

My understanding of what was eventually to transpire was that in the late 1980s, Bill Dore was involved in discussions with Reading Borough Council. I know not whether Allied Presentations Limited was in breach of the lease or if the council approached Bill Dore to sell back to them the ninety-nine-year lease I had negotiated.

The outcome was that the ninety-nine-year lease was rescinded. A new lease was signed, which expired in October 2008. The safe tenure for ninety-nine years for speedway and greyhound racing at Smallmead was reduced to just thirty-four years in total. With the renegotiation also went some 25 acres of the land back to the council.

Reading Borough Council, in turn, then sold or leased the land where the stadium stood to the Prudential Assurance Company which would move onto the site, demolish the stadium and eventually construct offices.

In the dying years of the stadium, Pat Bliss did a deal with a company named Stadia UK Reading Ltd. This company took over the remainder of the lease on Smallmead, with Pat continuing to promote the speedway until she sold the rights in 2006 to the Grand Prix entrepreneur, John Postlethwaite.

He, in his wisdom, with no experience of domestic speedway racing, was going to show everyone how it should be done. This turned out, in reality, to be just how it should not be done!

I am sure he alienated the Reading fans on day one when he changed the name of Racers to Bulldogs. We had been Racers since 1968 – yes, nearly forty years – named, as I explained earlier, after the famous Harringay Racers.

Exit John Postlethwaite after eighteen months and £500,000 the poorer.

It was then welcome to the Swindon duo of Malcolm Holloway and Mark Legg, who reverted to the name Reading Racers. I was, of course, delighted. They took over in the hope that after the lease had expired on Smallmead, a new stadium would be built by Stadia UK Reading Ltd, just up the road from the old site.

This has not materialised at the time of writing. I believe there has been a problem in getting a casino operator on board to make the project of a new speedway and greyhound stadium viable. The first interested casino operator bailed out. Stadia UK, which operates greyhound racing at Poole and Swindon, had announced a plan to spend £9 million on developing the new Reading site and had originally hoped to open in the spring of 2010.

It is the fans I feel sorry for. They have been short-changed of another potential sixty-five years of speedway at Smallmead under Allied Presentations Limited, who were in charge of their own destiny.

I saw and lived my dream at Smallmead, turning a former rubbish tip into a speedway track and a team into a household name. I hope that subsequently someone will follow in my footsteps and promote speedway racing once more in Reading. Whoever that proves to be, I wish them luck.

CHAPTER THIRTEEN

THE POOLE DISASTERS

A number of disasters have afflicted Poole speedway in its sixty-year-plus exist-ence. My own tenure, from 1979–84, ranks as perhaps the biggest disaster experienced by any of the promoters who, over the years, have been charged with being caretakers of one of the sport's best-known venues.

My gloomy recollections of Poole make it somehow appropriate to start this chapter with a record of those who paid the ultimate sacrifice with their lives on the Wimborne Road track.

When Poole opened its doors to speedway on 26 April 1948, the track claimed the life of Reg Craven on the first corner, of the first race, of the first meeting. It is a record which I am sure is as unique as it is appalling.

Reg, who was riding for visitors Yarmouth, was the eldest of three speedway racing brothers. Malcolm was adored by the West Ham fans and Gil was equally popular with the Cradley Heath supporters.

It was by no means the end of racing fatalities at Poole. Three more riders were to meet their deaths at Wimborne Road:

Johnny Thompson, a Poole-contracted rider who had made great strides in his racing career, received fatal injuries at the track on 9 May 1955, dying a few days later.

Malcolm Flood, racing for Norwich, crashed at Poole on 2 April 1956 and died that same evening.

Kevin Holden, again a Poole rider, crashed and died on the track during a match against Reading on 24 July 1977.

The curse seemed to spread to riders with strong Poole connections who died in track crashes elsewhere:

Gordon Guasco, an Australian who had made a big impact in British speedway and was a Poole-contracted rider, received fatal injuries on the track at Liverpool speedway, New South Wales, on 8 November 1970, dying eight days later.
Christer Sjosten, a popular Swedish rider, again contracted to Poole, had an ambition to race in Australia during the European winter. I arranged his contract with my good friend Bill Goode, promoter of the Brisbane Exhibition Ground in Queensland. Christer crashed heavily at the Exhibition Ground on 1 December 1979 and died five days later.
Leif Wahlman, another Swedish rider who was in the early stages of a promising career, although contracted to Poole, was on loan to Exeter when he crashed at Kings Lynn on 28 July 1984 and died the next day.

Another death involving a Poole personality, this time a non-rider, was that of Charles Foot. This sad event, which happened in controversial circumstances, was more than a personal loss to his family and friends and a blow to the sport.

It was the catalyst for my taking the reins at Wimborne Road – which you could fairly describe, with the benefit of hindsight, as being a tragedy in itself.

Poole Stadium in the 1970s.

Charles, an accountant by profession, was a director and shareholder with the Knott family in Poole Stadium Ltd, and also held the post of president of the BSPA. Charles, as president, myself representing the BSPA, along with Charles' daughter Sandy and my wife Joan, were invited to the pre-Wembley World Final Banquet at the Royal Automobile Club, Pall Mall, on Friday, 1 September 1978.

The Control Board, which was charged with staging the World Final by the international governing body of the sport, the Federation Internationale de Motorcyclisme (FIM), was entertaining the representatives of other controlling organisations together with members of the media.

In one of a number of speeches made during the banquet, Charles Foot made a scathing attack on the members of the SCB regarding the loss to Britain of the annual World Championship Final which, at one stage, had been held exclusively at Wembley Stadium. Charles was also critical of the Board's handling of domestic events.

The chairman of the Control Board at the time was Nelson Mills Baldwin, who had been awarded the MBE for services to speedway. He took me aside and said he thought that Charles had been completely out of order in using the banquet platform to deliver his criticisms.

Soon after this, the event came to a close. Before setting off home to Henley, Joan and I saw Charles (who was still quite agitated) and Sandy into a taxi to take them to the Strand Palace Hotel where they were staying.

The next day, which saw the staging of the World Final at Wembley (won by Denmark's Ole Olsen), would prove to be tragic in more ways than one. Joan and I had invited as our guest at Wembley Pam Warren, the then wife of the former Australian 'Blond Bombshell' Graham Warren, who had been the darling of the Birmingham fans in the 1950s.

Pam, on holiday from Sydney, was staying with her talented ballet dancer son, Leigh, in Chiswick. That evening, at the dinner in the Wembley Conference Centre after the World Final, I introduced Pam to many people, including Barry Collins, a Gulf Oil representative. They clicked, eventually divorced their partners and married. Graham blamed me and never forgave me. We had been pals for almost thirty years.

Just after twelve noon on that fateful day, Joan answered the telephone at home. The caller was Sandy, phoning from the Strand Palace Hotel to say that Charles had died. She had breakfasted with her father before going shopping. Charles returned to his room to do some writing and had a massive heart attack.

Sandy had tried to phone her family and the Knotts but they were all on their way to Wembley. I told her to take a taxi to the Eurocrest Hotel in the Wembley

Stadium car park where many of us, including the Foots and Knotts, had agreed to meet. Breaking the sad news to them was a tragic and shocking business.

There was still more tragedy to come that day. Harry Weslake, the pioneer of the Weslake Engineering Company at Rye, Sussex, who had had remarkable success with his speedway racing engines, collapsed and died walking from the Twin Towers to the Conference Centre for the dinner.

Poole Stadium Limited held the lease on Wimborne Road from Poole Borough Council, which owned the stadium, car parking area and surrounding land. There was a sub-lease between Poole Stadium Ltd and Poole Town Football Club, at that time a semi-professional outfit in the Southern League.

It was Poole Stadium Ltd that ran both the speedway and the greyhound racing at the venue. With the death of Charles Foot, who was a driving force not only at Poole but also at the BSPA, the Knotts decided to sell their interests in the company.

I was approached during the winter of 1978/79 and held a number of meetings with Charles Knott Junior who had made a name for himself in the immediate post-war years as a leading county cricketer. Charles Knott played as an amateur for Hampshire, on the county's old ground close to the Bannister Court speedway and greyhound stadium his family controlled.

His *annus mirabilis* came in 1946 when he took 122 wickets, a record for a Hampshire amateur. He played against the touring Indian team and also for The Gentlemen at Lords. He died in 2003 aged 88.

Charles Knott was insistent that our meetings to discuss Poole should be held in secret. The first took place in Southampton on 24 January 1979, with the transfer of shares from Poole Stadium Ltd and several members of the Knott family to me and my wife Joan. The deal was finalised in the south-coast port on 18 July of the same year.

On that date, I became the custodian not only of Poole speedway but also of the greyhound racing, which was staged by the company three times a week. I also became the landlord of Poole Town Football Club which, under the sub-lease, paid no rent or upkeep of the stadium.

With hindsight, there were a number of things I should have done during that period of January to July 1979. I should have insisted on a structural survey of the buildings and I should have read the leases more thoroughly (the small print in particular) before handing over £125,000 for the shares in Poole Stadium Ltd.

I tackled the new venture with all the enthusiasm I could muster. I had taken on board as a co-promoter Terry Chandler, a local who had worked at Poole Stadium and who at one time was a novice rider.

This proved in the long run to be a misjudgement. His classic quote when an England v USA Test match was about to be cancelled due to rain and a wet track was this: 'If we turn on the floodlights it will dry out the track.'

One of my first tasks was to make the speedway racing safer by moving the football pitch a few feet across the stadium so that the shale track would have a better approach and exit to the bends.

The old track lamp standards, always a danger to speedway riders, were cut down. The track was now indeed safer.

Prior to my takeover, the Knotts had done a deal with Poole Town Football Club under which the football floodlights, mounted on pylons in the four corners of the arena, would also be used for speedway and greyhound racing, with the upkeep being the responsibility of Poole Stadium Ltd.

This proved to be another disaster as the close proximity of the stadium to the sea meant that the salt air deteriorated the metal structures.

Towards the end of 1984 there was a major structural problem. The Knotts had moved into Poole Stadium and promoted the first greyhound meeting there in 1960. They later built the West Stand which housed the greyhound tote hall, tote machines and a small cafeteria.

It was a good viewing place for both speedway and greyhound racing. Unfortunately, it was built with reinforced steel rods which, over the years, deteriorated, expanded and caused concrete from the ceiling to fall among spectators.

After my tenure, it was deemed unsafe and the new tenants erected nets to catch the falling debris. Later, it was condemned. In 1997, a new grandstand and a 440-seat restaurant replaced the old West Stand and tote hall. This was built by Stadia UK, the public company that had by then taken over Poole Stadium. Stadia UK also owned Swindon's Abbey Stadium where it promoted the greyhound racing.

The major income from the venue was, of course, the speedway racing. Unfortunately the paying public, over a period of four years, became disappointed and disillusioned and many stayed away.

As in most sports, public attendance depends upon the success of the team. For a number of reasons, speedway at Poole had a lacklustre appeal during my tenure, despite my investing thousands of pounds on the team. In 1978 the average crowd was 3,662 but by the end of 1984 this had gradually dropped and was hovering around a figure of 1,900 people.

Overall, the on-track results were poor. The Poole captain, Malcolm Simmons, took it into his head at one stage to miss meetings, always getting his wife to phone to say he was ill or had broken down en route to a match.

One of the new signings I made for Poole was the Californian, Ron Preston, who was soon challenging for top spot in the team. On one occasion, he appeared to be bundled by Simmons into the safety fence by the pits corner just as he was about to make a pass.

Preston sustained severe knee damage which virtually finished his racing career. When Simmons returned to the pits, I heard him say, 'That'll teach him.' In fairness, I have to say that, much later in life, Preston exonerated Simmons.

Simmons was sacked towards the end of the 1980 season, which was not the most popular decision for the fans.

Simmons was no stranger to controversy. In March 1985, both he and Simon Wigg had a year-long international ban and suspension imposed upon them by a SCB tribunal. Simmons had been charged with being paid £2,000 to miss the British Final at Coventry so that Wigg, the reserve, could take his place.

In an interview with *Backtrack* magazine in May/June 2006, Simmons said:

I'd fixed the odd race before. I'd done favours for people and bought and sold a point here and there when necessary but I'd never deliberately thrown points when riding for my team in a team match. The only time I did it was in Swindon's final League match of the '85 season – and I'm ashamed of it now.

Malcolm Simmons turned his hand to promoting, with a partner, Bill Barker, for one season at King's Lynn in 1988. He was later banned by the SCB from holding an official position within the sport for a period of five years.

I mentioned previously major investment in riders during my time at Poole, some of which proved to be great disappointments. I paid a transfer fee of £25,000 to Exeter for the American, Scott Autrey. He had always excelled at Poole and was the captain of the US team.

When he came to Poole, he relinquished the leadership of the US side and seemed to go down a gear, seldom beating the visiting number one and rarely winning races. Other team investments were Kevin Smith, transferred from Rye House for £10,000, and John Davis from Reading for £20,000.

Perhaps the biggest disaster for me was the signing of Michael Lee. He came to Poole in 1983 from Kings Lynn for £39,000, the fee to be paid at the rate of £13,000 for each season he completed. The conditions were imposed as he had been a recognised drug user but had declared himself 'clean'. By his own admission, in subsequent interviews and his own published book, he was not 'clean'.

If I had hoped the signing would have a positive effect on the gates, I was to be greatly disappointed. The signing, in fact, had a reverse effect on the gates, with the average attendance down by 5 per cent on the 1982 figures. I can only suppose Michael Lee's reputation had travelled before him.

His on-track successes came early in his career. He made his first World Final appearance aged 18 in 1977 and finished fourth in Gothenburg. In 1979, he was third in the World Final at Chorzow, Poland. In 1980, he was crowned World Champion in Gothenburg, Sweden. In 1983, he was third again at Norden, Germany.

Michael Lee had few equals on the track but as an individual he was a law unto himself. He lived at Verwood, 15 miles north of Poole, in a link-attached house. He used his garage, which contained engineering equipment, as a workshop. He had a habit of working through the night in the garage. The noise was the cause of complaints from neighbours and eventually court injunctions were imposed upon him.

When racing for Poole at King's Lynn at the beginning of the 1984 season, he climbed the steps to the referee's box, was abusive and (in his own published words) put his hands around the throat of the referee, John Eglese.

At the starting gate, he appeared to move back and forwards several times. Eventually, at a time when he and his machine were rolling backwards, the referee let the tapes go. The other three riders made a good start but Michael rode to the first corner, turned around, rode back the wrong way to the start line and parked his machine. The referee then stopped the race as he considered the circumstances were dangerous.

Michael Lee's on-track action and assault on the referee resulted in him being suspended by the SCB from taking part in any motorcycle or automobile competition, nationally and internationally, for five years from 1 June 1984. Again, it is useful to refer to a *Backtrack* article to quote Lee's own words on the issue. In the September/October 2005 issue, Lee asked: 'Why was I banned for five years for something so f****** trivial anyway because I never rode the wrong way round the track?'

Putting hands around the referee's throat cannot be described as a trivial matter and this was taken into account in the sentence. In the same *Backtrack* issue, Lee said he was innocent of the charges. He was not found innocent of the charges, although the SCB did reduce his sentence to one year.

Lee continued in the *Backtrack* article:

My appeal was heard in London on the same day as the British Final and to show how hopeful I was that I'd be cleared to ride in that meeting, I even had my van, with all the bikes on board, parked outside the Court.

The facts are that I, as the Poole promoter, appealed against this sentence and engaged a top sports lawyer, Ronnie Teeman of Ronnie Teeman International, Leeds, to take on the case. He had been recommended to me by another speedway promoter, Ian Thomas, who had been successfully defended on a drink-driving charge by Ronnie Teeman.

The date for the hearing was set for Wednesday, 20 June 1984 (the date of the British Final at Coventry) and it was arranged that I would collect Lee from his home at 7 a.m. to drive to SCB headquarters in Belgrave Square, London.

When I arrived at his home, he and Poole teammate Neil Middleditch were in the garage/workshop. It was obvious that they had been working through the night. Lee said he would go into the house to get changed. I waited some time and was getting anxious so went into the house and asked his partner, Janet, to see where he was.

She came back from upstairs to say he was on the bed fast asleep. I went up to the bedroom and tried to wake him. I pinched and shook him but rousing him proved impossible.

I insisted that Middleditch accompany me to London for the meeting with Ronnie Teeman and subsequently the Court of Appeal. Before leaving Verwood, I telephoned a doctor friend, Charles Rees (who was also the track doctor at Poole speedway), to visit the Lee household and see what the problem was with Michael Lee. Middleditch and I then set off for Belgrave Square, London, for the hearing.

Lee was still asleep when Charles got there and he was unable to make any impression on him.

On page 244 of the book *Michael Lee: Back from the Brink* by Tony McDonald, Michael Lee states:

> I remember going inside the house, up to the bedroom and thinking I'll lay down here for ten minutes, sort myself out then get ready. But I laid down and didn't get back up … I remember Reg arranging for the Poole track doctor to come to the house to examine me. Although I was basically in a semi-coma, subconsciously I was aware of what was going on around me. I could hear Reg and the doctor talking and, because he was so angry, Reg was physically hitting me trying to wake me up. 'Wake up you f******* bastard,' I heard him say. He was really giving it some.

[Charles Rees and I were never in the same room together that day. Nor did I use the language Lee describes.]

> I knew what was going on but I wasn't going to wake up. I didn't want to know, so I just let them get on with it. In the end the doctor arrived and Reg pushed me back on to the bed … Then the doctor got hold of my hands and started sticking pins in them but it still didn't register with me. I thought, 'You carry on, mate, I ain't moving'.

Michael admits:

> I just didn't want to face the appeal hearing. I hadn't done what I'd been
> accused of (endangering other people's lives), so I didn't believe I should
> have to go there in the first place. It was all bollocks.

On page 233 of the book, Michael Lee admits that he was still using drugs during
his time with Poole: 'As well as cannabis, I was also on amphetamines by then,'
he says, before confirming his former promoters' claim that drugs had become rife
in British speedway by 1983.

On page 249, Michael Lee contradicts his interview with *Backtrack* thus:

> My appeal was heard in London on the same day as the British Final and to
> show how hopeful I was that I'd be cleared to ride in that meeting, I actually
> had my bikes prepared and ready to go to Coventry for the meeting that night.

Michael was convinced he would have re-emerged from his early morning stupor
to grab a top eight qualifying place from the meeting won in controversial fashion
by Kenny Carter.

There are many instances within the pages of the book confirming Michael
Lee's unreliability and addiction to drugs. His last line on page 303 in the book
says: 'One thing I will say, I am not ashamed of anything I've done.'

Drugs first became a problem for Michael Lee in 1981. In August that year,
he was stopped by the police whilst speeding on the M1 motorway and was
charged with possessing cannabis which had been found in his car.

He was sentenced to prison for three different drug offences, the first at the
end of the 1980s and then in 1993 and 1998. On 15 November 2007, he was
convicted of growing cannabis and sentenced to 160 hours of unpaid work and
a fourteen-month supervision order.

In the 40th anniversary book on King's Lynn Stars, Ivan Mauger quotes:

> Unfortunately he (Lee) was a victim of his time, when it was all rock and roll
> and drugs were coming into speedway. I have plenty of friends in America
> and none of them would deny that the Yanks started it in England and
> Michael got caught up in that scene. He was just overboard and it was a
> great shame.

Besides Michael Lee, there were many others in the speedway circle at that time
taking drugs. Some were also in the team at Poole.

I remember well Mrs Bridgett Middleditch – she and her husband Ken, the parents of Neil, ran the Bailie House Guest House at Sturminster Marshal in Dorset – asking me one day what the riders would be using dessert spoons for when tuning their speedway machines as she had so many burnt and blackened spoons in her cutlery drawer.

I had no answer. It was many years later that I learned of their use in the preparation of drugs. Many riders stayed at Bailie House – some for the season – and others who were travelling between fixtures.

Ronnie Teeman did a good job for the £3,500 that I paid him and had Michael Lee's sentence reduced to one year. Of course, he never raced for Poole again as by now the company was in debt to the National Westminster Bank for almost £100,000. With the interest rate at 20 per cent and with the country in recession, the bank decided it wanted its money back.

I had, of course, given a personal guarantee to the bank. The outcome was that it put the company, Poole Stadium Ltd, into receivership. Ernst Young were appointed as liquidators.

Many people were owed money, including tradespeople and riders, and Neil Middleditch, whose testimonial money was swallowed up in the liquidation. Many people believed that his testimonial money went into my pocket. Nothing could be further from the truth. My co-promoter and co-director in the latter stages of the Poole Stadium operation was Brian Maidment. It was he who was on the Neil Middleditch Testimonial Committee. With hindsight, of course, a separate bank account should have been opened up but we were not to know that the bank was going to foreclose.

My five-year tenure of Poole Stadium saw me, personally, lose more than £250,000 and also a great deal of esteem. I always remember Charles Ochiltree, the Coventry supremo, saying to me that I had got it right in renting stadiums to stage speedway. If it didn't work out, one could walk away.

This time I got it very wrong. There were all sorts of problems, by no means all connected to speedway. During my tenure, the football club directors had been a real pain with their demands. They were forced to leave the stadium by the borough council in 1994.

Greyhound racing was not without its problems either. The greyhound racing manager and handicapper, Ernie Welch, took early retirement, which left me with a big gap to fill.

Every greyhound stadium in the country had bookmakers standing as an alternative to the tote betting, with accepted restricted numbers. Although the official fee for a bookmaker to stand was three times the admission price, it was general practice for them to pay a fair rate to stand and run their business.

A betting man from Wimborne set up Peter Jolliffe, a bookmaker, to stand at Poole greyhound meetings. He came to my office to ask permission which I refused as I already had what I considered my quota. This was not legal and resulted in a court case against me but, of course, affecting every greyhound track in the country.

I took the problem to the National Greyhound Racing Club whose officials took over the case and fought it in the High Court in London. This eventually saw the conditions amended regarding bookmakers standing at greyhound tracks.

I suppose with that result in mind you could argue that something positive came out of my tenure at Poole. But it was poor consolation for all the other troubles and the effect the years at Wimborne Road had on my bank account and on my reputation.

CHAPTER FOURTEEN

SPEEDWAY INTERNATIONAL

I have spent all of my adult life at the heart of speedway racing. Given that speedway is a truly international sport, it has inevitably meant a great deal of travel and contact with riders, officials and supporters from every continent.

There may well be others with a speedway background who, when travelling extensively on the sport's behalf, have for the most part confined their interests to what has happened on the track and in the pits.

I have been blessed with an enquiring mind from an early age and, in the course of my speedway travels, I have always taken a great interest in the history and the lifestyles of the nations I have been privileged to visit and the individuals I have been fortunate enough to meet, on a social as well as a racing or a business basis.

From my earliest visit to Australia, followed by my spell living in New Zealand, to my experiences in Europe, both during the time it was divided into East and West and in its now much more united state, in the United States, in South Africa and Asia, I have observed and I have asked questions.

In case the reader might believe that this chapter is going to be a mere travelogue, let me assure them otherwise. My observations have extended far beyond the realm of speedway racing and my impressions have, on occasions, led to conclusions that have not always found favour with my speedway friends.

THE POLISH CONNECTION

Given the country's status with speedway, it is probably fitting to begin with my thoughts on Poland. My Polish connections certainly go back a long way.

They really begin when having spent almost eighteen months and two seasons racing in Auckland, New Zealand, Joan and I arrived back in England in March 1956. With no home of our own in the UK, Joan's parents welcomed us to their home in Leek, in Staffordshire, until we were able to settle down.

Whilst we were in New Zealand, Joan's sister, Doreen, had married a former Polish Army officer, Henryk Kranich, who had been living, with many other Polish troops, at Blackshaw Moor Camp, just outside Leek on the A53 Buxton road, formerly an American forces transit camp and home to the 565th US Anti-Aircraft Battalion.

When the Americans moved out in 1946, the camp was taken over by Polish troops returning from Italy and other European battlefields. Men and women who served in the Allied armed forces under British command, unable to return to their Polish homeland due to its occupation by the Soviet Union, made their homes at Blackshaw Moor and in other abandoned American camps.

During the war, Henryk had been a member of both the Polish Resistance and the Polish Army and had changed his name to Danilowicz to prevent reprisals to his parents, brother and sister left behind in the city of Torun.

He was taken prisoner by the Germans in the autumn of 1944 and was being transported to Germany when, with several companions, he escaped and made his way south to meet up with the advancing British Army which absorbed the escapees into a Polish unit.

I learnt a great deal from Henryk and from his close friend, 'Teddy' Ryczkowski, who had married Joan's friend, Doris.

The Germans had walked into Poland on 1 September 1939, effectively bringing the British Empire into the Second World War. The nation was occupied for some fifty years as the Germans were succeeded as oppressors by the Russians.

Despite Henryk's attempts to shield his family, all of its members were arrested and placed in a concentration camp, where his sister died from TB. Henryk and Doreen moved to London but during those days in Leek, I often used to go with Teddy to the Polish camp for the evening to meet his friends and enjoy both their company and their hospitality in the form of very strong liquor. They certainly had an excellent bar.

Reg Fearman's sister-in-law Doreen and Henryk Kranich, the former Polish Army officer she married, pictured on their wedding day.

I have always had a great admiration for the Poles who fought side by side with British forces during the Second World War and, in particular, for the Polish pilots who flew with the RAF and helped to defend our shores in 1940 during the Battle of Britain.

It is not so well known as it should be that tens of thousands of Poles escaped the German invasion in 1939 to fight alongside the Allies. Many escaped to France where they fought until that country's collapse, while others came to Britain from the USA, Canada, Argentina and other countries.

The Polish Air Force was re-formed in Britain in 1940. The Polish airmen fought alongside the RAF and 12 miles to the west of London, just off the A40 and adjacent to RAF Northholt, is a memorial containing the names of the 2,165 Polish airmen who lost their lives fighting alongside the Allies. Polish pilots and other aircrew are buried in no fewer than 139 cemeteries throughout Britain.

In all, some 17,000 men and women served in the Polish Air Force which comprised eighteen operational flying squadrons, each named after a Polish city. Northolt was the main base for Polish fighter squadrons during the Battle of Britain and the memorial was erected in 1948 from public donations.

The Polish Air Force memorial at RAF Northolt.

The sacrifices made by these Polish servicemen were not always appreciated or adequately commemorated. As is often the case, short-term political considerations intervened. This was brought home to me very forcibly in 1946, long before I had any family connections with Polish ex-servicemen.

On the night of 7 June that year, my pal Cyril Hill and I travelled from Plaistow to Trafalgar Square and slept under Admiralty Arch to ensure that we would have a good position for the Grand Victory Parade which was to take place the next day.

A large rostrum had been erected halfway down The Mall where King George VI took the salute, accompanied by

The insignia of the individual Polish fighter squadrons are inscribed on the Northolt memorial.

members of the Royal Family and Parliamentary dignitaries. Much later in life when reading *For Your Freedom and Ours* by Lynne Olson and Stanley Cloud I read that:

> The Allied troops marched, 12 abreast and in perfect step, through the heart of bomb-pocked London. American troops, in a place of honour at the head of the nine mile-long parade, were followed – in a kaleidoscope of uniforms, flags and martial music – by Czechs and Norwegians, Chinese and Dutch, French and Iranians, Belgians and Australians, Canadians and South Africans.
>
> At the end of the parade, in a crowd-pleasing, Union Jack-waving climax, came at least ten thousand men and women from the armed forces and civilian services of His Britannic Majesty, King George VI. Accompanying the parade was a fly-past of hundreds of aeroplanes – Spitfires, Hurricanes, Lancasters and Wellingtons.

What the tens of thousands of people who stood cheering, along with Cyril and me, did not know as they watched the parade pass by was that the Poles had been refused permission to take part.

The historian Robert Conquest later summed up the position in the following words:

This was one of the most disgraceful ethical horrors of World War Two. How, believing the need to support Stalin at all costs, we discredited, and later neglected, our oldest, bravest, and most trustworthy ally in order to conceal the truth of a revolting crime.

Britain and the United States had betrayed Poland. When Winston Churchill and General Wladyslaw Anders, commander of the 11 Polish Corps, met in Italy in August 1944, the British Prime Minister assured Anders that neither he nor US President Roosevelt would ever abandon Poland.

Despite these assurances, it was announced in February 1945, at a conference at Yalta on the Black Sea Coast of Russia, that Churchill and Roosevelt had formally ceded Eastern Poland to Stalin and had handed control of the rest of that country to a provisional, Soviet-bred, communist government.

It should be noted here that General Wladyslaw Sikorski, prime minister and commander-in-chief of the Polish Government in Exile, had been mysteriously killed in a plane crash off Gibraltar. Sabotage was suspected although never proven. Sikorski was succeeded by Stanislaw Mikolajczyk who in turn was assured by Anthony Eden, a member of Churchill's wartime cabinet and a future prime minister, that Poland would not be ceded to the USSR.

The Polish servicemen and women in Britain were stranded by this betrayal. Fewer than 20 per cent of the 30,000 Polish military in Britain decided to return to their homeland.

Part of the massive stadium in Katowice, Poland, where England won the World Team Championship in 1974.

After I became a speedway promoter in 1960, I made many trips to Poland, some as England team-manager and on other occasions as a back-up to the manager of the time. On many occasions, I was the official representative of the BSPA.

Two of my proudest moments came as manager of England at the World Team Championships in 1974 when, in Katowice, England with Peter Collins, John Louis, Dave Jessup, Malcolm Simmons and Ray Wilson, won the trophy, beating Sweden, Poland and the Soviet Union.

At the same venue in 1976, I was present in an official capacity when Peter Collins won the World Individual Trophy. It was on this occasion that I took the opportunity to visit the Nazi's extermination camp at Auschwitz where over a million Jews, Poles and other gentiles were first gassed by cyanide and then incinerated.

My experience at Auschwitz, illustrating man's inhumanity to man, was something one could never forget nor understand.

Reg Fearman with the World Team trophy won by England in 1974.

Despite the presence of the Iron Curtain separating the countries in Eastern Europe occupied by the Soviet Union from their western neighbours, the Polish speedway authorities did allow a small number of their riders to compete in speedway in Britain in the 1950s, with Leicester being one of the main beneficiaries of this policy.

A group photograph taken at the 1973 World Final in Katowice, Poland, won by Jerzy Szczakiel after a run-off with Ivan Mauger. From left to right: Bob Radford, Charles Foot, Ian Macdonald, A. Scribe, Gary Fearman and Speedway Control Board manager John McNulty.

Subsequently, many Polish riders were engaged to ride in the British League, formed in 1965 after the settlement of the dispute between the National and Provincial League authorities. One of the first to arrive was Antoni Woryna, who was signed by Poole.

The man responsible for the negotiations to bring Woryna to Britain was Ryszard (Richard) Lubaczewski, a businessman of Polish origins, who had offices in Poole and Westbury, in Wiltshire. He was friendly with the Poole promoting team of Charles Foot and the Knott family and subsequently became the unpaid agent and negotiator between the British League and the Polish Motor Federation for the import of Polish riders into the league.

Richard was born in Lwow – now in the Ukraine. His father was Lord Chief Justice of Poland who, in 1939, had escaped to Hungary and joined the Polish Army. Richard and his mother were transported to Siberia but released in 1942 under an agreement made by Roosevelt, Churchill and Stalin. They made their way to Persia (Iran) and finally to Lebanon, staying there until 1947 when they were able to take a boat to Southampton.

The main entrance to the notorious Auschwitz concentration camp. (Jochen Zimmermann)

World Team Cup press conference in Poland. From left to right: Richard Lubaczewski, Peter Collins, an unidentified young girl, Zbigniew Pietrak, PZM representative, Malcolm Simmons and Phil Crump.

Many of these Polish riders became world-class competitors although, ironically, the only one in that era to win the World Individual title, Jerzy Szczakiel, World Champion in 1973, never raced for a British team.

Some of the great names of Polish speedway who never won the World title crown included Zenon Plech and Edward Jancarz, who was murdered by his wife and who is now honoured by the naming of the purpose-built speedway arena in Torun.

Richard Lubaczewski was a great character. In return for the Polish riders and teams being allowed to race in England, he and I, on behalf of the BSPA, would occasionally organise a day trip from Heathrow to one or two of the speedway venues in Poland.

The drill was that we would take two teams, with machines, and fly by a chartered Polish LOT airliner. We would assemble at Heathrow at 6 a.m. on a Sunday morning, many of the riders having ridden on the Saturday night in far-flung places.

One Sunday morning, I encountered a problem when Dave Jessup and Chris Morton arrived, one

Official recognition for the role speedway plays in Poland. Back row: Zbigniew Pietrak, Richard Lubaczewski, and Marek Lubaczewski. Front row: Nobel Peace Prize winner and co-founder of Solidarity, Lech Walesa, President of Poland 1990–95, his wife Danuta and Janet Lubaczewski with, in front, the Walesas' daughter.

without a passport and one without a visa. I signed a document at Heathrow saying I was taking the two named persons out of the country on my own responsibility – something which would be impossible today. We arrived in Wroclaw and were met by the Polish Motor Federation (PZM) representative, Zbigniev Puzio – affectionately known as Charlie.

I immediately told Charlie that we had a problem with Morton and Jessup. His response, in his perfect English, was that this would not in fact prove to be a problem as the two forgetful riders could keep each other company in a secure room at the airport! Immigration, he said, would certainly not allow them to enter Poland.

I then asked Charlie and the immigration officials to telephone the British Embassy in Warsaw to allow me to speak to the Consul. I explained that we were a British speedway team on a day trip and urged him to contact his counterpart in the Polish Foreign Service department, explain the situation and ask for permission for Jessup and Morton to enter Poland on a temporary basis.

We certainly wanted to take both of the riders back with us to England and they had no wish to remain in Poland any longer than was strictly necessary. After a short while, the telephone rang. It was the Polish Foreign Service officer giving permission for the riders to be released into the custody and under the jurisdiction of Charlie Puzio.

Charlie was not at all pleased considering that Jessup was in one team and Morton in the other, with the teams going in opposite directions. Although Charlie was unable to keep his eye on both of them at the same time, it was realised that there was no fear of either Dave or Chris 'jumping ship' and remaining in Poland.

On another trip with Richard Lubaczewski to meet the PZM, we stayed at the Monopol Hotel in Wroclaw, in the Presidential Suite once used by Hitler. It was from a balcony at the Monopol, opposite the Opera House, that the Führer gave a wartime speech.

The room was massive with large and heavy furniture. The extra-large bathroom was tiled in green with a green bath, green washbasin and a green WC, all dating from the 1930s. It was quite unbelievable.

Another memorable trip involved taking the Polish riders' speedway machines (which belonged to the Polish speedway clubs) back to Poland at the end of the 1976 British season. Richard arrived at Reading speedway with one of his ex-coal lorries with some machines and personal items belonging to the returning riders already loaded.

Two or three more machines were loaded at Reading and he and I set off for Dover and our journey through Belgium and Germany to the Polish border. When we arrived at the border, Polish customs took the truck apart. All the equipment had to be offloaded, checked and reloaded, causing a couple of hours' delay.

All this time, the reception committee, friends of Richard, were waving and shouting messages from the restaurant/café on the other side of the border. We eventually drove through and Richard handed over the lorry to a friend to drive whilst we were chauffeured.

Customs, having carried out such a thorough search, had failed to discover any irregularities and I naturally asked Richard what all the fuss had been about. Did they think we were smuggling items? He coolly replied that in fact we *were* smugglers. He was leaving the lorry in Poland for a friend who had a farm and he had two tickets for us to fly back to Heathrow.

Because of the affinity Joan and I had with the Polish people, when the time came, we had no hesitation in sending our son, Gary, to the Divine Mercy College at Fawley Court, Henley-on-Thames, which was run by the Marian Fathers, a Polish Religious Order established in 1673.

Fawley Court was rebuilt in 1684, after the English Civil War, to the design of Sir Christopher Wren. It was sold to the Scottish banker and railway entrepreneur, Edward Mackenzie, in 1853. He retired to Fawley Court following

Gary Fearman at Fawley Court.

very successful ventures developing major stages of the railway network in France. It was requisitioned in the Second World War by the army and used by a Secret Operations Unit.

The Marian Fathers bought Fawley Court in 1953 from Miss Mackenzie, a relative of Edward, for £35,000. Initially, it served as a boarding school to educate the sons of Polish refugees who had taken up residence not only in Great Britain but also in the United States, Canada and South Africa after fleeing their homeland in 1939. Many local boys attended as day pupils as the school's reputation and educational results were exemplary.

Gary, who had been taught a certain amount of Polish, made several trips to Poland with me and at times acted as a manager for the day. Prince Radziwill, who lived in Henley-on-Thames and was a brother-in-law to Jacqueline Kennedy-Onassis, was a benefactor to the college and had a church built within the grounds. He is buried there.

The college closed in 1986 because of the lack of students. It was until recently a Retreat and Conference Centre, still run by the Marian Fathers. The Marian Fathers have now sold Fawley Court and its grounds to Aida Hersham of Eaton Square, London, for a reported £22 million.

THE SWEDISH INVOLVEMENT

Another of the great powers in the speedway world is, of course, Sweden, and, over the years, I have had a great deal of involvement with Swedish riders and with the sport's administrators in that country.

I have also taken a great interest in the history of Sweden and, perhaps because of my family connections with Poland, have been able to contrast the experiences of the two countries during the Second World War.

This interest, as we shall see later on in this chapter, has led to a sometimes fierce and as yet unfinished discussion with one of my best friends in the speedway game.

My first involvement with Swedish speedway riders occurred when Ove Fundin came to England in 1954 to race in his World Championship qualifying rounds at West Ham and Norwich.

Aub Lawson brought the young Swedish rider to the Fearman home for a cup of tea. My dad helped Ove in the pits at West Ham and was later at his side in his first World Final at Wembley.

Our friendship was to develop over the years and I am proud to say that it continues to this day, almost sixty years later.

When Joan and I embarked for New Zealand on the SS *Oronsay* in October 1954, there were some forty speedway personnel on board, bound for Australia. Among that number was Jack Parker, who was travelling with three Swedish riders, Ove, Ulf Ericsson and Goran Norlen, all contracted to race down under.

My involvement as a promoter with Swedish riders, over a period of twenty-five years, was particularly good, with many of the top boys from Sweden racing for my promotions.

Ove Fundin who, by that time, had won four of his eventual five World Championship titles, joined me at Long Eaton in 1966. His stay at Station Road was extremely short, due to him being banned by the Swedish Motor Federation, SVEMO, for refusing to ride in a championship event in Sweden.

Ove Fundin, left, in the Long Eaton pits with young Archers star Ray Wilson.

Ove returned to England in 1967 for a short period, to race for Belle Vue, and won his fifth World Title. Ove recommended several riders to replace him at Long Eaton. Niels Ringstrom and Leif Enecrona duly had spells in the Archers team although neither of whom stayed the pace.

The third rider to be recommended by Ove hit the jackpot. Anders Michanek was an overnight success at Long Eaton in 1967 and went on to race at my tracks at Leicester, Newcastle and Reading. He was a promoter's dream – good looking, almost shy, and a tremendous hit with the girls. We became very good friends.

Anders, in my book, was one of the nicest speedway riders one could meet. Honest, charming and polite, he remains to this day one of my favourites. At Long Eaton he immediately made a mark with his ability and skill.

He had an excellent command of English with just a slight Swedish accent. We shared many jokes and laughs in those early days, especially when I gave him a lift to Heathrow after meetings for him to catch a plane back to Stockholm.

The Long Eaton team, promoted by myself and Ron Wilson, moved en bloc to Leicester in time for the 1968 season, a move which was based purely on financial judgement. Anders was a driving force that first year at Blackbird Road and was an excellent team man.

Swedish riders were banned from British speedway by the BSPA in 1969 (and again in 1974) due to the costs involved, mainly where the air fares were concerned.

In 1970, Allied Presentations Ltd, of which both Ron Wilson and I were directors, bought Newcastle from Mike Parker, who took Ole Olsen with him to one of his other interests at Wolverhampton.

Anders Michanek replaced Olsen in the Newcastle team in no uncertain fashion. But even the popularity of Anders could not rekindle the lost popularity of the sport on Tyneside. And so in 1971, Newcastle's British League Division One licence and riding assets were transferred to Reading, also owned by Allied Presentations Limited, and where, up to this point, the team had raced at the second tier of speedway in the UK.

Anders never raised any objection to these moves and was always co-operative. At Reading, he quickly became a firm favourite and was extremely popular not only with the fans but also with his teammates – he truly led by example.

For a short time, he lived with Joan and me at Henley until he was fixed up with accommodation in Reading. I believe the only time we ever had cross words – there were never any about money – was when he would be cleaning his machine in the garage beneath my office and would use petrol for the cleaning purpose. The fumes would come up through the floorboards and just about knock me out.

On another occasion, a small disaster resulted from Anders' determination to keep his bike clean. Most speedway riders at that time would soak the chains of their machines in a container full of oil. On this occasion, somehow or another, the oil caught fire in the workshop with my new Rolls-Royce standing nearby.

Anders evidently grabbed a fire extinguisher and, of course, once he pushed the plunger, he couldn't stop it. The extinguisher put out the fire but also covered the whole garage and the Rolls-Royce with white powder. Joan happened to walk in at that moment, saw the devastation and said, 'Anders, I think we should clean this lot up as I don't think Reg will be very pleased when he gets home.' I am happy to report that they made a good job of it.

Swedes have trouble pronouncing the English letter 'J' and Joan used to pull Anders' leg unmercifully in trying to get him to say 'Joan' instead of 'Yoan' and 'Jumbo Jet' instead of 'Yumbo Yet'.

One winter, I arranged for Anders to spend the season at Claremont Speedway, at Perth in Western Australia. He raced for my friend, Claremont promoter, Con Migro, who wrote to me afterwards with glowing reports of Anders' racing skills, his co-operation with the media and sponsors and his overall conduct on and off the track.

Anders was more than a World Champion and a great rider. He was an ambassador, both for Sweden and the sport. I was privileged to meet his parents and his brother and sister, both in Stockholm and when they visited the UK.

Yes, I have some great memories of Anders Michanek. I am pleased to call him a friend and I am sure he left many broken hearts in England when he decided to retire from the world of speedway racing. The last time I saw him was the day Princess Diana was killed in Paris and the Golden Greats were to be staged at Coventry. He was a legend in legendary times.

Anders won the World Title in 1974, the year the Swedes were banned from racing for British clubs. The reason for the ban was the insistence by SVEMO on the Swedish riders commuting between England and Sweden for their Swedish club matches, something which could happen two or three times a week.

A return air fare at that time was in the region of £250. The British promoters, in their wisdom, decided that if they banned the Swedes for a season, SVEMO would come to heel and agree to a compromise in the future regarding the commuting. SVEMO stood its ground and, in the Swedish riders, the tracks lost a tremendous drawcard for the British public.

The Swedish club system has no individual promoters. All the clubs are involved in several disciplines of motor cycling and some also have links with car racing.

Of the other Swedish riders I have known, Gote Nordin, whose best performance was when he finished third behind fellow Swedes Ove Fundin, the winner, and Bjorn Knutsson, the second-place rider, was a hard racer but a real gentleman off the track. Bengt Jansson, one of the most stylish riders ever to stand on the

World Final rostrum (he finished second in 1967 behind Ove Fundin), was a quiet man but a very determined racer.

Christer Sjosten, the younger brother of Soren, was a rider with a tremendous future in the sport, but was tragically killed on the track at Brisbane in December 1979. It was with shock, sadness and disbelief that I received the telephone call at my home in Henley just before Christmas from the promoter, Bill Goode. It was I who had arranged for Christer to spend the season in Australia.

I mentioned earlier in the chapter that my speedway connections with countries such as Poland and Sweden have inevitably widened to take in an interest in the nations themselves and their recent history.

My wife Eileen and I have often had dinner with Ove and Joanna Fundin and our conversations and discussions covered a whole range of subjects.

On one such occasion, Ove mentioned the question of Sweden's neutrality during the Second World War. This has proved to be a discussion we have not yet finished!

It was only later in life that I had learned of Sweden's wartime involvement. I knew that Sweden, like Switzerland, had claimed neutrality during the conflict. Some time after the end of hostilities, the activities of both countries during the war years were exposed to the general public.

In the case of Switzerland, the accusations against the country centred on the banking of Nazi gold, stolen from the oppressed, and the storage of art collections, also stolen by the Nazis.

In my view, Sweden was perhaps even more involved than Switzerland in helping the Nazi campaign.

Swedish iron ore was an important economic factor in the European theatre of the Second World War. Both the Allies and the Third Reich were keen on the control of the mining district in the northernmost part of Sweden surrounding the mining towns of Gallivare and Kiruna.

The importance of this issue increased after other sources of iron ore were denied to Germany by the British sea blockade during the second Battle of the Atlantic. Both the planned Anglo-French support of Finland in the winter war and the following German occupation of Denmark and Norway (Operation Weserubung) were, to a large extent, motivated by the wish to deny their respective enemies the iron critical for wartime production of steel.

Prior to the Second World War, Germany was able to supply itself with only a quarter of its total iron ore consumption per year, with the rest being imported from other countries. Sweden provided up to almost 60 per cent of the iron ore that was imported into Germany. In 1940, iron ore imports from Sweden as well as Norway constituted 11,550,000 of the 15 million tons Germany consumed that year. Norway had of course been invaded and occupied by Germany on 9 April 1940.

Sweden was able to remain neutral throughout the war. According to Erik Boheman, the Swedish Secretary of State during that period, the main reasons for being able to maintain neutrality were luck and the way the conflict developed, in combination with Germany's knowledge of the Swedish people's spirit to resist an invasion, together with the Scandinavian country's diplomatic skilfulness.

Another angle on the situation is supplied by German contemporary sources which believe Hitler considered Swedish neutrality as beneficial to Germany. Hitler did not want to commit the amount of troops that would have been necessary to invade and occupy Sweden and, at the same time, he was afraid that Norwegian partisans and Allied Special Forces would cross into an occupied Sweden and attack mines and railroads.

Indeed, Sweden supplied 10 million tons of iron ore per year to Germany from 1940–43, a similar figure to the amount supplied in the pre-war year of 1938, in addition to vast quantities of manufactured ball bearings. In compensation, Germany exported to Sweden coal, iron and fertilizers at affordable prices. The Swedish trade with Germany was terminated in the autumn of 1944, without any Swedish deficit.

It has been claimed that the massive deliveries of iron ore and the granting of other facilities from Sweden to Nazi Germany lengthened the Second World War. Casualties of the war have been estimated at 20 million killed in Europe alone. How many of them died due to Sweden's material support to Nazi Germany is not known.

It was not only through the supply of iron ore that Sweden assisted the Nazi cause. Stockholm's Enskilda Bank, owned by the powerful Wallenberg family, helped German corporations like Bosch, IG Farben and Krupp to hide their foreign subsidiaries in order to avoid confiscation by the Allied governments.

Documents from the Second World War contain evidence that Jacob and Marcus Wallenberg used their bank to help Nazis dispose of assets seized from Dutch Jews who died in the Holocaust. Whilst the family bank was funding Hitler and helping to hide Nazi investments, Raoul Wallenberg, a Swedish diplomat in Budapest, was saving an estimated 20,000 Jews from deportation by providing them with special Swedish passports.

When the Red Army liberated Budapest in January 1945, Wallenberg was arrested as an American spy and vanished.

There are several estimates of the number of Swedes who fought for the Germans, ranging from 150 to 330. The truth is that no one really knows as few Swedes would admit to having volunteered after the war ended. In reality, the figure could have been as high as several thousand.

It is known that Swedes served in at least three Panzer Divisions and that eleven Swedish SS men went through the SS Officer Training School at Bad Tolz. Several Swedes worked as SS war correspondents and the 3rd Company of Nordlands Armoured Reconnaissance Battalion had so many Swedes in the 4th Zug (platoon) that the company was known unofficially as the Swedenzug.

Swedish Prime Minister, Per Albin Hansson, admitted to German troops crossing Sweden by train. Officially, the train in question transported wounded soldiers and soldiers on leave. All in all, close to 100,000 railcars had transported 1,004,158 military personnel through Swedish territory, on leave to Germany, and 1,037,158 to Norway, by the time the Transit Agreement was disbanded on 15 August 1943.

CHAPTER FIFTEEN

NEW FRONTIERS
FOR SPEEDWAY

The speedway community, as I write this chapter, is getting excited about the prospect of watching the 2013 World Cup.

As things stand, well into the second decade of the new millennium, speedway is truly an international sport.

As is the case in football, Great Britain may be the home of speedway as a fully professional sport, with a league structure first developed more than eighty years ago, but many of our traditional rivals, notably Sweden and Poland, are now arguably ahead of the game in terms of facilities and spectator numbers.

New Zealand staged its first highly successful Grand Prix round in 2012 in Auckland. Young Australians continue to flock into British speedway with great success. Chris Holder became World Speedway Champion at the conclusion of the 2012 season.

Although South Africa, once seen as a potentially powerful speedway nation, is no longer a major player in the sport, the results section of the *Speedway Star* now regularly features meetings in Argentina, Italy, Holland, Ukraine, Croatia, Estonia and Lithuania.

In the last chapter, I looked in detail at my dealings with the great riders from Poland and Sweden, many of whom have made exciting contributions to British speedway.

During my promoting career, I had many opportunities to be involved in speedway in these well-established homes of the sport. I also became involved, to a greater or a lesser degree, in attempts to widen the frontiers of speedway by establishing the sport in new regions of the world or in places where, sadly, it has failed to make a mark on any number of occasions.

MIDDLE EAST SPEEDWAY

Taking speedway racing into the Middle East, where its only foothold had been the rough and ready circuits raced upon by British servicemen waiting for demobilisation after the Second World War, was an amazing experience and a venture which enjoyed considerable success.

On the other hand, I have watched as several vain attempts have been made to popularise the sport in Spain where, despite the advantages of climate and the presence of both a sport-mad native population and plenty of British tourists, nothing has to date ever succeeded.

Interestingly, it was the not-uncommon situation of turmoil in the world of English football that originally pointed my thoughts in the direction of the Middle East.

Reg Fearman in Arab garb ready to break new ground by taking speedway to the Middle East.

In 1977, Don Revie walked out of his job as manager of the England national football team and took up a position with Dubai in the United Arab Emirates. It was because of his defection that I thought there might be an opening for speedway racing in the Emirates. There had been much publicity about the number of stadiums owned by oil-rich sheiks.

Early in 1978, I decided to send a colleague on a fact-finding mission to the Middle East. He came back with many photographs of stadia and some very useful information.

As is usual during the British speedway season, I had a phone call from a journalist on a national newspaper asking if I had any news for him. I thought hard and said I was in negotiation to take speedway racing to the Middle East.

The story was printed and, within a short time, I received a phone call from Ian Gow of the leading tobacco company Rothmans of Pall Mall. He told me that Rothmans were very big in the Middle East as a whole and had already sponsored a top car rally event.

I agreed to meet Ian Gow in Aylesbury, where he was based, to discuss my proposals for speedway in the region. Our initial meeting was also attended by several others involved with the promotion of the Rothmans' brand, including Peter Tolfrey and Brian Roach.

Les, Peter and Phil Collins head for Kuwait to launch speedway's Middle East venture in 1978.

Several other meetings followed and it was agreed that, as the company had a large task force on the ground in Kuwait, we would start our Middle East venture in that country in November 1978, with sponsorship from Rothmans. The company appointed Peter Tolfrey as its liaison officer and organiser, with the speedway arrangements to be looked after by myself.

The venue for the first meeting was to be the Kuwait Sporting Club Stadium at Keefan. It had a large athletics track around the outside of a football pitch and would prove ideal for our purpose once some modifications had been carried out under the direction of Eric Boothroyd, my co-promoter at Halifax.

Eric oversaw the track preparation and the installation of the equipment needed to run speedway. An existing metal rail fence between the track and the spectators was covered in plywood for safety reasons. Not surprisingly, given that we were in the Middle East, the surface of the 400m track was sand, very different from the red shale of British tracks.

The logistics were quite challenging. To avoid any complications with visas, we contracted sixteen British riders to take part in the meeting including the 1976 World Champion, Peter Collins.

A vital member of the British party was the highly experienced announcer, Dave Lanning. It was his task to impart to a translator the basics of speedway racing and, in particular, all the details of the scoring procedure to ensure that the Kuwaiti crowd understood what was happening out on the track.

The British party flew out to Kuwait from Heathrow Airport on 19 November 1978, returning on 26 November. Our base in Kuwait was the Messilah Beach Hotel where one of the riders, Dave Morton, spent the practice day in the care of a local doctor after he complained of being ill.

The sixteen speedway machines had been taken to the cargo section of Heathrow Airport to be placed in crates, with the methanol fuel and oil having been drained from the tanks. Footrests and handlebars were removed and strapped on the side of each machine ready to be air freighted to the Middle East.

Methanol, the racing fuel, was available in Kuwait but not the Castor (vegetable) racing oil. This we had to take with us along with the starting gates, flags – yellow for the last lap, chequered flag for the finish and several red for danger.

Leading up to the two meetings on Thursday, 23 November and Friday, 24 November, a press conference was held at the Messilah Beach Hotel. A display and personal appearances were staged at car and motorcycle showrooms in the city.

At the start of the first meeting, which was called the Rothmans Speedway Spectacular, we were introduced to the general secretary of the Kuwait Sporting Club, Mishari Al Anjari, who said it was a great honour to be the first stadium to stage speedway racing in the Gulf region.

The opening ceremony for Kuwait's first speedway meeting. Reg Fearman introduces
the riders to the general secretary of the Kuwait Sporting Club, Mishari Al Anjari, who is
pictured shaking hands with the then World Champion Peter Collins. The thoughts of John
Davis and Jim McMillan (far right) seem to be miles away.

At the first of the two meetings, Peter Collins was unbeaten in his five races. On the
second day he was beaten twice, once by his brother Les and also by his Belle Vue
teammate, Chris Morton. Peter Collins was thus crowned Kuwait's first champion
with 28 points, second was Les Collins with 25 and third John Louis with 24.

The other scorers were Chris Morton 21, Dave Jessup 18, Tom Owen 18,
Barry Thomas 17, Jim McMillan 15, Craig Pendlebury 13, John Davis 13, Bernie
Leigh 13, Reg Wilson 12, Ian Cartwright 11, Dave Morton 5, Neil Middleditch 3
and Richard Greer 3. The whole event was hailed as a great success.

For a second venture to the Middle East in 1979, Rothmans again agreed
not only to sponsor but to extend the speedway racing with meetings first in the
Egyptian capital city of Cairo, followed by events in Kuwait and a third and final
venue in Abu Dhabi. The tour and championship would be known as the Craven A
Masters Tournament.

I decided to send an advance party out to the Middle East consisting of Eric Boothroyd once again joined, on this occasion, by Peter Jarman, a former rider with a number of British tracks who had moved over to work in track preparation and safety.

Eric and Peter were to arrive a few days before each race meeting to make sure that all arrangements were in hand for the scheduled two meetings on successive days at each venue.

The main party arrived in Cairo on Sunday, 4 November and checked into the Nile Hotel Restaurant and Club, Omar Khayyam. It gave us plenty of time for press and publicity appearances before the first meeting which took place on Wednesday, 7 November.

The programme cover for the Rothman's-sponsored meeting.

Before it could go ahead, we had to face our biggest challenge of the Middle Eastern adventure to date. The Egyptian customs officers at the airport impounded the speedway machines and equipment that had arrived in Cairo on a Kuwait Airlines flight.

I spent hours filling out forms and documents but to no avail. Customs then decided that they required a bond of several thousand Egyptian pounds to ensure that the machines and equipment left the country. Time was running out fast as it was now the day of the meeting.

Rothmans managed to supply the necessary bond and the machines were released at noon. We then faced a mad

Dave Lanning, highly experienced as an announcer and a TV commentator, was a vital part of the team in the Middle East. Here Lanning (centre) gets a chance to relax on deck with Reg Fearman and rider Dave Jessup.

drive across Cairo (where the traffic was horrendous) to the stadium where the riders were in the pits, changed into their racing leathers and waiting for the machines to arrive by truck.

There were 15,000 people in the stadium, waiting expectantly for the racing to begin. The crates were broken open and all hands went to work to assemble the machines. We just made the scheduled 3 p.m. start.

It doesn't bear thinking about what might have happened if the speedway machines had not been cleared in time by customs.

The large crowd was in a state of amazement at their first sight of speedway racing, so much so that they wanted to carry the riders shoulder high at the end of the racing. They climbed over fences and broke down gates and at least one person was impaled in the leg by a spike from the metal fence.

The success of Kuwait in 1978 led Rothmans to back an extension to Egypt for the Middle East venture in 1979, with meetings in Cairo. Track preparation is in progress at the impressive stadium where Eric Boothroyd was again in charge joined, on this occasion, by Pete Jarman.

The first race gets underway in Cairo after the desperate efforts to free the machines impounded by Egyptian customs officers.

Riot police were on duty in the Cairo stadium for the next day's racing to control a full-house crowd of 28,000, with more locked outside.

For the following day's racing the Cairo police riot squad were brought in and sat on benches along the centre of the football pitch to control a full house of 28,000 people, with many more locked outside.

The leading scorer for the Craven A Masters was Chris Morton with 14 points followed by Dave Morton with 13 and Phil Collins with 13.

Before we left Cairo for Kuwait, we did manage a visit to the Pyramids and the Sphinx. Some of us were able to visit the Coptic Museum which houses the world's largest collection of Christian artwork, providing a link between ancient and Islamic Egypt.

Success in Cairo for leading Craven A Masters' event winners Chris Morton, Jim McMillan (left) and Peter Collins.

World Champion Peter Collins during a visit to the Pyramids.

We had time to visit Old Cairo and the City of the Dead where thousands of people had made their homes in a cemetery using wood, metal and cardboard to make their shelter.

On arrival in Kuwait, we made the Marriott Hotel our base. The two race meetings took place on Tuesday, 13 November and Friday, 16 November. We added to the publicity that Rothmans had achieved prior to our arrival by giving radio and press interviews.

In between the two race meetings, we were regally entertained with tours to the Doha water towers, a reception, cocktails and supper for 200 people at the Marriott Hotel, a garden party at the British Embassy and a visit to Jafra, a Bedouin village. We also attended a Craven A barbecue for sixty people. We had truly been well looked after and entertained.

The result of the second round of the Craven A Masters in Kuwait was a win for Chris Morton, with second place going to Dave Morton after a run-off with Dave Jessup.

Moving on, our midnight flight from Kuwait to Abu Dhabi was cancelled due to fog so we were taken by bus to the Messilah Beach Hotel for the night. We eventually arrived in Abu Dhabi late on a Sunday afternoon.

The timing for the speedway meetings in Abu Dhabi was not good. Important Asian football matches were taking place at the time and proved to be significant competition. The press and publicity arrangements in Abu Dhabi also left a lot to be desired and we were given a lot of free time to enjoy ourselves, swimming in the Gulf, wind sailing and surfing.

Don Revie, who unknowingly had inspired the whole Middle East speedway venture, was staying at the Meridian Hotel in Abu Dhabi. Several of our group took the opportunity to introduce ourselves and learned that he was really enjoying his new coaching appointment.

The first meeting was on Tuesday, 20 November. The track was narrow and the surface was composed of tarmac, with some sand sprinkled on top. It was not quite what we had been used to but the riders put on a show for the poorly attended meeting.

Several expatriate Brits made themselves known to us after the meeting and invited some of us to join them in their work. They were helicopter pilots and ground maintenance crew whose jobs consisted of ferrying oil industry workers from land to the rigs.

The next day, several of us went out to the land base of the oil rigs and met up with the chaps we had met at the speedway the night before. Several of us

Lunch in Kuwait with Hussein, one of the officials of the Kuwait Sporting Club at Keefan.

climbed on board a thirteen-seat Bell 216 helicopter for a trip around the Gulf. What we didn't know was that the helicopter had just had a service and certain procedures had to be followed. One movement that left us horrified was when they cut the engine and it dropped a couple of hundred feet before recovery.

The final meeting of the Craven A Masters series took place on Thursday, 22 November. The meeting was delayed for 1 hour as someone had forgotten to arrange an ambulance to cover the event. We eventually got under way in front of a pathetic number of people in the audience. This was a shame as Cairo and Kuwait had been so well attended by the local public.

The meeting was won by Phil Collins with Dave Morton second and Chris Morton third. The overall result of the Craven A Masters was a win for Chris Morton with 40 points followed by Dave Morton with 39 and Phil Collins with 37.

The other scorers in the championship were Bernie Leigh 32, Peter Collins 31, Dave Jessup 27, Jim McMillan 26, Les Collins 24, Joe Owen 22, John Davis 19, Reg Wilson 14, Craig Pendlebury 12, Richard Greer 11, Barry Thomas 8, Ian Cartwright 8, and Neil Middleditch 4.

After the meeting, we crated all the equipment ready for departing the following day from Abu Dhabi to London Heathrow. Rothmans arranged an excellent reception and cocktail party for us after the meeting, bringing to an end an exciting series. On Friday, 23 November, our flight to London was delayed as Heathrow was fog-bound. We eventually arrived at our destination at 10.30 p.m., 4 hours late.

The Middle East and Kuwait, and Cairo in particular, proved very receptive to speedway, at least for a short period of time, and gave both riders and officials a memorable experience.

Spain, a nation where the sort of dashing and flamboyant courage traditionally displayed by speedway riders is embedded deeply in the national psyche, should, at least in theory, be fertile ground for the sport.

In practice, since the early days of speedway, a succession of promoters, from Johnnie Hoskins in the pre-war era, through to Johnnie's son Ian, and others, have experienced immense frustration and have lost considerable amounts of money trying to establish the sport in the Spanish sunshine.

THE PAINE IN SPAIN

My own experience of being a close observer of one of the later attempts to promote speedway in Spain did not involve any personal loss. As someone who has largely fulfilled his own ambitions of promoting the sport, it did, however, highlight to me the heartache involved when things go badly wrong.

This particular Spanish episode involved a broken speedway dream that cost the dreamers a very great deal, both financially and emotionally.

Spare a thought here for Russell Paine, a former Wimbledon rider, and his partner, Claire Evans. Their dream started back in 2003 when they purchased some land with the intention of building their own speedway track in Spain.

They found land south of Murcia, just off the motorway, at Huercal Overa, not too far from Almeria and Mojacar. They bought the land and through their agent, applied for planning permission. The agent in time told them permission was in place, allowing them to go ahead with their plans.

They brought in earth-moving equipment, shaped the track, built an outer fence and so much more. They had already driven from England in an articulated lorry with about twenty-five speedway machines, dozens of pairs of riding boots, leather and Kevlar riding suits for the proposed training school.

My own involvement came many months later, in fact during the weekend of 29/30 October 2005. A group of ex-pats in Spain, formed by Alan Brett and John Chaplin and known as The Amigos (those of us in the South of France were kindly included), were invited to the 'pseudo-opening' of the track.

The event was largely for the benefit of BBC TV cameras filming a series called *Living in the Sun* (what wonderful potential publicity) which was due to be broadcast the following January.

A tape was duly cut for the 'opening' and a few races were staged for the cameras. Many former riders attended, including the legendary Split Waterman, formerly of Wembley, Harringay and New Cross and a resident of Nerja in Spain for more than twenty-five years.

Speedway amigos: ex-riders at the grand opening of the speedway in Spain, 2005.

Russell and Claire had done a fantastic job of turning a wilderness into a speedway track of first-class shape with banking on the outside for spectators. Their long-term aim was to encourage the motorcycle-mad Spanish to take up speedway racing. In the short term, they wanted to offer facilities to all speedway riders for training and testing and to operate their own training school. What could be better with Spain's 300 days a year of sunshine?

We spent a wonderful weekend, full of hope for the future, leaving behind our good wishes for Russell and Claire. Shortly after, the couple were served with a stop notice that meant a cessation of work. They were told that they did not have certain permissions in place.

They stopped the physical work and ever since have been working on trying to get the 'right' permission, complete with rubber stamp. Anyone who knows anything about the Spanish hierarchy will know that can be very difficult. I know Russell and Claire are indebted to their families and friends for support through this harrowing period of their lives.

The financial cost has been enormous and the strain of living under this cloud is immeasurable. Hopefully, their dream will one day come true.

Speedway, both at home in the UK and in farther-flung regions, can offer immense pleasure and considerable rewards to promoters. It can also go wrong, as was proved in Abu Dhabi in the 1970s and in Spain on many occasions, and can shatter both dreams and lives.

CHAPTER SIXTEEN

HEROES

Over the course of my life, I have been privileged to meet a great many outstanding people, some of whom have been my heroes, my mentors and, in so many cases, my great and enduring friends.

Many of these people have already been mentioned in these pages as my life story has unfolded – great names of speedway, like Lionel Van Praag, Eric Chitty, Aub Lawson, Lionel Wills and many more.

Others have come into my life and vanished again, such as the great boxing champion Randolph Turpin, a figure I encountered during my army days.

Although speedway racing, for almost all of its existence, has been very much a male preserve (with a huge female fan following), that has not always been the case. Women riders were popular at tracks in the early days of speedway and in a subsequent chapter I shall be telling the story of one of the greatest (and a controversial character to boot).

Before mentioning ladies and the seamier side of life (I am not suggesting the two are in any sense connected), I want first to mention in a little more detail some of the people who have enriched my life both within and outside speedway.

LIONEL WILLS

I mentioned in the introduction to this book the prime role played in the introduction of speedway racing in the UK by Lionel Wills, a graduate of the University of Cambridge.

In July 2011, at my request, Peter Wills, Lionel's son, wrote the following:

Thomas Wills, like generations of his family before him, was a yeoman farmer on Dartmoor, in Devon. In 1849 two of his sons, George and Richard, sailed for Australia, where they established the business of G & R Wills, which a century later had grown into one of the biggest companies in Australia.

Ten years later, George came back to England and ran the business from London for the rest of his life. He married, and of his four sons one became a barrister and Member of Parliament, the other three went into the family business, which in London became George Wills & Sons.

The youngest of these sons, Charles Percy – who was always known as Percy – married the daughter of an Army officer and in 1903 their eldest child was born. He was christened Percy Lionel, but was always known as Lionel. After that came three more brothers, Philip, Peter and Richard, who was always known as Dick!

Lionel was educated at the Royal Naval College at Dartmouth, but his eyesight was not good enough for a career in the Navy, so in 1920 he went to Trinity College, Cambridge, where his father had been. There he was able to indulge in motorcycling, a sport to which he had taken with enthusiasm. He rode for the Cambridge University Motor Cycling Club against Oxford, and took part in many trials and competitions, including the ACU six days trial in 1923, London to Land's End in 1924, and the Colmore Cup and Scottish Six Day Trials in 1925.

In 1926, Lionel and his brother Philip were sent to Australia to learn about that side of the business, and there he saw Speedway for the first time, visiting Smithfield, Speedway Royal and Claremont on his trips. There, too, he met Johnny Hoskins, with the results for the establishment of Speedway in Britain that are well known.

In the first ever England Australia Test at Crystal Palace in 1928, Lionel and Roger Frogley beat Ron Johnson and Steve Schlam to win the match.

After breaking his arm in a crash, he abandoned Speedway, and on another trip to Australia in 1930 – he went on business there frequently – he married a girl he had met on his first trip three years earlier.

His father died while he was on his honeymoon, and on his return to England he had to take a more demanding role in the firm, especially as his two uncles also died in the next few years. He became more involved in motor cars – his family moved to a house near Brooklands – and participated in a Monte Carlo Rally starting from Talinn. During the war he was in the

N.F.S., first putting out fires in London, then, as a column officer, employed in Regional H.Q., Tunbridge Wells, and later training AFS Despatch riders at Aldershot.

After the war he went back to the family firm, where he worked until he retired in 1960 and moved to Trieste, Italy, where he had many friends and business contacts. He died there in 1967.

Lionel's brother, Philip, took up gliding in 1932 and became internationally famous for the many records he achieved for height and distance. He was World Champion in 1952. Richard gained the Military Cross during the heroic raid on Dieppe in 1942 when he was taken prisoner. He was awarded the CBE in 1961 for services to export.

Lionel married Edythe Winifred Stapledon (1905–1982) in Perth, WA, on 30 December 1930. She was formerly engaged to Alfred Morgan of Broome, WA. Lionel and Edythe had three sons – Peter, John and David. Lionel and Edythe spent the Second World War years in England in the National Fire Service, their children having been taken to Perth, WA, for safety in 1940 and returning to England in April 1945.

Lionel Wills in action at Crystal Palace in the very early days of the sport.

Lionel Wills pictured at his marriage to Edythe Winifred Stapledon in Perth, Western Australia.

Quite soon afterwards, Lionel and Edythe were divorced. Edythe married Lynden Wynne-Tyson in August 1947. Lynden was divorced from actress Estelle Wynne-Tyson whose stage name was Esme Wynne (1898–1972). She was also a playwright and authoress and a great friend of Noel Coward. Edythe and Lynden were divorced and Edythe married James Thom in January 1950. Lionel married Madge Eunice Game, a divorcee, in February 1948. Lionel Wills was born in London in 1903 and died of throat cancer aged 64 years.

Garry Baker writes that by the time Lionel reached Australia, the Wills' family operations had offices in Perth, Fremantle, Kalgoorlie, Melbourne, Sydney, Brisbane, Broken Hill, as well as Singapore and a variety of Asian centres. The company also had European offices, including the London and Manchester focal points for the supply of goods vital to the huge merchant trade being conducted by the firm.

There had been several points at which the company, in its various guises, had taken advantage of major events. At the outbreak of the First World War in 1914 the British Government contracted to buy the entire Australian wheat crop, and George Wills and Co. secured the shipping contract, which at times saw as many as 100 of their vessels at sea – such was their scale of operations. When the great railway lines of Western Australia were built to service the goldfields, Wills' companies were involved in the nation-building exercise.

In the merchant and soft goods business, the Wills name was widely known across Australia, where local manufacture had become part of their operation. Indeed, name the product or commodity used in Australia, and Wills probably had dealings with it.

By the 1920s, the Wills organisation was one of the largest corporations in Australia, also having dealings with Broken Hill and the vast ore concentrates mined there, which were being transported off to England in George Wills and Co. ships.

Although there is no doubt that Lionel Wills' arrival in Australia in 1926 was business-motivated, and was not as has sometimes been suggested a motorcycling holiday, two-wheeled sport played a major role. His own pictorial record suggests that he rode a Harley-Davidson at Sellicks Beach in Adelaide, competed in a number of motorcycle trials elsewhere in Southern Australia and then, at the Sydney Show Grounds, had his momentous first meeting with Johnnie Hoskins.

Lionel watched speedway at Penrith, Maroubra and, in the latter months of 1926, went to Brisbane where he witnessed the opening day at the Exhibition grounds.

The Wills family business, which, like most corporations of that size, operated under a variety of subsidiary titles, celebrated its centenary in 1949. By the mid-1980s the company was the subject of a corporate takeover and today no longer exists in its past form, save for a few remnant businesses, of which members of the Wills family today have no connection.

Lionel Wills was universally respected within speedway racing. *Motor Cycle* magazine in March 1929 summed this up succinctly, when it said:

> To say that a man is the greatest sportsman in any particular branch of sport would probably arouse a most heated controversy. But this I will say – that there is no greater sportsman connected with speedway racing than P L B Wills. This is no private view, but the opinion of everyone who has come in contact with him. It is not generally known that Lionel Wills was largely instrumental in bringing dirt track racing from Australia to England.
>
> During the two years Lionel was in Australia on business, he contracted the speedway fever to such an extent that although his Cambridge and ex-Cambridge friends have tried to cure him ever since his return to England, they have not succeeded the man's enthusiasm for the sport is absolutely unbounded.
>
> And yet Wills has no financial interest in the sport. At the beginning of last season, one promoter at least had the hardest job in the world inducing him to accept any prize money, while such things as appearance money were flatly refused. His efforts both on and off the track are the outcome of a sheer love of the game.
>
> When he saw the sport down under he immediately thought how the lads at home would love it. Since then he has not left a stone unturned to give it to them.

AUB LAWSON – MY MENTOR

I was only 14 years of age when Aub Lawson came to stay with my family in Plaistow for the 1947 speedway season. Even after I had become an established rider myself and ridden both with and against Aub in meetings in Britain and in Australia, I suppose that to him I was still 'Junior', the name he had bestowed upon me at the very start.

Today, sixty-five years and more after our first meeting at my parents' home, he remains my speedway hero. My entire life, since that first encounter, has largely revolved around the sport and the many years of pleasure I have had out of racing, promoting and team managing (including two Test series' wins in Australia), can largely be attributed to the encouragement I received from Aub.

What a mentor for any budding speedway rider!

Aubrey Lawson (1915–1977), was born on 5 April 1915 at Kelly's Gully, Warialda in New South Wales, Australia, the second son of Blanche Ethel (*née* Atkinson) and John Stafford (Jack) Lawson. The family were farmers until the Great Depression took them to Sydney in 1924 where Jack found work in a tannery at Willoughby.

There was an older brother, Cyril, born in 1911, and a younger sister, Joyce, born in 1920. Throughout their marriage, both at Warialda and in Willoughby, Ethel and Jack Lawson fostered a number of children, including those of Ethel's brother, Sid, who had married a girl of 16 when he was already 60 years of age.

Three children were born to Sid and his teenage bride – Sid, the eldest and the twins Lynie and Laurie. Eventually this marriage broke up when Sid's bride ran off with another man. Sid took his children to Ethel and then went home, put a gun to his head and blew out his brains.

Another child to be fostered by Ethel and Jack Lawson was Donald Horsley who, in 1947, changed his name by deed poll to Lawson. The act was witnessed by Allan Quinn. With a change of name, Don basked in the reflected glory of Aub Lawson for a lifetime. Both Don and Allan, lifelong friends from childhood, became Australian international speedway riders in the late 1940s and 1950s.

It has been reported in many places over the years that Don was a half-brother to the Lawson family, but this was not the case. I understand that Don contacted his father later in life, when his father was in his 90s.

Life in the Lawson household was happy but Ethel was a very strict Presbyterian churchgoer and would not allow alcohol in the house. Jack would buy a couple of bottles of beer on his way home from the tannery and hide them in the garden, to consume later in the evening.

Aub attended Naremburn School and took his first job as a telegram delivery boy with the then Postmaster-General's Department, riding a heavy red bicycle around the Sydney, Redfern and King's Cross areas.

He began his speedway career at Shepherd's Bush, near Mascot, in 1937 and signed his first contract with World Speedway Pty Ltd on 18 September 1937. It was the start of a record-breaking career in which he was considered one of the best speedway riders never to win the World Championship.

Aub made an immediate impact with a flamboyant leg-trailing style and a long tartan scarf that trailed in the breeze behind him. His exploits attracted the attention of the Wembley management who sent him a contract. He arrived in England in March 1939 and, at the insistence of his strict mother Ethel, was accompanied by his sister Joyce, acting as chaperone.

Wembley initially loaned Aub to Middlesbrough, at that time operating in the National League Division Two. Aub was an overnight sensation in Britain, qualifying for the 1939 World Championship Final at Wembley, putting him in the list of the best sixteen riders in the world. The Final was never held due to the Second World War being declared that September before the meeting could be staged.

Aub returned to Australia with Joyce and in July 1940 joined the Australian Imperial Force as a despatch rider with the 8th Division Signals. He served in Malaya and Borneo and rose to the rank of lieutenant, being decorated for distinguished service.

Two days before the fall of Singapore, Aub and other key personnel were placed on a ship in an attempt to withdraw to Sumatra where it was hoped to hold the Japanese. The ship was sunk by enemy bombs and Aub survived 4 hours in the water before being picked up and taken back to Australia.

On arrival in March 1942, he linked with the 7th Division Signals. He was stricken with malaria and affected by other tropical diseases during the war which slowed his return to speedway racing after peace had been declared.

Aub Lawson, who originally joined the Australian Imperial Forces as a despatch rider with the 8th Division Signals, rose to the rank of lieutenant and was decorated for distinguished service.

In 1946, Aub raced at the Sydney Sports Ground for a promotional company named The International Speedway Club, which he had formed with other renowned riders such as Lionel Van Praag, Vic and Ray Duggan, Max Grosskreutz, Frank Dolan, Cliff Parkinson and Clem Mitchell.

Aub was a director and a financial investor in the speedway. At this time, the style of speedway racing changed to accommodate slicker track surfaces (less dirt) and Aub, like his rivals in the late 1940s, switched to a foot-forward stance with his left leg. While others struggled to adapt, Aub was spectacularly successful and went from strength to strength on the track.

England called again in 1947 and Aub returned to Britain to join West Ham, promoted by ex-riders Arthur Atkinson and Stan Greatrex, who had beaten pre-war Hammers chief Johnnie Hoskins for the promoting rights at Custom House.

At the centre of Australian speedway. Aub captained the Aussies' side that won the opening test of the 1951 series in England by 60–48 at Harringay. Back row, from left to right: Junior Bainbridge, Bob Leverenz, Dick Wise (manager) and Graham Warren. Front row: Jack Biggs, Cliff Watson, Aub Lawson, Jack Young and Ronnie Moore.

The arrival of Aub and Cliff Watson to live with my family in Plaistow, just a short distance from West Ham speedway, saw a major change in my life. Aub rode for West Ham from 1947–51 inclusive, being the team's top scorer in his final season.

In 1952, Aub took a break from international speedway and bought his own 240-acre farm at Quirindi, NSW. It was the only year during his professional

The Lawson family on the track at The Firs, Norwich.

career in which he did not compete overseas. However, the persistent call of British promoters was strong and in 1953 he was lured back to racing by the Norwich track. He rode for the Stars from 1953–60 inclusive and was the team's top scorer in 1953, 1957 and 1959.

While under contract to Norwich, Aub simultaneously dabbled in promoting for a second time – at Ipswich in 1957 and 1958, during which time a young Bob Sharp, later to become twice Australian Champion, raced for the Witches. Bob died from a heart attack at his home in Tara, in Queensland, in September 2012.

Aub qualified for twelve World Championship Finals (all at Wembley), including the cancelled 1939 event. He made his World Final debut in 1949 and was in the line-up again in 1950, 1951, 1953, 1954, 1957, 1958, 1959 and 1960, making more appearances and scoring more final points (73) than any other Australian rider.

He also qualified in 1955 and 1956 but was injured and unable to compete. His best result was a remarkable third place in 1958 at the comparatively advanced age for a speedway rider of 43.

His Test match record for Australia produced 680 points in eighty-four matches. Aub at one stage shared the record for Australian Championship wins (five) with the late Billy Sanders and also shared the record for New South Wales Championship victories (again five), this time with Jim Airey.

Aub retired from speedway racing in 1960. He made a one-off comeback at Kembla Grange in 1963 to win the NSW Championship at the age of 48, capping one of the longest international careers in the sport.

Having retired as a rider, Aub became a promoter once again, this time at Westmead Speedway, Sydney, in the early 1960s. From the late 1950s, he had been manager at Claremont Speedway in Perth whilst continuing to race. He settled in Perth in 1967 and later purchased a farm at Northam.

It was on this farm that he died of a heart condition on 20 January 1977, just short of his 62nd birthday. He is buried in Karrakatta Cemetery in Perth – the same resting place as another famous Australian international speedway star, Ron Johnson.

Aub married 19-year-old Mary Pullbrook in July 1940 in Sydney. They had five children, Rosemary Anne (born 26 August 1941), John Michael (23 December 1946), Sandra Emily who died in infancy, Lionel Aubrey (14 April 1950) and Patricia Jean (20 May 1954). Aub and Mary were divorced in 1969 and Aub married Roma Gasman in November 1972 in Perth, West Australia.

I am still in regular contact with some of Aub's family, including his daughter Rosemary and his sister Joyce who is now in her 92nd year.

ERIC CHITTY

Eric was born in Toronto, Canada, in 1909 and died in Florida on holiday in 1990 aged 81. He raced in several different types of motorcycle disciplines before coming to race at West Ham in 1935. He made his base in the London area with his wife Jeannie (Eugenie), daughter Carol Ann and son Raymond – who was born in London. I knew the family from 1948 onwards. Carol Ann died prematurely in 1983 at the age of 48, Jeannie in 1999 at 87.

Eric was forced to retire from racing in 1952 after he fell from his horse in Epping Forest and badly broke his leg. During his career he fractured some forty-four bones. At the outbreak of war, the family went to Canada (as did so many British evacuees for the duration of the war). Eric stayed in England doing war work. Towards the end of the war he joined ENSA (Entertainments National Service Association – formed in 1939) and entertained the troops in BAOR (British Army of the Rhine). During the war he managed to race at Belle Vue – like so many others – and won many 'unofficial' titles. The family returned to London in 1947.

As happens in life sometimes, you lose contact with people and the Chittys and I lost contact until March 2005. It was then that Raymond was looking, via the West Ham website, for information about his father's racing career – he and Eric had become estranged and Ray was looking for some photographs. We were put in touch and the reminiscing has been joyful ever since.

Ray left England for Canada in 1957 to join the Royal Canadian Air Force, in which he made his career, retiring in 1985. Coincidence and life are strange. Eileen and I had already booked a holiday by train right across Canada which started in Toronto and ended in Vancouver in May 2005, which is before the contact between Ray and me.

We exchanged several emails and arranged to meet at our hotel in Toronto. We had a marvellous three days with Ray and his wife, Traudl, showing us the sights of Toronto including Niagara Falls.

Eric Chitty in action on West Ham's silver sand surface.

When we returned to the UK, I telephoned an old pal from schooldays, Cyril Hill, who also went to West Ham Speedway in the immediate post-war period. I told him that I had met up with Ray Chitty in Toronto.

He couldn't believe the coincidence as, a couple of days previously, he was clearing out his attic at home and found a record made by Eric just after the war – a 78rpm. Eric Chitty made two records and had a readymade market with West Ham's 40,000 fans. Sometimes Eric would sing to the fans during the speedway interval. In the late 1930s Eric would supplement his racing income by singing in London clubs – he was quite a crooner.

Reg presents a framed copy of one of Eric Chitty's recordings to his son, Ray.

My pal Cyril had several CDs made from the record and I sent a couple to Ray who was emotionally surprised at hearing his father's voice again after such a long time. The songs were 'Was it Rain That Fell or Was it Tears' and 'Moon at Sea'. We have a copy and it is compulsory listening along with the story for anyone visiting our home for the first time.

Cyril gave me the record and Eileen and I had it framed in gold. Ray and Traudl, at that time, spent three months of the year in Portugal, escaping the worst of Canada's winter weather.

The next plan was for Eileen and me to drive to the Algarve and present the record to Ray as a surprise – which we did in February 2006. A few years later, the second record came to me from a former West Ham lady supporter. The songs are 'A Door Will Open' and 'When I Grow Too Old to Dream'. Both records are extremely rare.

RONNIE MOORE MBE

Ronnie and I have been pals for some sixty years or so. Our friendship started when his mother, Clarice, who died a few days short of her 100th birthday, wrote to me in January 1950, enclosing photographs and cuttings from the programme published by the Aranui speedway track at Christchurch in New Zealand.

A letter from New Zealand was the start of Reg Fearman's friendship with Ronnie Moore and his parents.

Ronnie Moore (left) with his mother, Clarice, Reg Fearman and another New Zealand speedway legend, Geoff Mardon, and his wife Val, pictured in Christchurch.

New Zealand is well known for its distinguished citizens. So many famous people have come from such a small population, including Sir Edmund Hillary, the first man to climb Everest; pioneering plastic surgeons Sir Harold Gillies and Sir Archibald McIndoe, who performed amazing surgery on RAF flying crew who had been badly burned and who became known as The Guinea Pig Club; Ernest Rutherford, who split the atom; Russell Crowe, the actor; Kiri te Kanawa, the opera singer; Peter Snell, runner and three times Olympic champion; Grand Prix drivers Bruce McLaren and Chris Amon; Bert Munroe, immortalised in the film *The Fastest Indian*, and many more.

No true speedway fan will need to be reminded of the fact that Christchurch must be the only city in the world to be home to three World Speedway Champions – Ronnie Moore, Barry Briggs and Ivan Mauger.

Ronnie, being the trailblazer, was racing before the really big money that came in to the sport at the time of Barry and Ivan. Their racing careers also lasted much longer than Ronnie's and they subsequently progressed into promoting speedway with their World Champions' Troupe.

It was Ronnie's father, Les Moore, who built the Aranui Speedway. Ronnie himself stormed onto the British speedway scene at Wimbledon in March 1950, at the age of just 17, and qualified that year for the World Speedway Championship Final and scored 7 points.

Ronnie Moore in his earliest racing days.

In 1954, at 21 years of age, he was World Speedway Champion for the first time. His success as a twice-World Speedway Champion, team rider and captain are well documented elsewhere. All the superlatives belong to Ronnie – the original Wonder Boy who everyone still loves, super star, giant of the sport, legend in his lifetime.

He was a Wall of Death rider, a Grand Prix racing car driver and a gold prospector along with his father and Trevor Redmond. In the winter of 1950, they dived for gold at Skipper's Gorge which is over the snow-capped mountains from Queenstown, New Zealand.

The Gorge is only 20ft wide and the water flows as a torrent and is extremely cold from snow melting in the mountains. Les wore his home-made diving suit with

Ronnie Moore's father, Les, pictured during his own racing days.

Ronnie and Trevor manning the air pump and holding ropes to prevent Les being swept away. They made a number of unsuccessful attempts before giving up.

It is said that at that time there was enough gold in the Shotover River to pay off the New Zealand National Debt. It is also said that in the Gold Rush of the late 1800s, a dog fell into the river and came out with its fur covered in gold dust.

In 1951, Les and Ronnie bought in London two 1930s Alfa Romeo road-going racing cars from Roy Salvadori, a former Grand Prix driver. (It has been reported elsewhere that one of the cars was a Lagonda.) The P3 Alfa had won the Italian Grand Prix with Nuvolari at the wheel in the 1930s. The two Alfas were shipped back to New Zealand and won the New Zealand Grand Prix three years in succession. Eventually they were sold.

Recently, the P3 Alfa changed hands in Australia for well over £1 million.

By 1954, both Ronnie and Les were racing Cooper Climax cars, built by John Cooper in England. I saw both Ronnie and Les in action at the Ardmore Grand Prix in Auckland. Racing on the same programme were Prince Bira of Siam (now Thailand) and Ken Wharton, Tony Gaze and Jack Brabham. Regrettably, Les lost his life in a racing car crash in 1959. He was just 48 years of age.

Ronnie married Jill in 1958 in London where their twins Kim and Lea were born. Shani and Gina were born in Christchurch. Jill died in 1985 from cancer. Ronnie has seven grandchildren who keep him busy, along with his hobbies of gardening, sailing and driving his 4x4 Land Rover into the mountains, plus, of course, overseeing his junior speedway racing track at Moore Park.

Prince Bira of Siam (now Thailand) in the helmet and overalls, pictured at the Ardmore Grand Prix in New Zealand in 1955 which was watched by Reg Fearman.

Ronnie took a break from speedway in 1957 and spent two years racing Grand Prix and Cooper Climax cars in particular. He returned to speedway racing in 1959, the year in which he won his second World Championship.

He retired from speedway in 1963 after a compound fracture of his left leg. After spending the next six years in New Zealand, he was lured back to Wimbledon in 1969 at the age of 36 by Wimbledon supremo, Ronnie Greene (a wartime controller of fire operations in Blitz-hit London, who had been awarded the MBE for services to the Fire Brigade Benevolent Fund).

Ronnie returned as captain of the Plough Lane Dons, qualified for three more World Finals and won his first World Pairs title with Ivan Mauger at Malmo, Sweden, in 1970. He finally retired from British League competitive racing in 1972 and during his twenty-two-year speedway career raced only for Wimbledon, the team he captained for many years.

In 1974, Ronnie was coaxed out of retirement by Ivan Mauger and Barry Briggs to tour with their World Champions' Troupe. It was at Newcastle, New South Wales, that Ronnie (then aged 42) crashed, suffering severe head and internal injuries.

The surgeon drilled into Ronnie's skull to relieve pressure on his brain and there was a 100-mile ambulance dash with a police escort to the North Shore Hospital in Sydney. Ronnie was in a coma for a month. It was many weeks before he could be repatriated to Christchurch for further hospitalisation. He had lost the sight of one eye (this did recover) and suffered a total loss of hearing (which has only partially recovered in one ear).

Aranui Speedway was bulldozed more than thirty years ago and a new track built at Ruapuna which was called The Ronnie Moore Stadium. Later, the speedway moved to a new venue and that is now called Moore Park.

Ronnie was absent from England for many years. Then, in 1998, I had the idea of inviting him as guest of honour to the 1999 Veteran Speedway Riders' Association Dinner.

I telephoned Ronnie and asked him if he would come if I could arrange it? He replied that he would be there 'like a shot'. I put the proposal to the VSRA Committee, who agreed, providing I could raise the money to pay his return air fare and expenses whilst he was in the UK.

I raised the sponsorship from a number of members who were delighted at the chance to see Ronnie again and, due to their generosity, he was able to come to England for some three weeks. Ronnie was grateful to Pete Saunders (ex-Crewe and Peterborough) for the loan of a car for the whole period.

At the VSRA dinner, I proposed the toast to Ronnie and, in my speech, included a message from Ivan Mauger, part of which I quote:

I am sure Ronnie has never realised exactly what an influence he had on my career, but I want to reassure everyone present, and Ronnie himself, that to all the kids in Christchurch, and especially in my district, he was our idol. We used to go to Aranui Speedway hours before the gates were due to open, just so that we could be on the street corner when Ronnie arrived.

In later life, one of my proudest moments ever was winning the World Pairs' Championship at Malmo with Ronnie. He was the original whiz kid and is still a hero of all the young riders, as he was for me and many others.

Ronnie Moore was also present at the End of Era Banquet at Wembley in September 2000 before the Empire Stadium was finally demolished. Wembley staged a number of farewell events for sporting stars who had graced the arena over many decades.

Barry Briggs was contacted regarding such an event for speedway. He decided to involve the VSRA and I assisted, along with others, in planning the evening.

It was hoped that as many World Champions as possible would attend and part of my remit was to organise their attendance. Unfortunately, a fuel strike prevented Hans Neilsen and Eric Gundersen from travelling from Denmark and kept Anders Michanek in Sweden.

On a visit to England Ronnie was reunited with the Allard midget car he had tested at Wimbledon in the early 1950s. Pictured with Ronnie is former rider Jack Taylor who discovered the midget in a Wiltshire garage and restored it as a museum piece.

Ronnie Moore and his fellow World Champions pictured at the Wembley End of an Era Banquet. Back row, from left to right: Gary Havelock, Ivan Mauger, Greg Hancock, Ole Olsen, Michael Lee, Sam Ermolenko and Peter Collins. Front row: Freddie Williams, Ove Fundin, Per Jonsson, Barry Briggs, Ronnie Moore and Bjorn Knutson.

I was fortunate, however, in that three speedway personalities came together to sponsor Ronnie Moore for the event. The three were John Harrhy, the VSRA host for the 'Rider Cup' at the West Midlands Golf Club, Jack Taylor, who restored the Atom Midget Car in which Ronnie Moore raced (and in which he broke his collarbone at Wimbledon when practising in the mid-1950s) and Pete Saunders.

In all, thirteen World Champions were present, each sitting at a different table and later mingling with the 1,000 guests.

The last time speedway machines roared inside Wembley Stadium was on 14 October 1996 when I joined forces with Alan Wilson of Edinburgh to promote awareness for the Guide Dogs for the Blind Association, a registered charity. The regional manager, Anne Thair, attended with her guide dog, Helena.

There was a good turnout of former speedway riders who rode – not raced – around the greyhound track. Good coverage was obtained from the media and BBC Radio.

My third success in bringing Ronnie halfway around the world was on the occasion of his installation as president of the VSRA in March 2003. The date of the dinner, 7 March, coincided with his 70th birthday. Ivan Mauger and his wife

Freddie Williams, Anne Thair, regional manager for the Guide Dogs for the Blind Association, and Reg Fearman at Wembley Stadium.

Raye were delighted to sponsor Ronnie's return air fare from New Zealand for this occasion. The dinner was extremely successful and drew a record attendance of 334 guests.

JACK WILLIAM GATES 1926–2012

I have mentioned in an earlier chapter the great friendship that Jack and I had for more than sixty years and the good fun we had when he raced in England and I raced in Australia. Jack's 80th birthday was on 3 December 2006. Around April that year, Eileen and I discussed the possibility of organising a secret and surprise birthday lunch for Jack near to his home at Burleigh Heads on Queensland's Gold Coast. We thought we could so we went into action and first contacted Bluey Scott, ex-rider with Glasgow, Long Eaton and several other tracks. Bluey lived not far from Jack (who lived on his own) and with his wife, Ann, a Scottish girl, kept an eye on Jack as he had been suffering a few ailments over the previous few years. Bluey found a good waterside restaurant, Elevations, and we took over from there.

Jack Gates listens intently as Reg Fearman reads from the special book compiled to tell his life story. Two former riders to the left are Bert Kingston and Nigel Boocock.

We looked at Elevations on the Web and liked the look of it and its position. We then emailed the manageress to make an open numbers booking for 3 December. We obtained several menus and the wine list and made our choice. We then set about emailing and telephoning many ex-riders who live on the Gold Coast. There are very few who have not moved from Sydney up to the year-round warm climate found there. All those invited were sworn to secrecy so that it would be a complete surprise for Jack on the day. We asked Bluey and Ann to tell Jack that they wished to take him out to a nice restaurant for lunch on his 80th. He asked them more than once why they couldn't have a BBQ in their yard as they usually did.

We made time to assemble a 'Red Book' of 'This was your racing life Jackie Gates' containing write-ups and photographs from his days racing in England and as an international rider for Australia.

Reg Fearman is on hand to help as Jack Gates cuts his 80th birthday cake.

The secret was well kept. I spoke to Jack on the telephone two weeks before the event and told him I would talk to him on his birthday. A few days later Eileen and I left for Australia, stopping off at Perth where we spent a week with Colin and Trish McKee, catching up with many of my former contracted riders and former Ipswich promoter, John Berry.

The guests at Jack Gates' 80th birthday lunch. Back row, from left to right: John Titman, Eric Williams, Bill Goode, Bert Kingston, Martin Rogers, Ian Hoskins, Ivan Mauger, Bill Bryden, Allan Quinn, Nigel Boocock, Kevin Torpie and Greg Kentwell. Front row: Jim Shepherd, Bob Sharpe, Reg Fearman, Jackie Gates, Bluey Scott, Adrian Guest and John Torpie, Kevin's son.

We flew to the Gold Coast with a couple of days to spare and were met by Bluey and Ann and taken to their home in Burleigh Waters. We had thirty-six friends of the speedway fraternity sit down for lunch including Ian Hoskins (Jack's former promoter at Glasgow) who flew in from New Zealand, Allan Quinn and some of the Lawson family from Sydney. Also from Sydney were Jim (speedway historian) and Judith Shepherd and, from Mackay, which is 600 miles north of Brisbane, Eric Williams, a former Wembley teammate of Jack's.

You will see from the photographs the surprise on Jack's face and the good time that was had by all those present.

It gave Eileen and me great pleasure in arranging such a wonderful event, without a hitch, in a very lovely location for such a good pal.

IGOR PLECHANOV (1933–2007)

I was also delighted to have been able to arrange for the great Russian star Igor Plechanov to be guest of honour at the VSRA dinner on the evening Ronnie Moore was installed as president.

Igor Plechanov, Igor Kalashnik and Ronnie Moore at the Veteran Speedway Riders'
Association Dinner at which Ronnie was installed as president.

Igori Plekhanov (his name in Russian) was born in Nijegorodka, at the foot of
the Ural Mountains.

During 2002, long-time Russian and world speedway fan, Igor Kalashnik of
Kishinev in Moldova, asked Ove Fundin (they had been in touch for some time)
if it might be possible for Plechanov to come to England for the VSRA event.
It was at the next VSRA committee meeting that I put forward the idea which was
accepted, the one stumbling block being that the Association's funds would not
stretch to such an expense.

I told the committee that I would raise the funds through sponsorship. I made
telephone call after telephone call and the close-knit fraternity of the VSRA opened
their hearts and wallets. Eventually, enough money was raised to bring Kalashnik,
Plechanov and his grandson to England for ten days.

Eileen and I met them at Heathrow and took them to the Coventry Hilton for
the Veterans' Dinner. Plechanov received a tremendous reception from fellow
riders and the whole evening was a great success. On the Sunday, we took them
back to Henley-on-Thames where we had arranged for them to stay in a hotel.
We arranged day trips to the usual London and Home Counties' tourist spots for
the remaining days of their visit. Eileen and I enjoyed being their guides as much
as they enjoyed the sights.

It had taken Igor Plechanov three days on the train from Ufa to reach Moscow to catch his flight to London. His grandson, Kirill, was at that time living in Moscow and was a member of the Moscow State Circus.

On the Sunday before taking the party to Henley-on-Thames, we travelled to Stonebridge for the Speedway Promoters' Exhibition Day which included memorabilia stands. The Russians had not seen anything like it and loaded themselves up with parcels of goodies. That evening, we were present at the Allesley Hotel, Coventry, where Plechanov was part of a public talk-in with Ove Fundin, Barry Briggs, Ronnie Moore and Freddie Williams.

In addition to the London sightseeing, we took a trip to the Midlands, taking in the British Motor Heritage Museum at Gaydon, the National Motor Cycle Museum at Coventry and Coventry Cathedral before attending a Saturday evening meeting at Coventry Speedway.

The next day we drove to Newport Speedway where Tim Stone and Neil Street made us most welcome. We also visited Reading Speedway although not for an actual race meeting.

All too soon it was time for Igor and Kirill to depart Heathrow for Russia. The five of us had had a wonderful time together despite the language barrier and we enjoyed several dinners at the Fearman home in Henley and several at

Igor Plechanov pictured on the London Eye.

nearby restaurants. On one such occasion, we were joined by former rider Stan Stevens. With every alcoholic drink there was a toast, Russian-style. (Not quite Russian style, actually, as this involves throwing the glasses into the fireplace!)

Before taking Igor and Kirill to Heathrow, we visited the Phyllis Court Country Club in Henley to meet Tony Gyselynck, an eminent grass track racer in the 1930s who had turned his hand to speedway just as the Second World War broke out in 1939.

In the late 1940s/early 1950s, Tony was a junior at Coventry but realised he was not going to break into the team so returned to his grass track roots. He later became a flight engineer and pilot with BOAC. In 1967, he started a still-thriving flying club at Wycombe Air Park where I learned to fly and pilot single-engine Cessna aircraft.

I remember one occasion extremely well in my early training. I was sent on a triangular course from Wycombe to Coventry Airport to Cranfield Airport and back to Wycombe. On the way to Coventry, I strayed off course and went into the restricted air space of the United States Air Force at Upper Heyford.

An American voice came over the radio saying, 'You are an unidentified aircraft. Please identify yourself,' which I did. 'Make a manoeuvre to the right and then a manoeuvre to the left.' The voice then said, 'OK Buddy, I now have you on radar. Where are you from and where are you going?'

Back on a machine. Igor Plechanov, with former Australian star Neil Street, at Newport's Hayley Stadium.

I told him I was going to Coventry on a training flight. He said he would put me back on the correct course, which he did. I travelled just another minute or so then called up the American voice and said, 'I want to go home! Please put me back on the course for Wycombe Air Park.' He told me to do a 180 degree turn and set me on the way. I understand people have been shot down for less!

During the time we spent with Plechanov, there were many opportunities for discussion about his career and life.

He told us that as a top Russian speedway rider, when he raced abroad, he had to collect the money due to himself and the other riders and take it to the Ministry of Sport in Moscow. He was allowed to retain 10 per cent.

At one time, he had an apartment in Ufa and a dacha in the country by a river where he grew his own vegetables. Under the Communist regime, as a top sportsman, he had a good pension which was lost when the Soviet Union disbanded and Russia became a democratic state.

Some little time after his visit to England in March 2003, he became ill with heart problems. He had several strokes, was paralysed down one side and lost his speech. He spent his time in hospital and at the home of his daughter, Veronika. At the end, although he was one of Russia's elite sportsmen, the state failed to serve him well. He died almost destitute, leaving a son, Igor, in Moscow, Veronika, who is a doctor in Ufa, grandchildren and great-grandchildren.

Igor Plechanov qualified for seven individual World Speedway Finals, at Malmo, Sweden, in 1961, as the first Soviet racer to appear in the Final, at Wembley (in 1962, 1965 and 1967), and at Gothenburg, Sweden (1964, 1966 and 1968 – the latter as reserve without any rides).

His best placings were as runner-up twice, in 1964 to Barry Briggs and in 1965 to Bjorn Knutson.

His personal honours were many and varied. He was Master of Sport of the USSR in 1959, Honoured Master of Sports USSR for motorsport in 1965 and International Master of Sport on track motor races (1965).

He graduated from Leningrad State Institute of Physical Culture of Lesgaft in 1969, was bronze prize winner of Europe Championship (1961–67), Champion of the USSR Nations Sport Festival (1965) and silver prize-winner of the USSR Nations Sport Festival (1967).

His other speedway honours included being Champion of the USSR in 1960, 1961, 1963, 1965 and 1968; silver prize-winner of the USSR Championship in 1959, 1962, 1964 and 1967; and Champion of the Russian Republic (1960–62), winning silver in this event in 1964 and 1966, and bronze in 1967.

Igor was a USSR Team Championship winner in 1962, 1964 and in 1967–69, and winner of the Gold Helmet of Czechoslovakia at Pardubica in 1964 and 1966.

Igor Plechanov's grave in his homeland, inscribed with his many achievements.

His World Championship appearances were raced on nineteen tracks in eight countries and altogether he appeared on more than 130 speedway tracks world-wide, establishing track records on ten of them.

He was a coach of the speedway national team of the USSR from 1970–72, and was decorated with the Order of Bashkira (Friendship of Nations) in 2004, awarded honorary diplomas of the Presidium of the Supreme Court of Bashkira in 1959, 1968, and the medal for Notable Sportsman of Bashkira in 1993.

ROY EDWARDS AND BUTTERSCOTCH

Roy and his wife, Sue, bought Park Farm on the edge of The Potteries in 1959. They came from a small village, Llanfechain in Wales, not far from Oswestry. Joan and I were introduced to Roy and Sue by our local bank manager, Eric Johnson. We became good friends. Roy was already a National Hunt jockey and, after two years at Park Farm, they bought a 75-acre farm in Shropshire to which they eventually added more land to make 200 acres in total. They turned the farm into a bloodstock and training establishment.

Roy Edwards mounted.

Roy rode over 500 winners in a riding career from 1956–71. He suffered many serious injuries but always bounced back.

In 1964, he was third in the Grand National on Peacetown. In 1967, at the Cheltenham National Hunt Festival, he rode the 6-year-old Saucy Kit, to win the Cheltenham Hurdle at odds of 100–6. In 1971, Roy and Sue moved full time into bloodstock and the training of horses.

By this time, Joan and I were living in Henley-on-Thames. Roy would often call into our home for a cup of tea on his way to the racehorse sales at Ascot from his 'Yard' near Shrewsbury.

One day in 1971, Roy suggested that Joan and I should buy a horse and he would train it. We readily agreed and accompanied him to the Ascot sales where he bought, on our behalf, Butterscotch, a 5-year-old mare. Joan and I became the owners and were registered at Weatherbys.

We already had two horses we used for 'riding out', Sabre, a former showjumper, and a pony named Crackers, which we had bought from Vic Gooden, himself a former rider in showjumping events, speedway rider and promoter.

We travelled to many race meetings where Butterscotch was jumping. She finished in the 'frame' several times but was never a winner. At Haydock Park, she unfortunately fell and was killed.

Roy and Sue had several stallions at the stud. Our hope was to have had at least one foal from Butterscotch – but it was not to be.

Roy and Sue Edwards.

One of Roy and Sue's stallions sired the 1999 Cheltenham Gold Cup winner, See More Business.

Roy died in December 2010 aged 77 years.

Roy's two brothers and sister were all involved with horses and the racing world. Roy and Sue's grandson, Charlie Huxley, is fast making a name for himself on the racecourse.

CHAPTER SEVENTEEN

A HEROINE AND A
COUPLE OF VILLAINS

In the introduction to the last chapter, I promised an account of the most famous (and in some ways the most notorious) woman to ever ride the speedways.

There is also an account of this particular East End boy's encounter with two of the greatest villains that ever walked the streets of London.

FAY TAYLOUR 1904–1983

The lady who qualifies for the title of speedway heroine was Fay Taylour, indisputably the female champion of the sport in the late 1920s and early 1930s, the period when women were allowed to participate in racing both at home in the UK and abroad.

Fay was the first speedway rider to arrive in Australia after the initial 1928 season in Britain, beating the men by several weeks. I met her on two occasions, the first in 1947. She was a guest at West Ham Speedway and, as a 14-year-old fan, I obtained her autograph.

The second meeting came when she was guest of honour (brought along by Johnnie Hoskins) at the Veteran Dirt Track Riders' Association Dinner at the Rembrant Hotel in London in 1973.

It was while I was doing some research on Fay that I learned of a lady from Kent, Ninette Gray, who had lunch with Johnnie's son, Ian, while she was on holiday in Harare, Zimbabwe.

Ninette had inherited from her mother all of Fay's papers and manuscripts. Fay and Ninette's mother had been very good friends. Fay was a prolific writer and wrote tens of thousands of words covering her life story. I contacted Ninette Gray, who allowed me to borrow the several boxes of papers.

From these papers, Dr Brian Belton was able to write the biography *Fay Taylour: Queen of Speedway.*

Fay Taylour's achievements in the world of dirt track racing have thus been well documented over the years, both in Dr Belton's book and in numerous magazine and newspaper articles and other media. What is not generally known is Fay's turbulent personal history.

She was born Frances Helen Taylour in southern Ireland in 1904, into a family whose members followed a variety of professions. Her father, Herbert Fetherstonhaugh Taylour, came from the long-settled Irish families of Wolseley and Fetherstonhaugh. He was an officer in the British forces. When the southern part of Ireland gained its independence from Britain, first as the Irish Free State and later as Eire, he left the country and made his home in England.

Fay's mother, Helen Webb, was born in Dresden when her parents were spending a vacation there. Her grandmother was cousin to Lord Wolseley, Commander-in-Chief of the British forces and a favourite of Queen Victoria. Her maternal grandfather was Surgeon General Randolph Webb, RAMC who had seen much service in the Crimean War.

Helen had been the belle of many glittering balls held at the seat of British power in Ireland, Dublin Castle, where her maternal grandfather served in Ireland.

Fay Taylour in Auckland at the wheel of a midget car.

Fay's other grandfather was a Headford, an Irish marquis whose family name was Taylour. Fay's uncle, the late George Webb, was a professor and Fellow of Trinity College, Dublin.

When Fay finished college in Dublin in the mid-1920s, she moved to her parents' home at Burghfield Bridge Lodge, Burghfield, near Reading. There she met Frank, a garage owner who used to ride his motorcycle with Fay riding pillion. Very soon she bought her own motorcycle, sowing the seeds of her racing career.

Fay later recalled:

It was Lionel Wills, a young ex-Cambridge student on a trip to Australia in 1926, who urged the Australian promoters to bring dirt track racing to England.

He was in Lewis's, the shop where I went to buy my helmet and leathers. He drove me and my bike in the family's old open Rolls-Royce to Crystal Palace for practise. Lionel also raced and drove me to many tracks all over England.

Although initially welcomed, it did not take long for women riders to be banned from the speedways. Fay turned her hand to car racing. She competed in the Monte Carlo Rally and at the iconic banked Brooklands track near Weybridge in Surrey, driving a 105 Talbot owned by Fox & Nicholls, lapping the track at 108mph.

She won the Leinster Trophy in Dublin in 1934 in an Adler Trumpf, the only woman in the race. She drove at the International Hill Climb Contest at Shelsley Walsh in 1934, driving a factory-supplied super-charged six-cylinder MG Magnette which she shared with George Eyston and Italy's ace driver, Count Lurani. She carried off first place at her first attempt.

Later at Brooklands, Fay smashed the record held by Sir Malcolm Campbell and the ace driver, Raymond Mays. She also competed with great distinction in midget car racing on the speedways in England (Walthamstow 1952), Australia, New Zealand, USA, South Africa and in Sweden.

Her life was soon to take another turn. As Fay explained:

As a child, I'd been taken to Holloway Gaol to visit a suffragette aunt. In 1935 came a chance to see it properly from the inside. I was told that if I didn't pay a £1 fine for speeding, I'd spend a week in prison so off I went to Holloway, unannounced, having told one friend.

It leaked out somehow and the *Daily Express*, to get a better story, sent a man to pay the fine and take me out of prison. I refused to go out with a man unknown to me, saying it could be white slave traffic. The man left with his receipt for the £1, but without me.

I was suddenly called to the Governor's office and turned out of the prison abruptly on orders from the Home Office. Apparently, it was a breach of Habeas Corpus for me to be there once the fine had been paid. A few years later, Habeas Corpus failed to work when I wanted it to.

Fay was often asked why she remained unmarried. Her response was usually to say, 'I never found a man as difficult as a racing car' or, 'I never managed to stay loving one person for long enough'.

She later admitted that the plain answer to the question was that the right man did not cross her path. This, she felt, was because she was 'On the wrong track or rolling too fast', or 'maybe the men I didn't marry were the right men and I didn't know it'.

In the late 1930s Fay did, however, find herself pregnant. As she described it:

Back in London, a medical student confirms I am pregnant. I know of one gynaecologist and tell him of my predicament. Hush, he warns, such an operation as I suggest is illegal in England. Nevertheless, it is arranged and I find myself in a private nursing home in Bayswater under a strange name.

A really life-changing experience for Fay resulted from a trip to her mother's birth-place in Dresden. When returning from racing in the South African Grand Prix in 1939, she embarked at Cape Town upon a German ship, disembarking not at Southampton as originally planned but at Hamburg.

After visiting Dresden, she attended the motor races at the Nuremburg Ring. She later wrote:

Previous trips to Germany and deep friendship with a young German Baron had made me love the country, but war is now only a week away and I hurry back to England.

Letters to my father and aunts decrying the war are opened by the police who visit me. I tell them my views and they ask if I am a member of the British Union of Fascists, Oswald Mosley's movement. I know nothing of it but go to their offices where I see my views in their paper and join the organisation.

Later, when walking through Hyde Park, I am arrested by two policemen. Two tatty communists had pulled my small British Union brooch from my raincoat and had signalled to the police. I was taken to the Park police station and faced with a gabbled (and false) charge of struggling with a man in Hyde Park, causing a breach of the pease (*sic*) and public speaking.

Two days later, when the case came to court, the presiding magistrate said I was entitled to wear any badge I wished and dismissed the case.

At the beginning of the Second World War, many people in Britain considered to be a security risk were interned for the duration of the hostilities. Among these people were members of the British Union of Fascists. It was reported that Lady Diana Mosley was the principal channel of communication between her husband and Hitler.

Fay Taylour's papers reveal, again in her own words:

On May 22 1940, an amendment was made to the British Defence Regulations by which British citizens could be rounded up and held indefinitely in prison without trial or conviction. This amendment was called 18-B. Overnight and during the following weeks, hundreds of women of British nationality were flung into Holloway Prison without warning. No preparations regarding treatment or accommodation had been made. I was one of them. Following the Hyde Park court case, I was rounded up, the police breaking down my door in a hurry. The charge sheet had 'public speaking' on it as charged in the Hyde Park police station. It was also stated that I was pro-German and a member of the British Union of Fascists. I found myself in the dark, drab, disused F-wing of the gaol. Lady Diana Mosley was there and she certainly set an example. I would say she was the model prisoner and she managed to remain looking like a model, maybe because she was so natural and did not use make-up anyway. I went to a dinner party in her cell, the dinner made from a cabbage from the prison garden. It would take a very clever cook to do what she did with the cabbage. Later, when her husband, Sir Oswald, joined her at Holloway in an extension building, I smuggled across some pastry that I'd made from my two pats of prison grease (margarine). Mosley's endorsement of my cooking had a curious repercussion later. Lady Mosley was, by the way, flung into prison while she was nursing a new-born baby and the baby left behind. Then, without drawing the milk from her, they set her at once to clean lavatories.

Sir Oswald Mosley was without warning arrested with his staff, immediately following the creation of Amendment 18-B. Our cases, which might be better termed views, were heard by secret tribunals, presided over by three especially appointed KCs (King's Counsel) whose duty it was to advise the Home Secretary of release or further detention – although the Home Secretary reserved the right not to act upon such advice.

My case was heard underground because the Blitz was in progress. I was questioned about my views, which were known to the KCs through letters I had written to my father and aunt. Possibly I received such attention because I had been in Germany for the Nuremburg Ring motor races just before war broke out …

A little while later I had received a casual visit from two plain clothes policemen who told me that the man living opposite my flat had reported that I had said Germany was a beautiful country and that Poland and Czechoslovakia hadn't existed before World War One, but had been built up after that war to hem Germany in.

I was reported as saying that I didn't believe in declaring war on Germany to save the Polish Corridor. I had also said that the Germans didn't want war with England. When questioned I replied that Germany was my favourite foreign country, just as France had been my mother's.

When asked if I loved Hitler, I was too amazed and amused to form a suitable answer for these legal brains. What would I do if a German parachutist landed at my feet? I replied that I would run if he chased me and run for help if he was wounded.

Before my hearing, it was made clear to me that changing my views might gain release; retraction was the word used. But if simple, straight-forward answers tightened a noose around one's neck, the reverse would have choked me.

Fay Taylour was in Holloway Gaol from 1 June 1940 till the autumn of 1942 and was then detained for a further year in the Women's Internment Camp in Port Erin, Isle of Man, for another year. In fact, hotels and guest houses

An official photograph of Fay Taylour taken when she was interned by the British Government.

The last photograph ever taken of Fay Taylour, with a favourite cat.

were requisitioned by the government. The detainees were billeted and the cost of keeping them borne by the government. The army and police provided security although the detainees were free to shop, walk and go to the beach. It was a 70-mile swim to the mainland!

Fay may have been misguided in the views she expressed at a time of great wartime stress.

After the war, in 1949 Fay went to the United States to race motor cars and to sell sports cars for a Hollywood dealer. She sold cars to film stars including Clark Gable, Gary Cooper, Elizabeth Taylor, Tony Martin and Henry Fonda. At one time, Universal Studios were considering making a film of Fay's racing achievements with Rosalind Russell taking the part of Fay Taylour.

Fay died in Dorset in 1983.

THE KRAYS

At the start of this chapter I promised a glimpse of two real villains, who tried during their infamous careers to 'muscle' a well-known speedway rider and promoter.

My own encounter with the Kray twins came many years after their reign of terror in London's East End, which reached its peak in the early to mid-1960s.

It was in March 1995 that I took my 92-year-old mother to Moorfields Eye Hospital, in London, where she had to have double cataracts removed.

Mum had to stay at the hospital overnight so I stayed in her flat in Ilford, Essex. The next day, as I was driving through London's Bethnal Green, I saw a great many people standing on the pavements behind barriers.

Being curious, I found a parking place and then walked back to the crowd and followed them to St Matthew's church, Bethnal Green, where even more people were standing around. There were also a great many police officers and about eight tough-looking men, all very tall and wearing long black overcoats with Courtneys' Security tags on their lapels.

The occasion turned out to be the funeral of Ronnie Kray who had died in Broadmoor at the age of 61. As I watched, a prison car drew up, with Ronnie's brother Reggie visible in the back, handcuffed to warders. The crowd was shouting 'good old Reggie'.

When the hearse bearing Ronnie Kray's body arrived on the scene, I saw that it was pulled by six black horses. Another hearse followed, carrying a multitude of floral tributes. Behind the hearses came twenty-six limousines, carrying underworld gangs and rich and famous people from television, stage and screen.

It was like a film star's funeral. The upheaval to traffic was unbelievable as thousands lined Bethnal Green Road. The cortège then moved off for a 6-mile journey to the Chingford Mount Cemetery in Essex.

I left the pavement early in the proceedings to collect my mother from Moorfields. The operation was a great success so we had a drive all around the parts of London my mother knew but had not seen for years. There was to be no such joyride for Reggie Kray.

Reg pictured with Vic Gooden, who stood no nonsense from the Kray twins.

Reggie himself died in October 2000 aged 66. Both Ronnie and Reggie had been sentenced in 1968 to life imprisonment, with a minimum term of thirty years, for the murders of George Cornell (at The Blind Beggar public house in the East End) and Jack 'The Hat' McVitie.

They were the perpetrators of organised crime in London's East End in the 1950s and 1960s. Vic Gooden, the former speedway rider for Rayleigh and Aldershot, and one-time former promoter at Rayleigh, Ipswich and Poole, once told me that he had a visit in the early 1960s from the Krays (he did not know who they were then) at his plush car showrooms in Manor Park.

The twins 'offered' to look after the premises and make sure that no damage was done – their version of an insurance policy. Vic's response was to tell them to go on their way. He said he was not afraid of them as he had faced thousands of nasty people on the front line in the Second World War.

He added that if they came back, they had better make sure they killed him, because if not, he would certainly kill them. He never heard from them again. Vic was president of the VSRA in 1996 and died on Boxing Day 2010 aged 89 years.

CHAPTER EIGHTEEN

THE TWO
PETERS

The World Speedway Riders' Association (WRSA), formerly known as the Veteran Speedway Riders' Association (VSRA), of which I had the honour to be president in 1992, is proud of its declaration that its objects are purely social or benevolent in character.

Full members of the WSRA are former riders who have held contracts with speedway teams but, reflecting speedway's family status, the Association also welcomes into associate membership many who have played their part in the off-track roles without which the sport could not exist.

There is no question that the members thoroughly enjoy the social role enshrined in the WSRA objectives. They also take very seriously the benevolent aspect of the Association's activities.

I have had the privilege of being at the heart of two activities which seem to me to fully illustrate the way in which the speedway family is bound together through the WSRA, in many cases long after the members have ceased to play an active part in the sport, either on or off the track.

The activities with which I was closely associated both involved men called Peter; the fact that one was a rider of the highest class, a track legend in his own lifetime, whilst the other was a journalist and commentator, again in the highest class, illustrates the inclusiveness of the VSRA.

Peter Craven and Peter Arnold followed different career patterns in speedway. Peter Craven quickly developed into a high-class performer and was a double World Champion – the only English rider to achieve that feat. As a budding racer, Peter Arnold never made it past a few second half rides.

What is indisputable is the fact that both men left a lasting mark on British speedway.

Signed photograph of Peter Craven at the height of his powers and fame with the Belle Vue Aces.

Peter Arnold formed the Veteran Speedway Riders' Association (initially known as the Veteran Dirt-Track Riders' Association) in 1957, laying the foundation for an association that has brought pleasure (and in many cases, much-needed support and assistance) to a great many men (and women) over the years.

Had Peter Craven not been so tragically killed, I have no doubt that he would today be a leading member of the VSRA, an elder statesman, re-living his track duels with such contemporaries and rivals as Barry Briggs, Ronnie Moore and Ove Fundin, fellow World Champions who have all worn the Chain of Office as Association president.

It was in 1957 that Alan Baxter, known to all in speedway and in the much wider world of motor sport as a whole through his pen name of Peter Arnold, founded the Veteran Dirt-Track Riders' Association with just a few

Peter Arnold, founder of the Veteran Speedway Riders' Association (now the World Speedway Riders' Association) makes a presentation to Halifax and England rider Eric Boocock. Many years after this photograph was taken, Eric was to become president of the WRSA.

members. It grew very quickly and has had two name changes over the past fifty-two years. The first change was to the Veteran Speedway Riders' Association and more recently to the World Speedway Riders' Association.

We have so much for which to thank Peter. The Association holds reunions on a local scale throughout the year and stages two golf tournaments, one usually

Joan and Reg Fearman pictured at the VSRA dinner during Reg's year of office as president.

in the spring and one in the autumn called, tongue in cheek, the 'Rider Cup'. The WSRA Annual Dinner, usually held in March, is attended by some 300 members and guests.

Peter Arnold's original idea later gave birth to the VSRA of New Zealand, formed in 1979 and the VSRA of Australia, which came into being in 1991. All three are independent but all have the same objects. Each association has its own address and contact book so it is easy for us old boys to keep in touch, especially in this day and age of the computer.

Under Peter's guidance, the Annual Dinner was for many years held at the Rembrandt Hotel in central London. The Annual General Meeting was held in the afternoon before the World Individual Championship Final, usually at a pub near Wembley Stadium.

Those afternoon AGMs were always rowdy affairs, with presidents such as Bill Kitchen, Jack Barnett, Jack Parker, Wal Phillips, Len Tupling, Bob Lovell, Howdy Byford and Frank Varey trying to keep order.

Eventually, the Rembrandt closed for refurbishment and the Annual Dinner moved to a hotel in the Midlands. It has been difficult to find a hotel that could accommodate 300 people in one room. The relatively new Marriott Hotel in Leicester now seems to fit the requirements.

Joan Fearman at her final Association Dinner in March 1999. Pictured left to right are Ove and Joanna Fundin, Fred and Pat Williams, Merv and Sheila Hannam, Harry and Brenda Maclean, and Reg and Joan.

Peter Arnold was secretary of the Association until his tragic and untimely death in 1969. He was followed by Jack Barnett for ten years, George Greenwood for two, Vic Gooden for three and then Ron Hoare for twenty years.

The current secretary is Vic White who took on the role in 2001. The AGM is now held in the hotel in the afternoon before the dinner.

Peter Arnold was a brilliant journalist, broadcaster and announcer at speedway and other motor race meetings. In August 1969, whilst driving back to his home near Northampton from his announcing duties at Reading Speedway, he suffered a serious heart attack and crashed his car into a traffic island and lamp standard.

He was taken to hospital and the day after the accident I visited him there, where it appeared that he was going to recover – the effects of the actual crash were minimal. Unfortunately, he died a couple of days later from further heart attacks.

Peter's death left his 4-year-old son, Paul, an orphan, as Peter had lost his wife soon after Paul was born. The speedway and stock car fraternity (in addition to his speedway activities, Peter had founded and edited the magazine *Stock Car News*) set up a trust fund for Paul, to mature when he was 18, and in the meantime he was brought up by close relatives on a farm near Andover, Hampshire.

Through the sport of road racing, Peter had met Maureen Vinicombe, herself a widow whose husband had been killed on the track. Peter and Maureen were due to be married on 27 August 1969. As it turned out, Peter's funeral was held less than a fortnight after that date, on 8 September.

We certainly do have plenty to thank Peter Arnold for – his name, like many others of the speedway fraternity, 'will liveth for ever more'.

The existence of the Riders' Association, and the pursuance of its aim of benevolence within the speedway community, certainly helped make two subsequent events, this time involving the memory of Peter Craven, more certain of success than might otherwise have been the case.

Peter Craven died in an accident at the Old Meadowbank track in Edinburgh in September 1963, doing what he did best, entertaining the public with his spectacular racing style.

The accident happened in heat 12 of an inter-league challenge match between Provincial League Edinburgh and National League Belle Vue on Friday, 20 September, attended by more than 9,000 people.

Peter Craven won his first three races and in his fourth was chasing George Hunter, who fell. Peter took evasive action, crashed and was thrown heavily backwards into the solid board safety fence. He was just 29 years of age, married to Brenda and with two young children, Robert and Julie.

In 1997, a fan of Edinburgh Speedway, Allan Wilson, came up with the idea that a memorial plaque should be sited in the entrance hallway to the present-day Meadowbank Stadium in the Scottish capital city.

Old Meadowbank Stadium, which occupied the same site, was demolished to make way for a venue for the Commonwealth Games which, sadly, did not include a speedway track. The last meeting at Old Meadowbank was held in October 1967 and featured the Scottish Best Pairs event won by Reidar Eide, a Norwegian, and Scot Jim McMillan.

Allan Wilson worked extremely hard to obtain permission for a plaque from the authorities concerned, including Edinburgh City Council. My role was to arrange for Peter Craven's family and as many speedway riders as possible to attend the unveiling ceremony. I also acted as master of ceremonies for the occasion.

I cannot, I think, do better than to recall the occasion by reproducing my introductory remarks at the unveiling of the plaque in March 1998:

> Ladies and Gentlemen, it is my privilege to open this afternoon's proceedings. We are gathered here today at Meadowbank from all parts of the world to honour Peter Craven, a family man, friend, colleague and fellow racer and to witness Brenda, his widow, unveil the commemorative plaque in Peter's memory.
>
> Peter, a husband, father and twice World Speedway Champion and an inspiration to many, lost his life aged 29 here in Edinburgh thirty four and a half years ago. May we have a few moments silence in Peter's memory and for all other speedway riders – more than 180 worldwide – who have paid the ultimate price. Thank you.
>
> We are honoured to have with us Brenda and Peter's daughter Julie, Peter's sisters Sheila, Sylvia, and Pat and also sister-in-law Joan Craven. Unfortunately son Robert is unable to be with us.
>
> May I please ask Brenda to step forward and unveil the plaque?

Brenda duly unveiled the plaque and thanked everyone involved for attending and for what she described as 'a magnificent gesture'. Ian Hoskins said a few words in response, as did Ove Fundin. Allan Wilson presented Brenda with a bouquet.

There was a good attendance of former riders from both north and south of the border, including Willie Templeton, Jimmy Tannock, Brian Collins, Freddie Williams, Bert Harkins, Peter Collins, Merv Hannam, Harry Maclean, Roni Ferguson, Norrie Isbister, Fred Rogers, Ove Fundin, Gordon Mitchell and many more.

Ian Hoskins, who promoted the meeting at Old Meadowbank on the night of Peter Craven's fatal crash, addresses the crowd watched by Brenda and Reg Fearman. On the far left is Peter Craven's daughter Julie.

It was in April 2002 that I realised that in less than eighteen months' time it would be forty years since Peter Craven's tragic accident at Edinburgh on 20 September 1963. On a recent visit to Liverpool, I had visited the city's Anglican cathedral and thought what a fitting place this would be to hold a remembrance service for Peter, who was born and bred on Merseyside.

In May 2002, I wrote to Brenda (Peter's widow), who at a much later date had married Peter's mechanic, Leon Leat, to ask if she would give her permission for a service to be held. Both Brenda and her family were totally in agreement.

Time to relax in the shadow of the modern Meadowbank Stadium after the unveiling of the plaque. The group, from the left, are Joan Craven (widow of Peter's brother Brian, also a well-known rider), Pat Williams, Joan Fearman, Joanna Fundin, Sheila Hannam and, in front, Julie Craven and Peter Craven's sister Sheila.

My wife, Eileen, herself a Liverpudlian, was of great assistance in the planning and execution of this event. We wrote to the Dean of Liverpool, the Right Reverend Dr Rupert Hoare, who agreed that we should meet with Canon Noel Vincent in August 2002 to discuss our proposal. As Canon Vincent was about to retire, he passed our proposals on to Canon Mark Boyling, with whom we had a number of meetings at the cathedral to agree and finalise arrangements for the service.

More than 600 people attended the remembrance service on 20 September 2003, to remember Peter Craven and all the other speedway riders who had lost their lives on the track since the inception of the sport back in the 1920s.

The congregation included no fewer than fifty-six members of the Craven family. The service was a moving and emotional occasion and at times there was

Remembering Peter Craven at the Memorial Service in Liverpool Cathedral. World Champions Freddie Williams (second from left) and Ove Fundin (right) took part in the service and then were pictured with Peter's son Robert (left), daughter Julie (third from left), Brenda and Reg Fearman and a giant picture of Craven as the fans knew him.

not a dry eye in the congregation. The full choir gave a magnificent rendering of 'Now thank we all our God', 'Be thou my vision O Lord of my heart' and, lastly, 'Jerusalem'.

Ove Fundin, himself five times World Speedway Champion, gave personal reflections based on his own experience and knowledge of Peter Craven.

Peter Oakes, another Liverpudlian, journalist, speedway promoter and historian, also gave personal reflections. Freddie Williams of Wales, the first British double World Champion, gave the second reading from Corinthians and Timothy.

The Reverend Michael Whawell, the VSRA chaplain, gave a humorous and detailed address, entirely wrapped around speedway racing and the riders. Canon Mark Boyling, who conducted the service, gave the closing prayer:

We give thanks, Lord, for all engaged in professional sport as competitors, trainers and administrators. We pray for them. Help them to see their work as a part of a wider life and help them to remember that all life comes from You.

We give thanks for the skill and achievement of speedway riders and pray for them today. May they set for themselves the highest standards of professional and personal behaviour, both on the track and off, and for all who follow their fortunes may they provide an example to help make the heart of their country, county or city, sound. We ask this through Jesus Christ Our Lord, Amen.

We give thanks, Lord, for the pleasure and entertainment given to millions of people by the skill and achievements of sportsmen and women. We pray that they may be kept from harm and injury. We ask that through their knowledge of the laws of their sport they may see that there are greater laws, that through their experience of training and discipline they may see that there is a nobler discipline, that through their desire for victory they may be directed to the victory over sin and death won by Jesus Christ our risen Lord to whom be all praise and honour, glory and power, now and forever. Amen.

Some of the many former riders who gathered in Liverpool Cathedral for the Memorial Service for Peter Craven. The group includes Tony Robinson, Ove Fundin, Charlie Oates, Terry Stone, Fred Williams, Reg Fearman, Peter Williams, Merv Hannam and Jim Yacoby.

Also present in the congregation, in addition to the Craven family, were former Belle Vue director of operations Jack Fearnley, who was Peter Craven's Belle Vue promoter, and former rider Charlie Oates, who in the early 1950s discovered Peter Craven at Liverpool's own former track at Stanley Stadium.

The service ended with Belle Vue's signature tune 'Blaze Away', which, played on the cathedral organ, had everyone tingling.

It gave Eileen and me the greatest pleasure to see so many people at the remembrance service, a project that took us eighteen months to plan and organise.

Special thanks must go to Canon Mark Boyling for his co-operation and contribution to the service.

Peter Craven's grave.

CHAPTER NINETEEN

THE SCOURGE
OF CANCER

It is said that at least one in three people you know will be affected by cancer.

I remember, as an 11 year old in 1944, seeing my grandfather Aves – my mother's father – lying in his bed with a very yellow face. He died, as they said then, of a 'growth', later known as a tumour.

Happier days, before Joan's illness. She is pictured centre with my mother Sarah (left) and sister Doreen at High Beech, 1968 – speedway's 40th anniversary. My mother also contracted cancer but eventually died of 'old age'.

Dad and me at the same event – High Beech, 1968.

I well remember that the 'growth' description scared me, conjuring up all kinds of thoughts. The terminology of tumour and cancer for many of us is just as scary and difficult to live with today.

My mother also contracted cancer. Her father and her sister, Rosie, her half-brother Philbrook and half-sister, Winifred, all died from the effects of the disease. Strangely though, my mother died of 'old age' and a closing down of organs at the age of 95.

In 1974, she went into the Royal London Hospital at Whitechapel for a relatively simple operation for a gall bladder problem. I well remember my sister, Doreen, phoning me at Smallmead, Reading, where the new speedway and greyhound stadium was then under construction.

Doreen told me that Mum was in a serious condition and that the surgeon, a Mr Thomas, wished to meet with us. I raced up to London and met Doreen and the surgeon, who told us that when he had opened up my mother's abdomen, he was faced with a tumour the size of a grapefruit, attached to the outside lining of her stomach and lying in the cavity.

He removed the tumour along with half of her stomach. It took a long time but Mum made a full recovery.

Stella, my son Gary's partner of twelve years, was diagnosed with breast cancer in November 1997, at the Clementine Churchill Hospital. In December, she had a chest, liver and bone scan and in that month had her first chemotherapy treatment.

Reg and his mother on her 90th birthday.

Two more treatments followed and then in early February 1998, Stella had a mastectomy, followed by a reconstruction. There was a problem with the reconstruction and it was quickly removed. In April and May, Stella had five courses of radiotherapy treatment. From the time of a check-up in the middle of May 1998, she felt reasonably well until the first week of June 1999 when, on holiday in Tenerife, she felt unwell.

On 22 June, Stella was taken to Northwick Park Hospital, Middlesex. She had various symptoms of pain, sickness and fluid retention – which was drained. She was allowed out of hospital for the evening on 27 June to visit a restaurant for dinner with Gary. On 2 July, Joan and I spoke to Stella in hospital and she told us that three attempts had been made to insert a stomach catheter. On 4 July, Stella was in a serious condition and died at 10 p.m. two days later. This was a particularly stressful time for Gary, Joan and me.

Stella, Gary Fearman's partner.

On 1 March 1998, Ian Hoskins flew into Gatwick Airport from Harare, Zimbabwe, to attend the Veteran Speedway Riders' Association Dinner on 14 March at the Hilton National Hotel in Warwick. As was usual, several of us attending the dinner had lunch at the Lygon Arms, Broadway, on the following day.

Ian Hoskins came to stay with Joan and me in Henley before returning to his brother, Lionel, in Canterbury, on the same day that Joan and I attended the funeral of Tom Arnison, Eileen's husband, at Reading Crematorium on 23 March.

The first sign we had that something might be wrong with Joan was when she tasted bile in her mouth the evening before Tom's funeral. We put it down to having eaten out the previous evening but, a few days later, it happened again.

Joan saw her doctor, who arranged for her to have an endoscopy at the Berkshire Independent Hospital. The consultant Joan saw, in his report, said he 'did not like what he saw in her stomach', and recommended that a specialist, Mr Tom Dehn, should perform a laparoscopy.

Joan and Stella pictured together at a wedding.

We had an appointment with Mr Dehn on 28 April. He discussed with us the options of chemotherapy or/and surgery. There was no doubt in his mind that Joan had stomach cancer. Two days later, Mr Dehn performed both an endoscopy and a laparoscopy by keyhole surgery into Joan's abdomen cavity, a process involving four incisions.

In the evening after he had carried out these procedures, Mr Dehn told us there were too many secondaries in the cavity. An operation to remove Joan's stomach was out of the question. His prognosis was between three and fifteen months.

Joan had been an integral part of Reg's speedway life from very early days and played a full part in the sport's social calendar. Here she is pictured with Australian star Jack Geran, double World Champion Freddie Williams, and Reg.

A consultation with an oncologist was now recommended and during the following two weeks, this duly took place, with a number of tests being carried out, including X-rays, a CT scan, a test for granular filtration rate (kidneys) and an ECG, amongst others.

At the same time, Gary and I started to make positive enquiries regarding alternative treatment which resulted in Joan starting to take Benefin Sharks' Cartilage Powder on 16 May – a daily dose of 60gms.

I had talked to Cartilage Incorporated in the USA and also to a person named Joe Cartwright in Michigan. He had been on his deathbed several years earlier and told me he owed his life to Sharks' Cartilage. Dr I. William Lane had written a book entitled *Sharks don't get Cancer*. Joan also started drinking Essiac herb tea and taking vitamin supplements.

On 19 May, we travelled to London to the Royal Marsden Hospital in Fulham for a second opinion from the Senior Registrar, Dr David Cunningham. He told us that the oncologist Joan had consulted had previously been with his unit for six years before taking up a senior post at the Royal Berkshire Hospital in Reading. Therefore, he had every confidence in the oncologist's diagnosis and felt that the Royal Marsden could not add to this man's recommendations.

Joan was admitted to the cancer clinic at the Royal Berkshire Hospital on 8 June to be fitted with a 'Hickman Line', inserted in the chest directly into an artery to allow chemotherapy drugs to be administered. She was an in-patient for two nights and on the second day received her first treatment of Epirubicin, a 2-hour drip of saline and an overnight drip of Cisplatin.

A few days later, Joan had an external pump fitted for a seven-day treatment of Fluorouacil, with a repeat every seven days. On 2 July, it was an overnight stay, again to receive a repeat of the same drugs.

On 6 July, Joan lost all her hair as a result of the side effects of the drugs. She also had ulcers on her lips as well as red hands and fingers. Regular blood tests were taken and also the granular filtration rate to check her kidneys. On 9 July, the seven-day quantity of drugs was reduced by 50mg. Joan's third overnight stay was on 23 July when, unfortunately, the saline drip ran out and air entered the tube which resulted in the Hickman Line having to be disconnected.

The seven-day cycle continued. On 17 August, Joan had another CT scan. The Cisplatin, Epirubicin, Fluoroucacil, blood tests and granular filtration rates continued to be taken and, in between, we had started Joan on the New Zealand plant aloe vera, and paw paw. We had been reading and learning as much as we could regarding cancer and homeopathic alternative medicines.

On 7 September, Joan underwent another endoscopy and laparoscopy – a 50-minute operation – when Mr Dehn took a number of biopsies. We were told on 10 September that there had been some improvement in Joan's condition. The same day, the by-now routine overnight treatment took place, with the usual drugs over a period of 8 hours, plus two units of blood. By 14 September, Joan had been on chemotherapy for fourteen weeks.

On 17 September, we were told by the oncologist that eight biopsies had been taken on 7 September, five from Joan's stomach and three from inside her abdomen. No cancer cells had been found in any biopsy. The cancer cells had either gone or melted down. This was very good news for us.

By 19 September, Joan had been on Sharks' Cartilage Powder for eighteen weeks. During this period, my mother had been taken ill and I was with her when she died on 20 September – my sister Doreen's birthday. Doreen had predeceased her by ten years. She had been ill for a long time with a rare condition called mixed connective tissue disorder.

On 1 October, Joan had had sixteen weeks of chemotherapy and twenty on Sharks' Cartilage Powder. It was time for a sixth overnight stay at the Royal Berkshire Hospital for the usual drugs. On 15 October, the oncologist told us that six overnight treatments were sufficient and that further would show little improvement against general well-being. A check-up would be undertaken in five weeks.

On Monday, 19 October, Joan vomited (for the first time) which was accompanied by 'niggles' in her abdomen which continued to the Wednesday. On Thursday, 22 October, we were told that the pump and Hickman Line would be removed that day, after twenty weeks of chemotherapy.

There is a shrine to the Virgin Mary at Walsingham, Norfolk. It is said that a visitation was witnessed in the village by Lady Richeldis in 1061. She was the wife of the Lord of the Manor of Walsingham Parva.

Since then, regular pilgrimages have been made to the church and shrine, known as 'England's Nazareth'. There are more than 300,000 visitors a year. We made our journey on 22 November to pray, take the water and pin a message of help on a wall containing thousands of similar messages.

As Christmas 1998 approached, we armed ourselves with several parcels of presents for the staff at the Royal Berkshire Hospital who had been so kind and caring throughout Joan's treatments.

In between treatments, we had tried to live a normal life, with local visits to friends and restaurants. Over the Christmas period, Joan's sister Doreen and son Andrew came to stay and, with Gary and Stella, we had a pleasant time.

Our next appointment with the oncologist was on 19 January 1999. Joan's stomach, liver and neck glands were examined and the verdict was that all was well.

Our next appointment was made for 20 April 1999.

On 16 March, at 5 a.m., Joan told me that she had had 'niggles' in her lower tummy on and off since 1 March but had said nothing as she did not want to spoil the weekend of the Annual Dinner of the VSRA at the Coventry Hilton. We had Ove and Joanna Fundin staying with us and on 10 March, the four of us went to the Lyceum Theatre to see *Oklahoma* and we also enjoyed lunch at The Bear at Woodstock, near Blenheim Palace, where our guests included Ove and Joanna, Freddie and Pat Williams, Bjorn and Madeleine Knutson and Merv and Sheila Hannam.

Joan was very ill and had lost a great deal of weight when this picture was taken at the Veteran Speedway Riders' Association Dinner in 1999. Throughout her illness she never complained or asked 'why me?'

On 16 March, we visited our GP, Dr Collett, who had been excellent in her attention. She felt Joan's abdomen and could find no lumps. We made an appointment to see the oncologist a couple of days later. He felt Joan's abdomen, which was tender, and made an appointment for her to have a scan and laparoscopy at the Royal Berkshire Hospital, during which several biopsies of the secondaries were taken.

On 12 May we learned from the oncologist that the biopsies from 26 April proved that cancer was active. He gave us three options: to do nothing except take drugs, steroids and pain killers; to go back on chemotherapy, which would involve a Hickman Line and three weekly visits as an outpatient; to see a Dr Talbot at the John Radcliffe Hospital in Oxford to discuss testing new drugs and research.

We took option 3.

Pain killers were prescribed and on 19 May we introduced Joan to an additional homeopathic remedy – three daily doses of Maitake D Fraction Tincture from the Japanese mushroom.

On 27 May, we had an appointment with Dr Talbot at the Churchill Hospital, part of the John Radcliffe Hospital in Oxford. By 3 June, a three-drug trial of Hismitomycin at the Churchill Hospital was recommended but only for between four and six weeks because of the strength of the dosage and the fact that it destroyed white blood cells.

Throughout this period of time, investigations and procedures continued at the Churchill Hospital. On 26 June, I gave Joan the last injection of Fragmin at home. I had been taught to give injections directly into her buttocks. On 28 June, at the Churchill Hospital, Joan underwent an ultrasound scan and we were told of the seriousness of her situation.

On 29 June, 6.75 litres of fluid, equal to 15lbs in weight, were drained, and Joan's weight dropped to 7 stone.

On 15 July 1999, Stella's funeral service took place at Harrow-on-the-Hill, with interment at Greenford Park Cemetery and afterwards at Pinewood Studios Restaurant.

Joan's condition continued to deteriorate. In early August, she became very poorly and Dr Collett came to the house with a district nurse. Gary arranged for a wheelchair from the Red Cross. By 7 August Joan was hallucinating, her breathing was very difficult and a gurgling sound accompanied her breathing.

On 10 August, Joan was taken by ambulance to the Royal Berkshire Hospital cancer clinic and was admitted. An ultrasound showed ascites fluid on Joan's chest and in her lungs. Four litres of fluid were drained off on 11 and 12 August, and on 13 August a drain was put into her left lung.

Joan died on Sunday, 15 August, at 12.15 p.m., with family and friends around her. Not once did she complain nor utter the words 'why me?' She was a very brave lady. This was a particularly traumatic time for both Gary and me with Stella's passing just one month before. I had lost the last of the three most important women in my life – my sister, Doreen in 1988, my mother in 1998 and now Joan. We had been married for forty-five years.

Joan's funeral took place on 25 August at St Mary the Virgin, Henley-on-Thames, with interment at the Fairmile Cemetery in Henley-on-Thames and afterwards at the riverside at Phyllis Court Club, one of our favourite places.

People came from the Royal Berkshire Hospital cancer clinic and Joan's charity work in Henley was recognised by those who came as representatives. Many of the speedway racing fraternity attended, as well as family and friends. A great void was left in the lives of so many people.

Happy times to remember amidst all the sadness. Joan, Gary and Reg at Gary's 21st birthday celebration.

Joan and Gary in 1980. As Gary grew up he became a tower of strength in helping with the speedway business.

Times to remember. Legendary speedway photographer Alf Weedon and his wife Dot on holiday with Reg and Joan in Majorca.

It is said that a man needs a good woman at his side and I certainly had that in Joan. Although I was not a role-model husband, we had a good marriage despite my extramarital affairs. We had worked hard together, particularly in the promoting of speedway racing.

Joan kept the books – as she had done when we had the garage business – and collated the speedway riders' prize money, all whilst balancing Gary on her knee. We would take Gary in his carry-cot to the speedway office on race nights and, when he was old enough, Joan had him help her to count the cash by putting twelve pennies in a pile and asking him to make the rest of the pennies into the same height. He loved doing that. When he grew up he was a great help in the business and always a tower of support to me, as indeed his mother was.

We had a good quality of life and travelled extensively to the Mediterranean islands, South Africa, the Seychelles, Spain, France, Scandinavia, the Benelux Countries, Italy, Poland, Kenya, Zimbabwe, Egypt, Australia and New Zealand. Most winters, we would ski in Austria.

Joan always had plenty of time for people and especially those in need. To this end, she was a member of the Red Cross and very involved in Henley's voluntary work, especially one-to-one adult learning, meals-on-wheels and helping the blind with their personal affairs.

JUNE BRIGGS

It was on 11 June 2003 that four-times World Speedway Individual Champion, Barry Briggs, telephoned me in Henley from his home in Dana Point, California, to tell me that his wife, June, had been diagnosed with colon and liver cancer.

As I had been through similar circumstances, Barry asked if I would put him in touch with the specialist in England who had treated Joan. A number of telephone calls were exchanged over the following few days between us and the Briggs' eldest son, Gary.

The outcome was that I referred them to The Oasis of Hope Hospital in Tijuana, Mexico, run by father and son doctors of the family Contreras Rodriguez. I had made extensive enquiries and had spoken to Dr Ernesto Contreras of the Contreras procedures (metabolic therapy).

But for Joan being so desperately ill and unable to travel to Mexico, we would have gone there in 1999. I had first read about The Oasis of Hope Hospital when a friend of Gary's partner, Stella, came back from the United States in 1999 with a magazine which carried an article about Donald Factor, grandson of the cosmetic founder, Max Factor, who in 1986 had been diagnosed with lung and liver cancer in London. He was, at the time, living in the Cotswolds.

Donald Factor knew of The Oasis of Hope Hospital which specialised in homeopathic remedies as well as conventional treatment with chemotherapy and radium. Although extremely ill, he had made his way there and was successfully treated and was alive and well seventeen years later in 2003 when he gave an interview about his experience with cancer to Lucy Mayhew.

Max Factor was founded in 1909 by Maximillian Faktorowicz, a Polish Jew (1875–1938). He emigrated to America in 1904. He moved to California and became involved with the film industry. The Max Factor company was sold in 1973 for $500 million. Proctor & Gamble are the current owners of the company.

On 27 June 2003, Gary Briggs wrote to me by email to express his appreciation of my recommendation of The Oasis of Hope Hospital. He could not speak too highly of the hospital, where 97 per cent of people went as a final option.

He explained to me that June's initial treatment would follow the standard three weeks' protocol, slightly amended to suit her condition. He told me June was displaying a great determination in working towards better health and was, at that particular moment, walking down the beach with Barry and Tony.

On 6 July 2003, Barry telephoned to tell me that June was receiving treatment and was very positive in her outlook. His next telephone call was to tell me that June was feeling good and taking some homeopathic medicines. Later that month, June was actually putting on a little weight.

The Briggs family at The Oasis of Hope Hospital in September 2003.

In August, Barry sent me a lovely photograph of the family at the hospital and told me June was in good spirits – she certainly looked well. Although her blood tests were up and down, Tony Briggs telephoned me in October to say that June was now receiving chemotherapy directly into her liver by catheter. I next spoke to Barry on 5 December 2003 as, sadly, June had died on 2 December. June's quality of life over the previous six months had been much greater than expected, thanks to the care and treatment she had received at The Oasis of Hope Hospital.

CHAPTER TWENTY

WHEN THINGS GO WRONG ...

I have written earlier of the tragic deaths that have occurred on speedway tracks all through the sport's now long history.

We must always remember too that speedway riders suffer injuries, ranging from the relatively minor, which will keep them out of the sport for a few weeks at most, to those which are life-changing, condemning super-fit young sportsmen to a most restricted, if usually still amply fulfilling, life in a wheelchair.

So many riders over the years have been glad that the sport insists on adequate insurance. The story of my connections with the firm which, throughout my years in the sport, was inseparable from speedway in the insurance sense is well worth telling.

It was also through the company that I had perhaps the closest shave I have ever experienced – and that is saying a lot for a former speedway rider and promoter!

When George Burrows was demobbed from the Royal Navy after the Second World War, he invested his money in becoming an insurance broker, opening offices at 32 Cambridge Park, in Wanstead. The company he founded still bears his name.

The first group insurance George contracted was for the whole of speedway racing as it stood at the time, becoming responsible for the insurance of some 300 riders. The premiums were paid partly by the riders and partly by the speedway promoters.

To give some idea of the pre-eminence of his company, George was to provide group insurance cover for a number of police forces throughout Britain, for fire brigades and for staff working for the Mersey Docks and Harbour Board as well as for the Manchester Ship Canal, to name but a few.

I consider myself fortunate to have had a close working relationship with the firm and its staff. However, this also served to illustrate how the world of financial investment can go badly wrong.

It was in 1972 when the then joint managing directors of George Burrows Group Insurance Ltd, Peter Percival and Olive Pattenden, came to my home in Henley to collate my insurance policies – property, cars, personal, etc. They suggested that perhaps I would like to become a Name at Lloyds

To that end, I was introduced to Bob Groves of Steel Brothers, Underwriting Agents at Lloyds. The means test was a minimum of £75,000 but it wasn't necessary to put in any money, only to sign an unlimited guarantee. It did seem to me to be too good to be true.

They gave me the figures for 1967, 1968 and 1969 for Syndicate Number 727 – S.A. Meacock and Co. – which appeared to show a handsome return. (The accounts are three years in arrears and when one leaves a syndicate, one is still liable for the following three years.)

I had an excellent tour of Lloyds with Bob Groves and saw the chaps sitting at their desk, each of whom had a large box on its end, into which other underwriters would drop that part of the risk they did not want. I did not understand this process.

We walked around the Lutine Bell and had a delightful lunch, after which I got into the Rolls and drove home. I discussed the day with Joan and we studied all the papers which had been given to me, including a nice copy of Nelson's famous message from HMS *Victory* at the Battle of Trafalgar: *England expects that every man will do his duty.* I understand the logbook is in the Nelson Collection at Lloyds.

I decided that because I did not understand the system, it was not for me and Joan agreed.

Of course, when the crash came in the 1980s, more than 34,000 Names lost money. The total loss exceeded £8 billion. Half of that sum was from asbestos claims in the United States. I saw the interviews on television of people who had lost everything. They had put nothing in but had given a personal unlimited guarantee for which they were now liable.

We read in the newspapers of people jumping off Beachy Head. In total, there were fifteen suicides. I had sympathy for a few friends who found themselves in the predicament and who paid anywhere between £500,000 and £1 million to Lloyds of London.

John Berry, the former Ipswich speedway promoter, was one, and Ivan Mauger, the multi-World Speedway Champion, was another. In actual fact, the couple from whom Joan and I brought our last house in 1988 were Names at Lloyds and were forced to move to a much smaller property.

Peter Drummond (left) who succeeded Peter Percival as managing director of George Burrows Group Insurance is pictured with World Speedway Champions Barry Briggs, Ronnie Moore and Ove Fundin. Rob Hall, second from the right, succeeded Peter Drummond.

The fact that George Burrows Group Insurance Ltd had suggested to me that I become a Name at Lloyds did not affect my relationship with the company.

Peter Drummond succeeded Peter Percival as managing director and we were, and still are, good friends. We took part in many social events over the course of our friendship including the Henley Royal Regatta, rugby events at Twickenham and in Paris.

I was a social member of his rugby club at Brentwood, Essex, and made a number of trips to France to engage with clubs at Chartres and Chateaudun. We also sailed on the Lloyds' yacht *The Lutyens*.

SEXATIONS

I was about 11 years of age when Evelyn Hodgson said to me, 'Show me yours'. I replied, 'Show me yours first', which she did. I ran away – I should have kept running. However, I do remember earlier peering through the keyhole of the door leading from our living room into the kitchen/scullery and seeing my sister's friend, Iris Manche, standing in the tin bath, being bathed by my mother (her own mother was in hospital at the time). She was facing the kitchen door, naked. Doreen grabbed hold of me and told me to 'Come away or I'll tell Mum'.

The 1960s dawned and with it the contraception pill for women and also the Beatles, Jane Fonda burning her bra and declaring, with Germaine Greer and others, liberation for women which then meant sex was on tap – married or single. It seemed everybody was having sex with everybody! At least, it seemed that way in Stoke-on-Trent where I was living. There was a lot of social partying and there was always an invitation. I was weak and succumbed. I was not a role-model husband as far as extramarital affairs were concerned. There are people who know that and the subject needs to be part of my autobiography.

Some of those parties in the early 1960s were held at Leon the Barber's premises. Len had the barber's shop over a gents' outfitters in Burslem and, above him, his wife had the ladies' hairdressing salon. They lived in a terraced house with her mother and so a Saturday night party would be held in the ladies' hairdressing salon. Len would have got the drinks in and his wife would have organised the food. The drying machines and chairs would be pushed back around the wall and the record player wound up. It was good fun.

It was there that I met Joan Hammond and her husband, Stuart. He was a quantity surveyor and well-in with the clergy in Stoke-on-Trent and received a lot of work from them and the City Council where he had some major contacts. He was a good pal. Stuart had a strange quirk. He would say to his wife on a Friday evening, 'I'm just popping up to the pub for a packet of cigarettes' and would return three days later.

It certainly was 'all go' in the 1960s and I had several negligible flings with a couple of female hairdressers which are hardly worth recording.

I had opened Stoke Speedway in 1960 with Mike Parker and my promoting career took off with involvements with Stoke, Liverpool, Leicester, Newcastle, Wolverhampton, Middlesbrough, Long Eaton and Halifax (not all at the same time). In the winter of 1967/68, the Second Division was formed with me as chairman and I formed with Maury Littlechild, Danny Dunton, Len Silver and Ron Wilson (all had promoting interests in tracks in the British League) Allied Presentations Ltd which promoted a number of tracks over the next few years.

In December 1968, Joan, Gary and I moved to Henley-on-Thames where we bought a nice Georgian-style detached house with 25 acres of land. (I was pleased to leave Stoke-on-Trent behind, even if it was only to relieve the sexual stress and involvements.) I had taken responsibility for Reading Speedway for Allied Presentations Ltd and I also had a lot of meetings in London to do with the BSPA, British League and Division Two. Henley was a good commuting town to London.

Having moved to Henley, there was a lapse in extramarital activities until 1976 when I met Margery Wright (it just shows how either one's life is mapped out from birth or how circumstances which change can alter one's life).

During the 1970s, I was chairman of the Promoters' Association and had been successful, with an agent, Michael Addison, in bringing into the British League a considerable amount of sponsorship. The main sponsor was Gulf Oil, founded in 1901, who supported speedway to the tune of £120,000, in today's money equivalent to some £730,000. Many other sponsors were also brought in by Michael.

Gulf Oil's offices were in Chiswick and they came in for three years and stayed for five. James Wright's office was responsible for PR/marketing. The World Individual Final in September 1976 was at Katowice, Poland. I was there in 1974 as the England Team Manager when we won the World Team Cup. With all the riders, equipment and officials to be transported, we the management committee decided to invite our sponsors for the long weekend, 3, 4, 5 and 6 September. (We charted the aeroplane – Polish LOT Airlines.)

Wimbledon Speedway, 1975. Reg Fearman, chairman of the British Speedway Promoters' Association, with N. Pignatelli, president of the Gulf Oil Company, Eastern Hemisphere.

James Wright said he would come but only if his wife could also be invited. It was agreed but at the last moment, James was prevented from going but his wife, Margery, made the trip. Although my son, Gary, and my sister Doreen were also with me, it did not stop the chemistry which was apparent between Margery and me.

On our return, she wrote to me at Reading Speedway (Smallmead, which I had opened in March 1975) thanking me for the invitation to Katowice and enclosing a £5 note, the sum I had loaned her at the Polish customs. I telephoned her and that was the start of a long, on-off, affair.

James and Margery lived close to Richmond Bridge and had two children. It was another house I visited from time to time when her husband was commuting weekly to Edinburgh.

The Post House Hotel at the Heathrow junction of the M4 was a meeting place and a room could be taken there during the day (mainly for people who were in transit) for about £7.50.

I believe it was 1977 when Gulf Oil transferred James to their Edinburgh office. The house in Richmond was sold and the family moved to Edinburgh. It wasn't the end of the affair because when Margery was settled, she would sometimes take a day trip on the British Airways Shuttle, Edinburgh/London, and I in return sometimes did the trip in reverse.

Towards the end of the 1970s, Gulf Oil decided to move their office from Chiswick to Cheltenham and, a while later, the Wrights were transferred to Cheltenham.

My tenure at Reading Speedway Smallmead (1975–78) had come to an end due to a conflict of personalities.

During the period 1975–78, Dave Lanning who lived at Hornchurch, Essex – whose full time job was with *TV Times* – was employed at Reading Speedway as an announcer and programme compiler. His wife, Lee, would come with him every Monday evening and play the records between races and keep notes for him.

One of her sisters, Dawn Linford, who lived in Poole, would sometimes come to Reading with her boyfriend to meet up with Lee. This is how I met Dawn. She had been a dancer/chorus girl in the 1960s with a troupe and had spent a lot of time in France and Italy on engagements. She became pregnant by an Italian in the mid-1960s, which didn't interfere much with her dancing as her parents helped bring up her son.

When I bought Poole Stadium in 1979, she was one of the few people who I knew there and we would meet up occasionally just as friends. At the beginning, I used to stay in an hotel, the Post House Roundhouse, in Bournemouth. She was then working in Boots as a beauty adviser.

A close relationship between us continued for several years. I must have told her about Margery during our 'friendship' time and she said she didn't mind as long as Margery never came to Poole.

When Margery moved to Cheltenham from Edinburgh, our relationship fired up again. Margery had a friend in Verwood, which was not too far from Poole, who she used to visit on occasions. By this time, I had a flat in Bournemouth which I used on my weekly visits to Poole from Henley. The stadium staged the speedway on Wednesday nights and three greyhound meetings during the summer and two in the winter so I was commuting Henley to Poole.

In a period of madness during 1980, Margery and I decided we should live together and to that end, we would tell our respective spouses. Margery's marriage was already precarious. I went home and told Joan – the reaction to which I can't describe – and then told Gary. Margery didn't tell her husband, so I learned, as Joan rang her husband at Gulf Oil, Cheltenham, the next day to ask him what he thought about our affair.

Of course, the balloon went up. Margery stayed in Cheltenham and I moved – almost completely – for a while to the Bournemouth flat. The affair continued with her making periodic visits to Poole, which her husband knew about (I think he expected she would get it out of her system), and I think Joan knew.

Eventually, Margery did move to Bournemouth with her daughter in 1985 and rented a flat there, obtaining a post as a project manager raising funds at the Bournemouth College of Higher Education in Wallisdown which later achieved university status. Dawn disappeared off the scene as she said she would. So, the affair with Margery continued on and off until about 1990.

The affair had long ceased before Joan became ill in March 1998 although we did have some contact.

Sometime after Joan died in August 1999, Margery telephoned me in Henley and asked if we could meet up, which we did at Winchester. She asked if we could go away for a few days together to see if we had anything that might rekindle our former relationship and for the future. I declined the suggestion. It was the last time I saw or heard from her.

During its latter stages, the affair had become at times very stormy and although I had continued to see her since the 1980s, described as a period of madness, when we were going home to tell our respective spouses and she didn't, I never really trusted her again.

Her husband divorced her, married a woman in Cheltenham, sold the house and moved back to Scotland.

I suppose at the time of the foregoing, it was the excitement, the thrill and the adrenalin flowing but looking back, what an awful lot of grief, trouble and stress involved for so many people. If I had my time over again, there would have been no extramarital affairs. As I said at the beginning of this chapter, when Evelyn Hodgson showed me hers, I should have kept running!

CHAPTER TWENTY-ONE

LATTER YEARS AND NEW BEGINNINGS – EILEEN'S STORY

For eight glorious years at our home in Provence, Reg and I reminded ourselves each day that we were living in paradise.

In fact, the name of our street translated from French into English as 'Bird of Paradise'. Why paradise? The climate, the wine, the food, our wonderful French friends (and Swedish) and, most of all, the fact that we had each other.

Reg and Eileen's home in Provence.

One of Reg and Eileen's own favourite pictures taken on the terrace of their Provençal home.

How did this all come about? Let me tell you.

I first met Joan Fearman in the early 1970s when she was introduced to me by a mutual friend, Mary Wyatt, a widow. I used to travel from my home in Chester to Henley-on-Thames to visit my good friend, Mary, for the weekend.

On many of these occasions, Mary would invite Joan for supper on a Saturday evening as she was on her own most weekends, Reg being away at the speedway. 'Saturday night, after all, is race night!'

After supper we would settle down with a glass of wine to play scrabble.

If my memory serves me correctly, Mary remarried about 1973 and went to live in the United States. In 1974, I was head-hunted and moved from Chester to London with my future husband, Tom.

In 1982, Tom and I moved to Wargrave when my friendship with Joan was rekindled and in 1990 Tom and I moved to Henley-on-Thames. I used to meet up with Joan during the daytime and, occasionally, she and Reg and Tom and I were invited to mutual friends for dinner. I did not know Reg very well in those days.

Tom died in March 1998 after thirty-eight years together. We had enjoyed a wonderful and loving relationship and I had no thought of ever remarrying. Reg and Joan came to Tom's funeral and I later learned from Reg that at the time of Tom's funeral, he and Joan were awaiting the results of some tests which Joan had undergone because of a health problem.

The results of the tests were devastating. Joan was diagnosed with stomach cancer and it was necessary for her to start treatment immediately. Joan was given six months to live but in fact survived for eighteen months. During this period, Reg and Gary gave Joan all the love and care that anyone could give which, I believe, prolonged her life.

Reg and Joan's nephew, Mark, sought out alternative treatments and non-conventional medicines. In particular, Reg discovered that Donald Factor, grandson of Max, the founder of Max Factor cosmetics, had been told by London specialists that there was no treatment for his liver cancer.

Donald Factor had then travelled to The Oasis of Hope Hospital in Tijuana, Mexico, where he was successfully treated and had lived for many years after. Reg was anxious to take Joan to the hospital but, unfortunately, her condition had deteriorated so much that she would not have been able to make the journey.

As an aside, when Junie Briggs was diagnosed with cancer, Barry rang Reg from their home in California to ask him the name of the consultant who had attended Joan, as he was taking Junie to England as soon as possible. Reg advised him to take her to The Oasis of Hope, which he did.

Whilst the doctors there were unable to cure Junie, their treatments gave her at least three months longer to live, with a much better quality of life. After Junie's death, Reg received a most moving email from Tony, thanking him for pointing the family in the direction of The Oasis of Hope.

Joan died in August 1999 and I attended her funeral. For several Sundays after Tom's funeral, I had attended St Mary the Virgin church in Henley, as I knew his name would be remembered in prayers.

I therefore rang Reg and told him that I would be attending church the following Sunday when Joan's name would be remembered in prayers. Would he like to come with me? He said he would.

That really was the beginning of the New Beginning, although neither of us realised it at the time.

Our friendship flourished and, as Reg tells people, we started 'walking out' – a really old-fashioned expression. Our first 'public appearance' was in March 2000, when we attended a lunch in Coventry hosted by John Chaplin and Peter Lipscombe of *Vintage Speedway Magazine*.

This was my first introduction to speedway. I enjoyed meeting people like Freddie and Pat Williams, June and Barry Briggs, Andreas Jonsson and others of the speedway fraternity. When Reg and I returned to Henley, he gave me six videos entitled *The History of Speedway* and told me that he would test me on them the following week. He tells me I passed with flying colours!

In 2001, Reg was thinking about making a trip to Australia and New Zealand to meet up with his friends from earlier days. He asked me if I would like to accompany him and I jumped at the suggestion, not having been to either country.

I remember counting that we had met up with fifty-six of his pals and their wives whilst in the two countries. In the six weeks we were there, we stayed in hotels for only three or four nights, the rest of the time staying with his friends who afforded us fantastic hospitality.

I believe we were the first of the speedway fraternity to climb Sydney Harbour Bridge.

When we were planning our trip, we discovered that the most economical

Eileen meeting a real live native Australian. This is not a statue!

air fare was a round-the-world ticket so, having spent three nights in Singapore on the way out, we returned to the UK via Los Angeles.

Eileen and Reg on the Sydney Harbour Bridge with the Opera House in the background.

Here we hired a car and drove south to San Diego, calling in on the way to have tea with June Briggs – Barry was away on business. Being so close to Mexico, we decided to take the bus from San Diego to Tijuana, having in mind that we might make a visit to The Oasis of Hope Hospital. As it happens, we didn't. I think Reg felt it would be too stressful.

Whilst we were in San Diego, we visited the Hotel Coromandel where many celebrities had stayed including most American presidents and the Duke and Duchess of York (Edward and Mrs Simpson). We didn't stay there ourselves, of course – it was far too expensive – but we did think we could afford a sandwich and a glass of wine on the terrace. We actually ended up having a free lunch.

Reg is impatient, to say the least, and after 20 minutes had passed and we hadn't even been given the menu, he said it was time for us to leave. On the way out, one of the receptionists asked if everything was satisfactory to which Reg retorted that it was not and that they wouldn't be seeing us again!

When the manager was called, he listened patiently to Reg's complaints and then explained the reason why we had not been served. He insisted we return to the terrace to have lunch on the house. At first Reg resisted, but eventually gave in.

Later that year, we planned a visit to my cousin in Seattle. On 11 September (9/11), we left Heathrow in the morning for Copenhagen where we were to change planes. We were taxiing up the runway in Copenhagen for take-off when the pilot announced that he had instructions to return to the terminal building. No reason was given.

After a while, we had to disembark because, we were told, there had been a major incident in the States and all airports had been closed. After several hours, it was announced that the plane would not take off that day and, in fact, all passengers who had travelled to Copenhagen from other airports in Europe would be given tickets back to the original airport of departure.

When we arrived back in Henley at about midnight, we turned on the TV to discover the horrendous happenings in New York. After a few days, we decided to jump in the car and drive down to the South of France to La Londe to see Ove and Joanna Fundin.

As they were planning a trip themselves, we rented a small apartment in La Londe. This was my second visit to La Londe, as we had previously spent ten days with Ove and Joanna at their home in Valcros, so I was getting to know the area quite well. In fact, whilst we were there, we looked at three or four houses with a view to buying one as a holiday home but didn't find anything to our liking.

In November 2002, the Australian Speedway Grand Prix took place in Parramatta, a suburb of Sydney, and this seemed an appropriate opportunity to make another visit to Australia and New Zealand. Again, we had round-the-world

Eileen and Reg Fearman by the helicopter that took them to the Fox Glacier in 2001.

airline tickets and having flown into Los Angles on the return journey, we hired a car, this time driving north to San Francisco, a city we both love.

In the spring of 2003, we again had the notion to purchase a holiday home and decided to fly to Alicante and drive down the coast to Marbella and Estepona, looking at various places en route.

The idea was that we would keep my house in Henley as a base and sell Reg's home. We looked at several locations, close to golf courses as both of us were now seriously into playing golf. We were very taken with two developments close to Estepona and came close to buying one of them but, at the last minute, decided the area was too busy for us so it was back to the drawing board.

Later that year, we decided to look again at the South of France, particularly as a golfing partner of Reg's, Rudi Kartal, had moved to Sainte-Maxime from Henley the previous year with his partner and little boy. We stayed with Rudi and Caroline for three days and Rudi showed us several properties he had investigated on our behalf. Rudi was keen for us to buy in Sainte-Maxime so that he and Reg could revive their golf relationship.

We were told that the population of Sainte-Maxime is 13,000 but that this figure swells to nearly 80,000 in the summer and life can become frustrating with so many people around. We decided Sainte-Maxime was not for us and that we would look elsewhere.

From Sainte-Maxime, we continued our visit to Valcros to stay with Ove and Joanna for about ten days. During this time, we thought it worthwhile to have another search in the area and looked at four houses in Valcros. The fourth one we looked at appealed to both of us but it was too large for a holiday home.

After much discussion, we both agreed that we should purchase the house, sell both our homes in Henley and buy a small flat in the town as our UK base. We completed the purchase of our house in France in February 2004. By this time, Reg's house was well on the way to being sold but mine was delayed because of complications with my neighbours over the boundary.

In March 2004, Reg's house was sold and his furniture transported to our house in France. In the interim, we had purchased a small flat in Henley with a magnificent view over the town. Meanwhile, my London solicitors, Streathers, were sorting out the problem over the boundary and in May 2004, due to their excellent advice, the sale was finally completed.

Whilst all this was ongoing, Reg proposed marriage to me as he said he wanted to make an honest woman of me and so we were married in August 2004. It was a small affair with Gary as Reg's best man and a guest list of twenty-four of our family and closest friends.

After the wedding ceremony in August 2004.

Gary Fearman, Reg's best man at his wedding in 2004.

Repaying some of the famous Australian hospitality. Bluey Scott, who rode for Reg at Long Eaton and Middlesbrough, and his wife, Ann, on the London Eye during their visit to Henley.

From that point up to the present time, we have travelled widely. In May 2005, we travelled across Canada, by train from Toronto to Vancouver, from where we cruised up the Inside Passage of Alaska for seven days.

In December 2006, we made another trip to Australia and New Zealand, primarily to celebrate Jackie Gates' 80th birthday at a surprise lunch party for thirty-six people which Reg and I had organised from France.

We stayed with Bluey and Ann Scott in Burleigh Waters. On this trip we visited many places in Australia which neither of us had visited before – Darwin, Alice Springs and Uluru amongst them and also places I had not visited previously. We were very sad to learn later that Ann had had a nasty fall and was in hospital. She has apparently developed a form of dementia and we have subsequently learned that Ann is now in a nursing home in Brisbane.

Before spending Christmas and New Year in Manly, we spent a great few days with John and Jacqui Boulger in Adelaide and three days with Ray and Marion Cresp in Melbourne. Ray took us on a tour to Philip Island where, at dusk, we watched the 1,000 or more miniature penguins coming ashore after their day's hunting for food.

We spent a marvellous Christmas Day with Jim and Judith Shepherd who had family and friends as guests.

On New Year's Eve, we celebrated by taking a dinner cruise in the harbour where we had front seats for the customary fireworks from the famous Sydney Harbour Bridge (built by English firm Dorman Long & Co. Ltd of Middlesbrough, in 1932).

After New Zealand, where we spent a week with Bob and Lynda Andrews, we flew to Hawaii for five days in glorious sunshine. We visited Pearl Harbour, the scene on 6 December 1940 of the attack on the American Fleet by the Japanese Air Force when twenty-two ships were sunk or damaged including the *Arizona*, with the loss of 1,000 men.

The relic of the *Arizona*, still leaking oil after more than sixty years, remains as a grim reminder of the damage that was done and the lives that were lost. This act brought the USA into the Second World War.

Arriving in San Francisco, we hired a car and drove north along the Pacific coast, through the Redwoods to Seattle where we met up with my cousin and her family and my niece and her husband who live in Vancouver.

In January 2008, we did a cruise around the South China Sea with Ove and Joanna. We were away for three weeks, two weeks cruising and a few days either side in Hong Kong. We stopped off at Manila, Borneo, Bruneii, Singapore, Da Nang, Saigon and Sanya before returning to Hong Kong. What a wonderful experience that was.

Then, in April that year, we travelled across the States by train, stopping off at various towns and cities for overnight or longer stops. We ended our travels in San Francisco to celebrate Reg's 75th birthday in style.

In November the same year, we spent two weeks in Barbados on Gary's recommendation, where we celebrated my birthday at The Cliff, a magnificent restaurant, built into the side of the rocks.

Dinner in style while cruising with Ove and Joanna Fundin.

Reg had said for a long time that he would like to take me to Egypt. We planned to go in February 2009 but due to the uncertain situation in Gaza and Israel, we decided it was not the time to make that trip.

The temperature in France dropped quite considerably in the winter of 2009 so in February we accepted the invitation of Ray Chitty (Eric's son) and his wife to stay with them in their holiday home in Venice, Florida. We were there for three weeks and during that time, we drove down through the Everglades to Miami and on to Key West.

On our return to Venice, we drove via Orlando, West Palm Beach and Jupiter, meeting up with ex-speedway rider Malcolm Brown and his wife. We enjoyed our stay in Florida so much that we rented a house there for three months for the winter of 2009/2010.

During the winter of 2010/2011, we rented a beach apartment in Venice for four weeks and we spent six weeks there in 2012 renting a house where our French friends, Andre and Domi, joined us for two weeks. All being well, we shall spend just under three months in Venice in 2013/14 and hope to play a lot of golf.

Yes, we have travelled extensively during the thirteen years we have been together and we shall continue to do so while we are fit and able. One never knows what lies around the corner so we have to make the most of life while we can.

During our time together, we have got to know each other pretty well and have grown to love each other. We laugh a lot, we do silly things together and sometimes I will say, 'we're daft' to which Reg adds, 'but not stupid'.

We talk a lot (at least, he does most of the talking), we enjoy good wine and, thankfully, he enjoys my cooking. Reg is a loving and caring person, a real English gentleman who takes good care of me and makes me feel safe and secure and we have a mutual respect for each other.

Although he is impatient and at times demanding, he is quick to acknowledge something which pleases him, attributes I imagine that contributed to his success in his speedway career.

When we lived in France, my main concern became the fact that the intense sun was not good for Reg. He was suffering because of it. This motivated our eventual return to Henley as well as the fact that the French inheritance laws are quite horrendous, going back to the Napoleonic Wars.

We now have a comfortable town house in Henley from where we can walk into the town for everything we need. However, neither of us really feels settled and we may just be on the move again. Watch this space!

APPRECIATIONS

Two men who knew Reg Fearman at formative moments of his life, during his teenage years and during his National Service in the army, contribute their own appreciations of his character.

CYRIL HILL

– Austerity-age youngsters were resilient and inventive

You asked me to jot down my memories of the early days of our friendship. Over the past few weeks I have tried to take myself back to the mid-forties around the time I first met you. Wasn't that a long time ago?

You must have been 12 years old and I was 13. You will recall the prefab I lived in, just off New City Road in the East End of London. My parents had been bombed out and we were homeless until allocated the prefab.

We all lived through a very austere period at that time which, with the

Cyril Hill, long-term pal from schooldays.

rationing and shortages, I believe made us young people very resilient and inventive. As the Second World War came to an end, we were also willing to look beyond our local horizons.

Relatively simple things provided us with great enjoyment. I recall paying 3d (in old money) to go into the old Greengate Cinema, which was almost falling down. Then, if we had the money between us, we would buy a hot pie to eat as we walked home.

I also recall that you played football on Saturday mornings (in West Ham colours, of course) for the Odeon Cinema Club football team.

Another treat and adventure was the 6d all-day tram ticket which took us, along with two or three other boys, anywhere in London. At that time, the Holborn Tramway Underground Tunnel was open, which made it a favourite.

The really big thing was bikes. If you had a bike you had made it and if I remember right, you were given a sports bike as a birthday present. You were envied as the machine had drop handlebars.

It was not long before cycling to Epping Forest was seen as quite easy, with Southend or Canvey Island taking a bit longer. A lot of time was spent oiling and cleaning and generally keeping our beloved bikes in good condition.

It must have been in 1946 that we went together to Wembley for the British Riders Speedway Championship. I managed to buy two tickets which included the coach fare for the trip. The coach was packed with Hammers' supporters but the title went to a Wembley rider, Tommy Price.

In the following year, 1947, our thoughts were all of plans for what became known as the great bike ride. At first it was all about a jaunt to Brighton for perhaps two or three days. As it turned out, the spirit of adventure kicked in!

Brighton, Worthing, Bognor, Portsmouth, Ryde – we just kept going, sleeping rough and with our money running out. It must have been 200 miles or more and proved to be a real adventure. Maybe we were the pioneers of sleeping on the beach? We both swam for hours at places en route as the sea water was so clear, unlike the Thames Estuary at Canvey.

As speedway became more popular, we actually cycled to New Cross and also made our way over to Harringay. Of course, we never missed our Tuesday nights at West Ham's Custom House. It was around this time when Aub Lawson and Cliff Watson arrived. It was wonderful to have two star riders living in New City Road.

When I spoke recently to our mutual friend of that period, Roy Horton, he told me about how the two of you went to the West Ham track before school to try and get a ride on the track spare.

He also mentioned the time New City Road School suffered severe bomb damage. You were both sent to Cave and then on to Burke School. Roy also mentioned swimming in the YMCA building in Greengate Street. I can just vaguely remember spending some time there in the pool. Roy sends his best wishes to you and Eileen and is pleased to know all is well.

You have a standing invitation to his shop – pie, mash and liqueur, genuine East End style.

Mavis, my wife, can go back slightly further than me regarding the evacuation to St Ives, Cornwall, mentioned early on in the book. Mavis remembers the Island School which all evacuees had to attend.

She remembers the long walks home from school, all wearing a long mackintosh which swept you along in the wind. She remembers too American soldiers giving out food and sweets.

Reg, you always walked home with Mavis and her sister Pat and then veered off to your own billet. That was a long time ago.

It is ALL a long time ago. I should imagine we went from year to year doing much the same thing. We enjoyed the freedom and looked forward to everything with lots of enthusiasm – no fighting or friction around our area and it really was a great time, growing up as teenagers in dear old Plaistow, especially with a friend like you.

It is wonderful that our friendship has continued to this day and Mavis and I always look forward to your visits to Essex.

DAVID WEEKS

– International speedway rider had not passed his test for a motorcycle licence!

In the very early 1950s, I was stationed at Kinmel Park Camp, Bodelwyddan, near Rhyl, with 80/81 Bty 31st Training Regiment, Royal Artillery.

During a re-organisation, I was moved from my existing job of looking after the battery's twenty or so motorcycles to running the Motor Transport Office, which involved looking after all transport for the Continuation Troop.

Continuation Troop was, as the name suggests, a continuation of training for drivers and gunners of the regiment. The best of the drivers were sent to the troop to learn how to drive Morris Quad Gun Towing Tractors, towing 25-pound field guns and limbers, and also to use the winching gear the Quads were equipped with.

The troop, as I recall, had fifteen Quads, three 3-ton lorries, one 15cwt lorry and three motorcycles. I was responsible for the everyday running and maintenance of the vehicles.

David and Amber Weeks with Reg Fearman.

The battery sergeant major, BSM Fisher, called me into his office and said he had just the right man to assist me. He said you should have been on your way to Korea but had been kept back at the regiment for reasons connected with missing mail (described earlier in this book).

BSM Fisher said I should get on very well with the newcomer as he was a rather well-known motorcyclist who rode speedway.

I was a very keen motorcycle rider myself, riding trials for the regiment, and I was also a member of the Motor Cycle Display Team. I assumed the newcomer – who, of course, turned out to be Reg Fearman – and I would have something in common.

My only doubt was that I had met several sporting celebrities during my army service and most had a 'touch me not – I am special' attitude.

A few days later, BSM Fisher and a tall, good-looking soldier came into the MT Office. BSM Fisher announced that this was the lad to assist me. He told the soldier that I was Bombardier Weeks and added that I would show him the ropes.

I remember vividly, after all these years, that the soldier broke out into a broad grin, offered his outstretched hand and said, 'I'm Reg Fearman and I am sure we will get on well – which of the chairs is mine?'

This broke the ice and I recall saying, 'Call me David or Dave, take your pick of the chairs but before we start, let's go to the NAAFI for a break!' This we did, with me being very keen to know all about his speedway riding.

Much to my surprise, Reg was also keen to know about MY motorcycling. This was the beginning of a friendship which still exists to this day – more than sixty years on.

As the days went by, we worked well together. Reg had by then acquired a motorbike. I cannot recall whether or not it was a 350cc Matchless or an AJS, but I remember he mentioned to me that he only had a provisional licence. I could not believe this. Here was a man who rode international speedway but had no road licence!

I was a qualified driving examiner, having passed the examination at the Army MT School. I duly gave Reg a test during our dinner break (me riding on the pillion) and presented him with his pink pass slip on our return.

There are so many memories to recall of those army days. During the winter months, our office was very cold. We had a coke stove in the office but no allocation of coke so we had the bright idea of utilizing what fuel was available – waste engine oil.

Two 1 gallon tins were fitted with lengths of copper pipe which went into the stove from the bottom of the tins. Taps were fitted to control the flow of liquid. At the bottom of the stove a metal plate, about 1in thick, was fitted, placed at an angle with a gap underneath and, with the aid of a blowtorch which we managed to scrounge, the plate was heated to red hot.

The tins were then positioned above the stove with the pipes entering the top. One was filled with waste engine oil and the other with water. The oil dripping onto the red-hot plate provided instant ignition and the water dispersed the flame into a cascade of heat, so much so that the stove would get red hot.

This was great until the BSM found out about it. No more red-hot office for us! I seem to remember this system was mostly thought up by Reg – I will blame him anyway.

Every six weeks, the whole troop would move to Sennybridge in the Brecon Beacons, where the practise ranges were situated, to fire our 25-pounders. On one particular trip, one of the guns and its limber became detached from the towing Quad. The gun and limber careered across the road into an oncoming lorry, causing a lot of damage but, fortunately, no injuries.

On our eventual return to Kinmel, a Court of Enquiry was held into the incident, with Reg and I having to hand in written reports. It was then that I found out how Reg was able to transfer his thoughts and recollections onto paper so accurately and quickly – a gift he retains to this day.

When on holidays in various parts of the world, Reg always sends me a detailed account of all he does, with descriptions of all the places he visits. It is so detailed that my wife Amber and I feel we have been there ourselves. I read them to Amber, who unfortunately has only 10 per cent vision. Thank you, Reg.

When I was transferred to Continuation Troop, I was newly married, living in an army flat in Rhyl, overlooking the sea. Reg often visited us and when I was on duty he would often ask if he could pop in and see Amber and perhaps take her to the pictures. I trusted Reg 100 per cent – he was the perfect gentleman and, as Amber says, treated her like a lady.

After Reg had been at Kinmel for a while, he got a temporary transfer from West Ham speedway to Stoke, which was within easy reach of the camp.

Reg would take Amber and me to some of the meetings. On one occasion, Reg hurt his foot and I helped him to the track medical centre, leaving Amber in the pits. Reg said we would not be long and that she would be OK staying where she was.

The treatment took longer than expected and there was no sign of Amber when we returned. In fact the pits were empty. After much searching, Amber was at last found. Did she tell Reg and me what she thought of us? She called us every name under the sun, although I did try to tell her that we both did have parents.

The next evening, there was a knock on the door at our flat. When Amber opened the door she discovered Reg, holding a massive bouquet of flowers and a large box of chocolates. What could Amber say except to thank Reg, say he was forgiven and invite him to have tea with us?

Reg had by this time acquired a Ford V8 car which was the envy of a lot of people at the camp, including most of the officers who were running Ford 8s, Morris Minors and similar vehicles.

This cut the travelling time to Stoke for Reg's speedway activities by a considerable amount. As the V8's speedometer went up so the fuel gauge went down, and rather rapidly. I wonder why our mpg figures for Continuation Troop went down suddenly as soon as Reg acquired the V8?

I once tried to get Reg to join the regiment's Motor Cycle Display Team, as we were desperately short of good riders. He declined, saying that it was much too dangerous for him. This was from the man who hurtled around a cinder track on a motorbike, much more powerful than ours, and with no brakes, no gears, one foot rest and a seat not much bigger than a pimple!

I think, in fact I am sure, that Reg would have joined us if it had not been for the fact that all practise for the Display Team had to be done in our own time. This would have meant that most of his free time would have been taken up.

The Display Team is still going strong today – named The Flying Gunners. The team was set up in 1948–49 by Captain David Miles who did so much for army motorcycling. Captain Miles himself was a very accomplished rider who won at least two gold medals and a bronze in International Six Day Trials. We are still in touch and I believe Reg has recently been in touch with him as well.

Our MT Office was remote from most other offices, being on its own right beside the road called Engine Hill, with only a small fence between the road and us. This road led past the Guard Room and up past Lowther College, a select college for young ladies (no, they were not allowed out).

However, staff employed at the college passed our office on their way to and from work. Reg would know the times of the comings and goings and would say, 'I am just going outside to watch the talent going past.'

He did get to know some of them. My wife, Amber, also worked there and is still in touch with one of the girls who still remembers Reg. She remembers him as a lovely, caring young man – and so good looking.

The road was also used by many young girls – and some who were not so young – all looking out for a bit of fun with the soldiers. I wonder if Reg still remembers Abergele Nellie, Engine Hill Lill and her daughter, Betty, Dyserth Dilys and others. These were a few of the regulars who frequented the camp.

The regiment also held regular dances which were very popular and a fair number of soldiers met their future wives at these events.

In early 1953, I returned to Civvy Street and as I had married Amber, a local girl, decided to stay in the area. It took a lot to settle down but, after several jobs, I finally found work I was happy with. This was at a new factory which had just opened, called Chance Pilkington, a division of Pilkington Glass, making optical and ophthalmic glass. I must have liked it as I stayed there for more than thirty years.

I had by this time lost touch with Reg but at times saw his name mentioned in *Motor Cycling* magazine. I knew he was back in speedway – and doing rather well.

After a number of years, we managed to afford a magic box, television, in the form of a 12in black and white set. I found that speedway was televised and on several occasions saw Reg. He was back to his winning ways and I used to boast to anyone watching with us that he used to be a great pal.

Some years later, on a Sunday evening, the telephone rang. On answering it, a voice asked if I had at one time ridden in motorcycle trials in the army? I said that the answer was yes. The voice then asked if I had been successful and if I had won a fair amount of events?

My response was that I had been fortunate enough to be a member of the very successful 31st Regiment Trials Team. A further question followed. Had I also belonged to the Royal Artillery Motor Cycle Display Team? Again, my answer was yes but, by now, I was feeling rather concerned and was impatient to know who was doing the questioning.

The voice on the telephone said he knew a lot more about me, including the fact that I had been involved in voluntary work for many years for the Marble Church and had also been a church warden.

By this time I was more than concerned. I was worried and it must have shown in my voice. The speaker obviously realised this and said that I had no need to worry, I knew him well, and we had worked together in the MT Office at Kinmel Camp.

'Do you remember me? This is Reg Fearman speaking.'

I was lost for words. There followed a lengthy conversation. I believe Reg had, by chance, met someone who knew me and that is where all his information about my later life had come from.

Reg had then decided to ring me and, as he said later, to get me going! This was the start of the renewal of our friendship. Reg was planning to come up to North Wales from his home in Henley-on-Thames and we planned a meeting.

I knew by this time that Reg had sadly lost his wife some years earlier, that Eileen, a great friend of Reg and Joan, had lost her husband around the same time, and that since then the two had become good friends. Reg explained that he would bring Eileen with him as she originally came from the Liverpool area, only some 40 minutes from our home, and had relations they planned to visit.

Coincidentally, Eileen knew of Kinmel Camp, the village of Bodelwyddan, and Lowther College, where relatives of hers had been educated. She was also involved in the building of Glan Clwyd Hospital, in Bodelwyddan, and altogether knew the area rather well.

Reg kept me informed of his whereabouts and all his many interests. By this time, he had moved to the South of France and he sent many photographs, not only of his new home both inside and out, but of the many improvements he was making. We found a lot of pleasure in this. It made us feel we had actually been there.

After many telephone calls and letters, the date of a visit by Reg and Eileen was finalised. As they still had a home in Henley-on-Thames, they would use this as their base. It was about fifty years since we last saw one another and I felt rather apprehensive. Reg had achieved so much in life and had been so successful in business, yet here he was wanting to meet up, finding time to visit us, his old friends from many years ago.

Came the day, the telephone rang and I heard Reg's voice. 'Hi David, I'm bxxxxx lost. I am by the Marble Church but all the roads have changed. Can't even find the old Kinmel Camp. Can you direct me to your home?'

This I did and after a few minutes, a BMW arrived and out stepped Reg and Eileen. Reg was much taller than I remembered – or had I shrunk? He had a little less on top and a little more in the middle.

Nevertheless, he was still the Reg I remembered. After embracing one another and being introduced to Eileen, the years just rolled back. There was so much to catch up on and so many memories to rekindle.

At Reg's request, I had booked a table at a local hotel for lunch where we all had a lovely meal and just talked and talked. Thankfully, Eileen and Amber got on really well together. As Eileen knew the area and Lowther College, where Amber had worked, they too had plenty to talk about.

After this meeting, we kept in touch by telephone and letter and for a few years, continued to meet up. On one of the visits to see us, over a coffee at our home, Reg said to Eileen, 'Shall we tell them?' Eileen smiled and rather shyly said, 'Yes.' Reg then announced: 'We've just got married.'

We celebrated by going out for another lovely meal. This was a real match made in heaven – two wonderful people and two great friends.

Reg then had the idea of trying to arrange a get-together with some of the old Kinmel Park 31st Regiment personnel. I tried to contact some that had retired to North Wales, but as I went through a list of the lads I remembered, I was shocked to find that so many had gone to the 'barrack rooms in the sky'.

Nevertheless, a few of us met up for lunch at the Ty Fry Inn, the local pub for Kinmel Park Camp.

In 2009 we met up again, at Reg's request. Taffy Roberts from London, Bill Adams, Don Warner, Brian Bucknall, Gwyn Roberts and, of course Reg and myself and our respective spouses.

Thank you both for these memories – we love you both.

Visit our website and discover thousands of other History Press books.

www.thehistorypress.co.uk